Catholicism Today

Catholics are not Christians. They worship Mary. They do whatever the pope says. They cannot divorce. They eat fish on Fridays. These flawed but common statements reflect a combined ignorance of and fascination with Catholicism and the Catholic Church. *Catholicism Today: An Introduction to the Contemporary Catholic Church* aims to familiarize its readers with contemporary Catholicism. The book is designed to address common misconceptions and frequently asked questions regarding the Church, its teachings, and the lived experience of Catholics in modern societies worldwide. Opening with a concise historical overview of Christianity in general and Catholicism in particular, the text explores the core beliefs and rituals that define Catholicism in practice, the organization of the Church and the Catholic calendar, as well as the broad question of what it means to be Catholic in a variety of cultural contexts. The book ends with a discussion of the challenges facing the Church both now and in the coming decades. Also included are two short appendices on Eastern Catholicism and Catholicism in the United States.

Dr. Evyatar Marienberg is an Associate Professor at the Department of Religious Studies at the University of North Carolina at Chapel Hill.

Catholicism Today

An Introduction to
the Contemporary Catholic Church

Evyatar Marienberg

Routledge
Taylor & Francis Group

NEW YORK AND LONDON

First published 2015
by Routledge
711 Third Avenue, New York, NY 10017

and by Routledge
2 Park Square, Milton Park, Abingdon, Oxon, OX14 4RN

Routledge is an imprint of the Taylor & Francis Group, an informa business

Library of Congress Cataloging-in-Publication Data
CIP data has been applied for

ISBN: 978-0-415-71942-1 (hbk)
ISBN: 978-0-415-71943-8 (pbk)
ISBN: 978-1-315-86738-0 (ebk)

Typeset in Minion
by Apex CoVantage, LLC

Printed and bound in the United States of America by
Edwards Brothers Malloy on sustainably sourced paper

Contents

Foreword and Acknowledgments

The core of this book is based upon my Hebrew work on the same subject, which was published in 2010.[1] Although I bear the ultimate responsibility, for better and certainly for worse, for this English version, my work on it was facilitated by the outstanding assistance of several individuals. Sharon Assaf and Matan Kaminer produced excellent translations of this previous work, nearly in its entirety. Matthew Hotham, a very meticulous English editor, helped later while I reworked this text. Two grants from the University of North Carolina at Chapel Hill, to which I am extremely grateful, made this translation project possible. I am thankful to the many people at Routledge who helped improve the final product including Andrew Beck, Laura Briskman, Emmaleigh Burtoft, Denise File, Tom Hussey, and Steve Wiggins.

Many people helped me directly or indirectly with this project. I thanked most of them in the Hebrew edition, and so will just hint to them here: I refer mostly to my many friends, colleagues, and students in the various academic institutions where I have spent many years, particularly those institutions in which I have been a student, a visiting scholar, or a teacher of Catholicism— The Institut Catholique de Paris, Tel Aviv University, The University of Notre Dame, and my current academic home, the Department of Religious Studies at the University of North Carolina at Chapel Hill.

Note

1. Evyatar Marienberg, *Katoliyut Akhshav: Mavo le-Havanat ha-Knesiyah ha-Katolit bat Yamenu* (Jerusalem: Carmel Publishing House, 2010).

Introduction

In the United States, or at least in some parts of it, one may hear at times quite surprising statements about Catholics and Catholicism: Catholics are not Christians. They worship Mary. They follow whatever the pope says. And they eat fish on Friday.

Unless one defines the words "Christian," "worship," "follow," and "they," in a unique fashion, these statements are all wrong. But the very fact of their existence shows, in a strange way, a relatively unique mixture of concepts about Catholicism that combines ignorance with a sense of fascination and exoticism. This book intends to familiarize its readers with Catholicism and Catholics. Such increased familiarity will certainly reduce the exoticism with which readers approach this group, while hopefully not decreasing their level of fascination with this huge and varied religious entity: a fascination that the author of this book, not himself a Catholic, shares with them.

This book is not about the history of the Catholic Church. Those wishing to learn about the history of this Church in particular and Christianity in general can find many other excellent studies.[1] This book aspires to describe the present state of things, not their historical progression, and to this end historical discussions regarding changes in ritual, hierarchical structures, ways of thinking, and beliefs have been kept to a minimum.

Scholars of the modern Catholic Church share an almost unanimous consensus that a new Catholic era commenced in the wake of the Second Vatican Council, also known as "Vatican II," a major meeting of the high hierarchy of the Church, which convened from 1962 to 1965 in Rome. The Council brought about many changes, theological[2] as well as practical.

Though perhaps not always categorically stated, this book, for the most part, focuses on the state of the Church since the Council.

The Catholic Church

This book deals with the Catholic "Church." Comparable terms in other languages for this word are worthy of mention. Thus, for example, the term for "Church" in German is *Kirche,* in Swedish, *Kyrka,* in Russian, *Cerkov.* In these languages, just like in English, the words derive from the Greek *Kyriakon,* "[the house] of the Lord" (*Kyrios*). The French term *Église,* or the Spanish term *Iglesia,* or the Italian term *Chiesa* derive, on the other hand, from the Latin word *Ecclesia,* which in turn comes from the Greek word *Ekklesia,* which stems from the verb *Ekkalein,* "to assemble," "to summon the people."

The fact that one of the original terms to designate what we call "church" refers to a physical or geographical location, while the other refers to a group of people, is significant. Indeed, the word "church" has a number of meanings. Sometimes, what is intended is the local church: the structure in which the believers gather, or the believers in a certain region. In other instances, what is meant is the Church as a large body, one that unites all the believers in a particular religion. In English, as is in some other Indo-European languages, it is possible at times to know whether the writer is referring to the narrower or the broader meaning by the writer's use of "church" or "Church" respectively.

If the meaning of the word "Church" is clear, the word "Catholic" may still need explanation. The source of this word lies in the Greek word *Katholou,* meaning "universal, general." It appears in a Christian context already in the second century. From the point of view of those who used the word in antiquity, the Church was entitled to be called "catholic," as it was everyone's Church, the universal and international Church. In addition, and probably already by the third century, the term also acquired the meaning of "The True Church," the Church that is "Orthodox," the Church which holds the true belief.

In point of fact, the "Catholic" Church never truly included all Christian believers. Of course, after the split between the Greek East and the Latin West, and the further divisions that followed as a result of the Reformation, the validity of the term became even more problematic. Nevertheless, even today the Catholic Church is characterized by exceptional universalism. While many Catholics feel a deep connection between their national and religious identities, most Catholics are very well aware that their Church transcends national and political boundaries.[3] Needless to say, deciding which group held the "true belief," and which groups did not, is the affair of theologians, not of historians: we will not even try to get involved in such debates in this book.

Because Catholicism means universalism and expresses the desire for the creation of a global Church, and because the word appears in early Christian statements of faith, a number of other Christian groups do not want to relinquish usage of the term. They define themselves as "Catholics" even though they do not recognize the authority of the pope in Rome. For this reason, there are those who use the term "Roman Catholic" (originally used by those opposed to "Roman" Catholicism) in order to avoid, among other things, uncertainties such as these. Others are not partial to the term, as in its essence it combines both broader and narrower definitions: Catholic being the broader definition, and Roman the narrower. Moreover, there are Christians who belong to the Catholic Church but who have patriarchs as their practical leaders, as for example Armenian Catholics, Greek Catholics or Maronite Catholics, and whose original liturgical languages are not Latin, the language of Rome: these are the "Eastern Catholics," some of whose particularities are discussed in a short appendix.[4] In this book, the term "Catholic" will be used with no other adjectives, referring by it to those Christians that, in addition to their many other characteristics, recognize the special authority of the Bishop of Rome. Similarly, although most every religious believer will claim that his or her community is "orthodox" ("follows the right path"), here, the borrowed meaning of this term is used: the "Orthodox" Churches are various Churches whose foundations generally, even if not always, lie in the eastern parts of Europe and in the Middle East: later we will briefly discuss the events that brought about a definitive division between them and the Catholic Church. They do not consider the Bishop of Rome as their leader.

Who Is Catholic?

According to Catholic doctrine, the answer to the question "Who is Catholic?" is clear: a Catholic is someone who was baptized in the Catholic Church, or someone who was validly baptized in another Christian Church but who has joined the Catholic Church at a later phase of his or her life. As long as that person has not officially and explicitly declared himself or herself as quitting the Catholic Church, or as long as the Church has not excommunicated him or her (either explicitly or as a consequence of certain actions he or she has taken), this person, as far as the Church regards, is Catholic.[5] According to these rules, more than half of the Christians in the world and about one-sixth of humanity—more than 1.2 billion men and women—are Catholic.

Scholars of religious studies cannot easily accept this theological-doctrinal definition, especially because the levels of involvement of many of these people in the life of the Church and their identification with it are quite diverse. Should someone whose last visit to a church was when he or she was baptized as an infant, and who perhaps defines himself or herself as religionless, be considered a Catholic, from a sociological point of view, just because of his or her baptism? Can we really say that he or she is as "Catholic" as (to use an extreme example) the pope is, because both were baptized in the Catholic Church? Obviously, the answer is no: we should not put all those that are formally Catholic in the same basket. So how can we distinguish between them?

One important objective factor that can help us is attendance at Mass, the central ritual of Catholicism. Various statistics show that in many countries today (including those that are considered "Catholic," like Italy, Poland, or Brazil), only about 10 to 20 percent of those who define themselves as Catholics consistently attend Mass on a weekly basis.[6] Those who attend Mass regularly can surely be in our basket entitled "Catholics." What should we do, though, with the other 80 to 90 percent? Some of them do not attend because of various personal circumstances: if they could, they maybe would. Others avoid participating in the public ritual life of the Church because they disagree with general issues in the universal Church, or with issues affecting their local parish or diocese. They do not leave the Church, but they express their disagreement with core issues by staying away. Those of them who actually care about the Church and hope for a change might see themselves as a "Faithful Opposition." They might feel that their parish or diocese is too conservative, or too liberal, or not in line with their own agenda in another way. With another type of leadership, maybe they would attend. And yet there are those who do not attend simply because they do not care much or at all about the Catholic aspect of their identity, do not feel a need to attend services, or are just bored by them. For some, this lack of attendance is a sign of their growing detachment with the Church. For others, the situation is more complicated. How should we treat those who indeed rarely enter a church, but who proudly identify themselves as Catholics? And what about those who call themselves "cultural," "lapsed," "surviving," or "recovering" Catholics? Sociologists of Catholicism will continue to wrestle with these questions, and the Church itself will continue to do the same. The only thing we can do is to keep in mind the formal definition mentioned above, while remembering that in real life the answers to the question are rather complex.

Catholic Geo-Demographics

Catholics are represented in almost every country, though naturally their percentage in the total population differs from place to place. The situation in the Vatican City State, where all citizens are Catholics, or in Argentina, the country from which pope Francis, the reigning pope at the time of this writing, comes, where about 90 percent of the population define themselves as Catholic, differs from Great Britain, where the number of Catholics is a little less than 10 percent, or Nepal, where only a fraction of a percent of its inhabitants define themselves as such. About 70 percent of the world's Catholics are concentrated in fifteen countries. More than a quarter of the world's Catholics reside in two countries: Brazil (with approximately 140 million), and Mexico (with approximately 130 million). In the other thirteen countries, the number of Catholics range (in descending order) from 70 to 20 million: the Philippines, the United States, Italy, France, Colombia, Spain, Poland, Argentina, the Democratic Republic of Congo, Peru, Germany, Venezuela, and Nigeria.[7] Catholics make up more than 75 percent of the population in eleven of these fifteen countries (with the exception of the United States, the Democratic Republic of Congo, Germany, and Nigeria). As mentioned above, one must remember that in all of these countries, only a small percentage of those defined as Catholics actively participate in Church life: what this participation or lack thereof means is, as we said earlier, an open question. Despite the high percentage of Catholics in many industrialized countries, one must also bear in mind that most Catholics today live in countries with a very low standard of living and subsist on only a few US dollars per day. The average Catholic is not white anymore. Of those involved in Church life, the percentage of women is significantly higher than that of men.[8]

The Current Pope

The pope reigning while this book was being prepared for publication was pope Francis, originally from Argentina. His two predecessors, Benedict XVI and John Paul II, are mentioned relatively often in this book as well. John Paul II had a tremendous impact on the contemporary Catholic Church. His influence is likely to continue to be felt for years to come through the thousands of bishops he appointed during his long reign, and through those appointed by his successor and right hand, pope Benedict XVI (also widely known by his civil name, Joseph Ratzinger, due to his strong presence in the Vatican as well as in theological circles before his election to the papacy). His memory is also likely to remain vibrant in the minds of Catholics and non-Catholics alike in the coming decade or two. His impact can be attributed not only to his magnetic and charismatic character but also to his unusually long reign of more than twenty-six years. Thus, any work dealing with the Catholic Church in the last decades of the twentieth century and the first decades of the twenty-first can hardly ignore him. Pope Benedict XVI was influential mostly by maintaining, in various ways, a certain status quo created during the reign of John Paul II. His reign, however, can hardly be considered a success story, regardless of one's leaning. It was marred with crisis and internal battles that were generally handled ineffectively. By far, Benedict XVI's most important act was his resignation, the first in about six centuries. It is very plausible that he will be remembered mostly, if not only, for this act. The reminder that a pope can resign like any other functionary, and that a smooth transition to a new one is possible, is likely to dramatically change the image of the papacy in the eyes of Catholics and put significant pressure on (or provide a way out for) future popes when and if their effectiveness seems limited.

It is very possible that, as you read this book, Francis is no longer pope, and both John Paul II and Benedict XVI are a fading memory. Still, one should not consider this a crucial fact that has an impact on the content of the book. Popes are important for the Catholic Church, but they are certainly not its essence. Popes come and go, with varying levels of influence and import. The Catholic Church and Catholic practice, however, except in rare moments, change slowly over larger time spans than a single papacy. When this book is read, another pope from Africa, or South America, or another part of the world might be in Rome. The Church might have already dealt seriously and effectively with various issues discussed in this book, such as cases of child abuse, remarriage, or homosexuality. Another challenge, the marriage of priests, might be less controversial. And maybe there will be also women priests. But, if history is any guide, the core elements of the hierarchical structure, the rituals, the doctrines, and the vague "mentality" of the Catholic Church, as described in this book, are likely to remain the same.

Additional Features of This Book

This book is intended as a coherent and useful introduction for nonspecialists interested in the field. In keeping with the book's introductory nature, scholarly references were kept to a minimum. References given in footnotes are generally of books, and not articles, published in recent years. As such, nonspecialist readers may find them relatively easier to access. Often, these books are not the sources of specific claims in this volume; rather, they are mentioned because they can provide a useful scholarly survey for further reading on the topic at hand.

Quotations from the New Testament are taken from *The New American Bible © USCCB,* widely used in the Catholic Church in the United States. Quotations of Catholic liturgical texts are generally taken from *The Roman Missal, Third Edition, for use in the Dioceses of the United States of America* (2011 Missal, © USCCB).

The Vatican is occasionally mentioned throughout the book, in sentences such as "the Vatican required," or "sources in the Vatican claimed," and the like. In fact, like many governments, various and even opposing views may be heard coming from the Vatican, particularly when the pope in charge is considered weak: this was obvious, for example, during the final years of the reign of pope John Paul II. With every reference to the Vatican, it is best at the outset to note who the speaker is and his title. An occasional statement by one or another member of the administration around the pope, his court ("Curia"), with regard to an issue about which he is not authorized to comment cannot be considered the official Vatican position. Despite this, in order not to cause further complications by mentioning names and titles that would most probably be unfamiliar to most readers, it was decided to dispense with such exactitudes. Nevertheless, it should be clear that when statements made by the "Vatican" are mentioned, the reader can be assured that these statements were made by members of the Curia who had the authority to comment on the specific topic.

Almost all of the important documents regarding instruction and doctrine that have been issued over the last few decades by the Magisterium, the Church's supreme hierarchy, are available online in a variety of languages. They can be easily found through their Latin title. For this reason, their titles are given in footnotes, so that those interested may locate and peruse the original documents.

To a certain extent, this book deals more with the "what" and the "how" of the Catholic Church, and less with the "why." As with other religions, Catholic practice is more fixed than are the explanations for it. In order not to adopt a particular manner of interpretation and thereby rule out another, it was decided in many cases to avoid lengthy commentaries regarding theological reasons for the existence of a particular act or reality, choosing instead to discuss the act or reality itself. The readers should be aware that if they are later given an explanation for the act or reality, it is likely to be one of several possible explanations.

The format of this book is not an "answers to frequently asked questions," which has become fairly common both in print and on the Internet. Notwithstanding, an attempt has been made in this book's structure, as well as in the topics covered, to provide answers to questions that, in the author's experience, are quite common when the subject of the Catholic Church is raised. After an extremely concise historical overview of Christianity in general and Catholicism in particular, this book explores what being Catholic might mean, the core beliefs of Catholics, the way the Church is organized, the variety of Catholic rituals, and the Catholic calendar. It ends with a discussion of the challenges the Church faces now and will face in the coming decades. It is suggested that the chapters of the book be read in order, but selective reading of specific chapters is possible as well.

Notes

1. It is obviously impossible to give even a limited list of such works in such a space. Still, a few relatively recent good examples, of very varied length, style, and depth, are the following: Gerald O'Collins and Mario Farrugia, *Catholicism: The Story of Catholic Christianity* (New York: Oxford University Press, 2003); Linda Woodhead, *An Introduction to Christianity* (Cambridge: Cambridge University Press, 2004); Linda Woodhead, *Christianity: A Very Short Introduction* (Oxford: Oxford University Press, 2004); Stephen Tomkins, *A Short History of Christianity* (Grand Rapids: William B. Eerdmans, 2005); Robert Bruce Mullin, *A Short World History of Christianity* (Louisville: Westminster John Knox, 2008).
2. The word "Theology" is made of two terms: *Theos,* which means "God," and *Logia,* which means "the study of." More broadly, theology is the name given to intellectual attempts to speak about God and many other aspect of religion. Among other things, theologians are different from scholars of "Religious Studies" in their explicit adherence to the faith in discussion and their style of speaking "from within" the religion in question.
3. The concern of some non-Catholics that Catholics may feel more loyalty to their Church than to their country is definitely related to that. The controversy at the beginning of the 1960s regarding Catholic John F. Kennedy's worthiness to be president of the United States of America, or, in a very different context, the Nazis' persecutions of Catholics, were no doubt connected to the not-entirely-mistaken understanding of this fact. For a discussion of the issue, see for example Christine Firer Hinze, "A Distinctively Catholic Patriotism?" in *God and Country?: Diverse Perspectives on Christianity and Patriotism,* ed. Michael G. Long and Tracy Wenger Sadd (New York: Palgrave Macmillan, 2007), 129–46.
4. See pp. 229–232.
5. The Church regards those in the process of preparing for baptism to be "in communion" with it in some manner or another. Those of them who die before having been baptized would, according to the Church, be considered Catholic. Nevertheless, because the number of those belonging to these groups is so small, they are of little importance in the context of the discussion at hand.
6. In some countries the situation is very different. Thus, for example, in France it is estimated that only about 5 percent of Catholics attend Mass regularly, while in Nigeria, about 90 percent do so. In the United States, the number seems to be around 25 percent. This might be yet another example of the unique religious characteristics of the US when compared to many other countries.
7. The fact that only five out of these sixteen countries are found in Europe, and none in the Middle East, the places in which Christianity emerged, is a good example of the demographic shifts challenging Catholicism today. For more on this, see pp. 184–185.
8. See, for example, the very enlightening table in Alicia Adsera, "Religion and Changes in Family-Size Norms in Developed Countries," *Review of Religious Research* 47, no. 3 (2006): 276.

A Very Concise History of Christianity and Catholicism

This book deals with the contemporary Catholic Church, and does not profess to offer a historical survey of Christianity in general or Catholicism in particular. The following lines are no more than a short "refresher" intended for those readers possessing at least a basic knowledge of the history of Christianity.

The Historical Jesus

Jesus, unquestionably a historical figure,[1] was probably born in the year that we now specify as four or five before the Common Era to a Jewish family from the Galilee, a region in the north of modern-day Israel. Although two of the Gospels (the four books of the New Testament that describe Jesus' ministry) assert that his parents were in Bethlehem (a city about seventy miles to the south and currently part of Palestine) at the time of his birth,[2] most scholars believe Jesus was actually born in the Galilee. They suggest that the mention of Bethlehem in his biography was intended to connect him to the lineage of the house of David, who came from that southern town, and to prophecies about the Messiah.[3] The Galilee then, and even now, was a rural area far from the centers of authority and wealth, where Jews lived alongside other peoples. It is possible that some of these Galilean Jews were descendants of nations that only a few generations earlier, during the Hasmonean kingdom, had converted to Judaism either by force or by choice.

During the period of Jesus' adulthood, a man by the name of John who preached ritual immersion as part of a process of repentance, or perhaps as preparation for a new era, was active in the Jordan River region to the south. Jesus was baptized by him when he was apparently in his early thirties.[4] At around this time Jesus started preaching in the Galilee, attracting a following, among them fishermen and tax collectors. His preaching probably included social themes related to the rights of the poor and those ostracized from society. Jesus also called for repentance, related to his absolute conviction that the end of time was near: during the lifetime of his disciples (and, probably, his also), God would found his Kingdom on earth, where evil and misery would no longer exist, and he, Jesus, would be its king. By believing in this, Jesus was not radically different from many other Jews of his time and place. And just like them, he was also wrong.

Around the year 30, during the important Jewish festival of Passover, Jesus and his disciples arrived in Jerusalem. According to one of the New Testament chronologies, Jesus preached, overturned merchants' tables in the Temple precinct, and perhaps even prophesied the Temple's destruction. It is reasonable to assume that during that same week he ate with his disciples. It is possible that during such a meal he uttered phrases that compared the bread they ate to his body, and the wine they drank to his blood. Later, Jesus was arrested by envoys of the Temple priests. For reasons not entirely clear, but seemingly related to the suspicions of the senior priests in Jerusalem (based on his violent behavior in the Temple) that he was trying to initiate some kind of revolt, or at the very least, some disturbances, Jesus was transferred, perhaps following a trial in which he was found guilty of some charge (possibly but not surely blasphemy), to the Prefect of the Roman Province of Judaea, Pontius Pilate, who was at the time in Jerusalem. The Prefect sentenced Jesus to death by crucifixion, a method of execution that was customary for certain crimes. Jesus was taken away for execution on probably a Friday, perhaps the afternoon of what we would call the 7th of April, in the year 30. According to the Gospel of John, the words, "Jesus of Nazareth, King of the Jews," were written in Hebrew, Latin, and Greek above his head. After several hours of suffering on the cross, Jesus died. His body was possibly transferred to a burial place within a cave. The Sabbath, the day when many activities are prohibited, was fast approaching, and his disciples were, therefore, not able to lay him in a final resting place.

The Historicity of the Events Described

Many of the details described up to this point may be considered historical information. It should not be inferred from this that all the information, down to the smallest details, indeed took place, or that there is agreement among scholars about one fact or another. Even the Gospels, the main source of information, almost the only source with regard to the events, are not in agreement with regard to many details (although it is worth noting that they are in complete agreement over a number of them).[5] Nonetheless, this is a type of information belonging to the realm of history, which can be studied using the historian's tools. In fact, much of what has been said above is indeed agreed upon by most scholars as "historical." There is not one serious scholar today who doubts the fact that a man by the name of Jesus did come from the Galilee, had a following of disciples, and was crucified by the Romans in Jerusalem. Many consider other details mentioned above to be historical fact as well.

The Christ of Faith

The rest of the story belongs entirely to the domain of faith, and it is this that separates the story of the life of Jesus from the life stories of so many other individuals. One must remember, though, that for believing Christians, the continuation of the story is as true and as essential as its previous parts. In fact, it is even more crucial: it is this part that created Christianity.

The details of the events are not identical in all four Gospels, but to a certain degree it is possible to present a simplified summary of them as follows: On Sunday morning, the third day after his death, women arriving to anoint Jesus' body with oil and ready it for burial discovered it missing. Some of the Gospels tell of a mysterious figure that related to them that Jesus had risen from the dead. He appeared to some of his disciples alive, sent his disciples to spread the news of his resurrection, and instructed them to baptize people in the name of the Father, the Son, and the Holy Spirit.[6] According to the beginning of the Acts of the Apostles, the book that continues to detail the lives of the disciples after the crucifixion, and which most probably comes from the same author of the Gospel of Luke, Jesus remained on earth for forty days, appeared to (some of) his disciples, and then ascended to Heaven,[7] where he continues to abide. Jesus was not only a man, a teacher, and a mentor, his disciples realized. He was something entirely different from anything they ever knew. He was the Messiah, the "anointed one," a Hebrew word translated to Greek as *Khristós*. He had something divine in him. He was the Lord.

Consolidation of Christian Communities

Ten days later, on the fiftieth day after the crucifixion, during the Jewish "Festival of Weeks" (*Shavu'ot*), which from a certain period was considered in Jewish tradition as the day of Godly revelation and the Giving of the Law to Moses, Jesus' disciples, or at least a number of them, gathered together in Jerusalem. The Spirit descended upon them, according to the New Testament book known as "Acts of the Apostles,"[8] and the community of believers was formed. They began adding new members to their ranks. Being Jews themselves, they turned first to Jews. Some of them nevertheless allowed members of other ethnic and religious groups to join as well. So as to "stop troubling the Gentiles who turn to God," they did not require circumcision of the males, a customary act among Jews and other groups, but which was considered unsightly in the eyes of many other peoples. They also did not demand fulfillment of the Mosaic Law in its entirety, but were satisfied with observance of some basic prohibitions, as well as, of course, faith.[9]

The lives of the first Christians were not easy. Jewish leaders in Palestine and the Diaspora made an effort and often succeeded at driving them from the midst of Jewish congregations. This was one of the reasons that Christians were defined by many peoples in the Roman Empire as believers in a new and strange faith and not as Jews. This status was a very troublesome one in a world that greatly respected ancient traditions. At times the Christians suffered violent persecutions, which were initially local, but after the mid-third century became more common;[10] at other times they were able to live in relative peace. They developed a broad network of communication between their various communities, defined their beliefs, and established their own methods of worship. The growth of these communities amid the Greek and Roman cultural traditions greatly influenced the terminology and ways of thinking they adopted, the customs they created, and the theologies they developed.

In the first centuries after the death—and according to Christian belief, the resurrection—of Jesus, the Mediterranean was engulfed by Christian communities. Despite the variedness within these communities/churches, at the end of the second century it was already clear to those observing the Christians from afar that there was one particular dominant Christian group: one "great Church," more or less, which was surrounded by many small groups. Among this "great Church's" characteristics were a particular hierarchical structure, an increasing trend towards uniformity in belief and practice, and the formation of a canon of sacred texts, among them the four Gospels we know today. Moreover, this "great Church," unlike many other Christian groups of the time—some of whom also had their own canon of books—considered the Jewish Scriptures as sacred, and the God of the Jews, described in these Scriptures, as the one only true and good God. Obviously, each group and sub-group considered itself to be following the right path, others being errant and even heretical. But in general, no one group had the power to force its views upon another.

The believers in Jesus lived in this way within their various groups up to the fourth century, when, as a result of a series of quite surprising events, the mainstream transformed from a persecuted religion to a tolerated one, and then from a tolerated religion to the official religion of the Roman Empire. These events transpired as a result of the support of a number of emperors, especially Constantine.[11] The communal nature, decentralization, and diversity of the Christian churches were restricted. The faction within the great Church, to which one or another emperor was predisposed, was considered "catholic," in other words universal, as well as "orthodox," meaning that it followed the true path. Whoever did not agree to the theology of this flexible "mainstream" was deemed a heretic according to imperial law. With imperial backing, the Christian faith set out on a process that was never perfected or completed, of paring down the differences among its divergent strains. Perhaps the most crucial in this process was the Council of Nicaea that convened in 325, in which the core of the Christian creed, accepted to this day and discussed at length later in this book,[12] was formulated.

The Middle Ages

The Middle Ages were a time of great development and change for the Christian faith. Some of these changes included additional formal splits between different Churches. Intellectually speaking, the great number of authors known as "Church Fathers," who were active between the late first and the early eighth century[13] in both the western parts and eastern parts of the (former) Roman Empire, shaped Christian doctrine. Their works are, to this day, at the background of all theological discussions.

In two councils that convened in the fifth century—in 431 in Ephesus and in 451 in Chalcedon (ancient cities in what is today Turkey)—theological debates about the nature of Jesus resulted in divisions, the repercussions of which are still being felt today. These seemingly pointed rifts were not only significant in and of themselves in the history of Christian theology, but also perhaps hinted at things to come: the anticipated break between East and West (even though this later division was not directly related to these earlier debates), and the fact that the political division of the Roman Empire into eastern and western parts already in the late third century was probably the moment when the division of the Church was started.

The religious division between East and West became clear as well as official in the eleventh century. Generally, the date given for this final split is 1054, but in fact it occurred in stages over a long period of time, beginning before and continuing after the date cited above. In that year, papal envoys excommunicated (or in other words declared to be outside of the Christian fold) the Patriarch of Constantinople as well as others in his retinue. In response, the Patriarch and his men excommunicated the papal envoys.[14] This ultimately led to a schism in the Christian world, though at the time many still thought that the situation could be mended quickly. The Christian communities in the eastern parts of the European continent and western parts of Asia, some of which were led in one fashion or another by the Patriarch of Constantinople,[15] continued to call themselves "Orthodox," those in possession of the true belief as well as the true worship. Before this break, they had called themselves thus in order to differentiate themselves from those they thought were in error. Now the name had come to empha-size their segregation from the Western, "Roman" Church, which was under the leadership of the Bishop of Rome. If, up to this point, some of the popes in Rome had thought, at least in principle, that the East saw in them the ultimate authority (something that was never true), it had now become clear to all that the Bishop of Rome was the de facto authority at the most of what had once been considered the western part of the Roman Empire. With the passing of a few hundred years, around the seventeenth century the concepts of "Catholic" and "Orthodox" more than any other terms car-ried the socioreligious meaning they have to this day.

These divisions are obviously only one aspect of medieval Christianity. During the Middle Ages, all the core elements that are associated today with many Christian groups came to existence: the creation of monas-tic life, the arrangement of the hierarchy, the complicated relationship between Church and State, Christian spirituality, Christian liturgy,[16] mas-terpieces of Christian thought and art, Christian architecture, and much more. The term "The Dark Ages," a term invented during the Renaissance and not used anymore by scholars, is quite distant from the medieval reality: life in the Middle Ages was definitely not easy for many, but the amount of creativity of all kinds during that time remains astonishing. The Middle Ages were not particularly "darker" than any other period of human history.

The Protestant Churches

Another major schism, this time in the West, began in the sixteenth cen-tury with the Reformation. The ideas of Luther, Calvin, Zwingli, and oth-ers, along with particularly complex political circumstances, brought about the creation and incorporation of separate Christian groups. Even if they did not necessarily intend so at the outset, these groups eventually rejected papal authority as well as many other features of the Catholic Church, such as the importance of priests and sacraments, centralization of power, and the existence of a single body responsible for establishing religious direc-tives. For both political and social reasons, the contemporary popes could not suppress the rising rebellion this time, as they had many times before. Later, those "rebels" would call themselves "Protestants": those who protested against the decisions of an assembly, a "Diet," convened in 1529 in Speyer, Germany, and which tried to halt the movement. Among the identifying characteristics of these Protestants one can find an emphasis on the centrality of the Scriptures for the individual believer, use of the vernacular in ritual, creation of a more flexible hierarchical system, rejection of rituals for which there is no basis in Scriptures, and refusal of loyalty to the Bishop of Rome.

Definitions of Christian Groups

From the moment this split became relatively clear and stable, we can speak about Catholics and Catholicism, leaving aside all other Christian groups that are not at the center of this book. It might be good to explain the terms used today when referring to Christian groups in general. It is customary to speak of three large groups in the Christian world of our times, this despite the variety within the Orthodox world, and despite the even more inclusive nature of the term "Protestant." Many varied groups came into being during the divisions of the sixteenth century, as well as during further splits that took place in the centuries that followed. Among these groups we may count the Lutherans, Calvinists, Anglicans, Presbyterians, Methodists, Baptists, and others. Thus the meaning of the term "Protestant" generally refers to all Christians who are neither Orthodox nor Catholics, and whose Church structure was conceived and designed in the last five hundred years. Some of these Churches came about from groups that branched off from the "classic" Protestant Churches. Today, one criterion used by some to distinguish between the vast numbers of these Christian groups is their liturgical structure. According to this division, "Liturgical Protestants" perform elaborate liturgical ceremonies during which specific dress is used by their clergy. "Non-Liturgical Protestants" espouse individual prayer and avoid formal, liturgical ceremonies (as well as, for some, formal clergy). There are many similarities between the first group (which includes Lutherans, Anglicans, Episcopalians,[17] and Methodists, among others) and Catholics, sometimes even more than things in common between them and "Non-Liturgical Protestants" (such as Baptists, Evangelicals, and Pentecostals, among others). One should also bear in mind that the three-way division does not take into account various ancient Churches, as for example the Coptic and the non-Catholic Syrian Churches, which split off at a very early stage from the other great Churches. These Churches, despite their theological and historical importance, are relatively small today. For this reason they receive little treatment in this book as well as in the global public discourse about Christianity. A growing number of Christian individuals and Christian Churches today declare themselves to be unaffiliated with any "denomination," and say they are "just Christians, following Jesus Christ." In reality though, the overwhelming majority of these Churches and their members can be counted as Non-Liturgical Protestants, similar in many ways to Baptists, Evangelicals, and Pentecostals.

Catholics in the Modern World

The Catholic Church was greatly shaken in the wake of the Protestant Reformation. Its leaders went on to define their faith, ritual, and laws to a degree of detail that was previously unheard of. They carried out this task mainly during the Council of Trent, which convened in the sixteenth century, but were further assisted by many powerful popes in the generations that followed. The "Counter-Reformation," or as some prefer to call it, the "Catholic Reformation," triggered as a reaction to the Reformation, was a time of new creativity, new Orders, renewed evangelization, improvement of education of clergy, building new churches, and renewed modes of spirituality and piety. When in the eighteenth century colonializing processes intensified and the Spanish and Portuguese empires expanded their control over growing areas with non-Christian populations, the Catholic Church, through its missionaries, was busy in spreading its gospel to these new recipients, whether they were interested in it or not. At the same time, the Church had to struggle with loss of power in Europe, culminating with the French revolution and the death of a pope under arrest by Napoleon's troops in 1799.

The First and Second Vatican Councils

The first major meeting of the Catholic hierarchy in the modern period was in 1869–1870, at a Council that took place in Rome in the Vatican. That Council became known as the "The Vatican Council," and later "The First Vatican Council." For various reasons, including the fact that it was suspended without ever concluding due to a war that erupted between France and Prussia, its output was limited, although not without impact.[18] The Council that followed it almost a hundred years later was by far more comprehensive.

The Second Vatican Council, also called Vatican II, was a meeting of the vast majority of Catholic Bishops and male Superiors of Catholic religious Orders, which convened in Rome during the 1960s. Without doubt, it was the most significant event in the history of the Catholic Church in the modern era.[19]

The Council's gathering was closely connected with pope John XXIII (and since April 2014, "pope Saint John XXIII"), born as Angelo Giuseppe Roncalli. In January 1959, three months after his election, pope John XXIII declared his intention to convene an ecumenical[20] council. He wanted this council to do what he referred to, in Italian, as an "*Aggiornamento,*" or updating, of the Church. After three years of preparation, on the 11th of October, 1962, in a festive ceremony in the Basilica of Saint Peter in the Vatican, the council officially opened. Around 2,500 Bishops and male heads of Orders from around the world were present at the ceremony. From among them, about 130 represented Eastern Catholic Churches. For the first time in history, a Council effectively included representatives from around the globe: more than 1,000 from Europe, 500 from South America, 400 from North America, 400 from Asia, and almost 300 from Africa. A historian by training, pope John XXIII attacked in his opening address those "prophets of doom," who always asserted that the past was far better and that the future portended disaster. He called for optimism and belief that the future holds the promise of good. For him the goal of the Council was to spread the Christian gospel to humankind, and not to deal with legal intricacies of doctrine. Even if the substance of the faith was preserved, how it was presented could, and perhaps must, change. The Church must avoid criticism of the bad and, rather, praise the good. It must forge a new path that would bring about peace between Christians as well as unity and peace for the world over.

The pope's words caused a sensation among those gathered: for some it was a pleasant surprise. In others it awoke deep suspicion. And indeed, already in the Council's first days it became clear that it was possible to divide most of the "Council Fathers" into two groups: the so-called "conservative group" that wanted to avoid far-reaching changes and sought to reinforce most of the Church's existing doctrines and practices, and the so-called "progressive group" that sought for the Council to set "pastoral" considerations as its priority. In other words, the decisions needed to aid in leading and counseling the believers. The fact that most members of the Council belonged to the "progressive" camp was also patently clear.[21]

The Council convened for four sessions, each lasting for a period of two months during the autumns of the 1962, 1963, 1964, and 1965. Pope John XXIII died shortly after the first session, but Cardinal Giovanni Battista Montini of Milan, who was elected the next pope, choosing the name Paul VI, immediately made the decision to continue the Council. Paul VI effectively steered the direction of the Council in its last three sessions, during which its decisions were formulated and promulgated.

The Council's decisions were, to a great extent, the prelude to many more changes that were to take place in the Catholic Church over the next decades.

Without delving into the contents of the sixteen documents promulgated by the Council,[22] it is probably fair to characterize them as displaying relative openness, optimism, flexibility, and permissibility of various types of changes in the life of the Church.

The greater part of Catholics living today did not know the Church before the Second Vatican Council. With the exception of historians, only a small portion of them are aware that Catholic culture was very different before the mid-twentieth century, and that things they take for granted today were not always so. The Council was accepted. Its decisions, at least in general terms, became the norm for the Church at the end of the second millennium and at the dawn of the third. For most Catholics, and, as far as they are concerned, rightly so, contemporary Catholicism is the natural and normal Catholicism. It is this Catholicism, for which the Second Vatican Council is a distant history, or at the very least is fading into the distant past, that this book addresses.

Notes

1. One can, at times, hear a small but vocal group that claims Jesus of Nazareth did not exist at all, that Jesus is a myth. Those defending this position are generally referred to as "Mythicists." One should know that this opinion is not accepted by any serious scholar today, and can be catalogued together with pseudo-scientific objections to other topics such as evolution and global warming. Serious scholars of the field, whether believers or not, have no doubt that a man names Jesus, regarding which early Christians speak, existed. As explained, though, this affirmation does not include a belief in any of his supposed superhuman qualities. For more on this issue, see Bart D. Ehrman, *Did Jesus Exist? The Historical Argument for Jesus of Nazareth* (New York: HarperOne, 2013).
2. Compare Matthew 2:1; Mark 1:9; Luke 2.
3. See, for example, Micah 6:1.
4. See Luke 3:23.
5. For two good introductions to the New Testament, see Raymond E. Brown, *An Introduction to the New Testament* (New York: Doubleday, 1997); Bart D. Ehrman, *A Brief Introduction to the New Testament* (New York: Oxford University Press, 2004).
6. See Matthew 28; Mark 16 (verses 9–20, which end the Gospel of Mark, are apparently of later origin); Luke 24; John 20–21.
7. According to Mark, or at least according to its current ending, Jesus' ascension took place close to his resurrection. See Mark 16:19.
8. Acts 2.
9. Acts 15:1–21; See also Galatians 2.
10. For a recent book highlighting that despite common perceptions propagated for centuries by the Church, the persecutions were in reality relatively rare and generally less horrendous than commonly believed, see Candida Moss, *The Myth of Persecution: How Early Christians Invented a Story of Martyrdom* (New York: HarperOne, 2013).
11. 272–337 CE.
12. See pp. 36–40.
13. This time frame is the one generally used in Western Churches. In the east, there is no clear "ending point" for the Church Fathers, and even contemporary authors and saints can enjoy this title.

14. On the annulment of these excommunications, see p. 222.
15. The three other Patriarchates that became part of the East, of Jerusalem, Antioch, and Alexandria, were already extremely weakened at the time due to internal schisms and other political factors.
16. The word "Liturgy" comes a combination of two Greek words, which mean together "Public Work." Later, it came to designate religious public worship. Today, it is generally used to refer to fixed religious systems of prayers.
17. The Episcopalian Church is the American faction of the Anglican Church (or "Communion"). I include both among the liturgical Protestant Churches even though there are some who would say that even their inclusion among Protestant Churches in general is problematic. Even more than the other groups mentioned, the Church of England's founding is connected, at least in its very beginning, to a historical-political confrontation with the Catholic hierarchy in Rome, and had initially slightly less to do with ideological-theological debates like those that brought about the creation of many of the other groups.
18. See a discussion of one of its most important decisions, in pp. 73–74.
19. The sheer amount of scholarly literature about the Council will make any bibliographical list lacking. The following short list begins with undoubtedly the most comprehensive work (in five volumes) on the topic in English, followed by a few other works of special interest or particular usefulness. The last four works mentioned in this list (by Wiltgen, McInerny, Lamb and Levering, and Marchetto) are, to some extent, examples of a certain current in the interpretation of the council that objects to the "narrative" of the first books listed below, considering it erroneous and at times marked by liberal agenda: Giuseppe Alberigo and Joseph A. Komonchak, eds., *History of Vatican II*, 5 volumes (Maryknoll-Leuven: Orbis-Peeters, 1995–2001); Xavier Rynne (Francis X. Murphy), *Vatican Council II* (1963–1966; reprint, Maryknoll: Orbis Books, 1999); Giuseppe Alberigo, *A Brief History of Vatican II* (Maryknoll: Orbis Books, 2006); Edward P. Hahnenberg, *A Concise Guide to the Documents of Vatican II* (Cincinnati: St. Anthony Messenger Press, 2007); Melissa J. Wilde, *Vatican II: A Sociological Analysis of Religious Change* (Princeton: Princeton University Press, 2007); John W. O'Malley, *What Happened at Vatican II* (Cambridge: Harvard University Press, 2008); Ralph M. Wiltgen, *The Rhine Flows into The Tiber: A History of Vatican II* (1967; reprint, Illinois: TAN, 1985); Ralph M. McInerny, *What Went Wrong with Vatican II: The Catholic Crisis Explained* (Manchester: Sophia Institute Press, 1998); Matthew L. Lamb and Matthew Levering, eds., *Vatican II: Renewal Within Tradition* (New York: Oxford University Press, 2008); Agostino Marchetto, *The Second Vatican Ecumenical Council: A Counterpoint for the History of the Council*, trans. Kenneth D. Whitehead (Scranton: University of Scranton Press, 2009).
20. In the sense of "universal," one that includes Catholic bishops of all nations and continents.
21. This reality enables careful scholars of the Council to use two objective, non-judgmental terms to describe these groups, by calling one "the majority" and the other "the minority."
22. All these texts are easily available online in several languages. In print, a rather readable edition in English is Austin Flannery, ed., *Vatican Council II, The Basic Sixteen Documents: Constitutions, Decrees, Declarations: A Completely Revised Translation in Inclusive Language* (Dublin: Dominican Publications, 1996).

relative peace within Catholicism's walls. In only the most extreme instances will Catholics engage in doctrinal confrontations or dispute issues related to the celebration of particular rituals without capitulating. This tendency to compromise at some point stems, among other things, from Catholicism's inherent flexibility. The Catholic legal system, its "Canon Law,"[2] is intentionally cushioned with clauses that permit flexibility in "special circumstances" and when there is a "particular need." One might say that the Catholic Church's ability to accommodate is an important factor in its universal appeal, and at the same time a result of that universality. This flexibility has allowed Catholicism to integrate itself into many cultures and for a long time has made its steady growth possible through the addition of new members to its ranks. The vast combination of cultures that are incorporated into the Catholic totality obliges, or some would say gives the great gift to, the Catholic faith and the community that holds it to be able to accept internal diversity.

Sensuality

The Catholic religion is a very "sensual" one, one that uses the physical senses in a particularly powerful way. Of course, it is not the only faith about which this may be said, but it is, it seems, one of the most apparent ones. Scholars of Catholicism will say that this is yet another aspect of belief in the Incarnation:[3] God can be found in this world. The faithful Catholic meets the Divine and Transcendent through the sense of sight: in Catholic architecture, in countless works of art, in gestures performed by those around him or her, in the light of candles, in the changing colors used in ceremonies throughout the liturgical year, in the varied vestments worn by the clergy, in the sculptures and decorations that adorn the churches, and in many other ways. The sense of smell is no less palpable. It is triggered through the use of incense at festive Masses and by scented anointing oil used in various rituals. The centrality of the sense of taste need not be elaborated on: the center of the Catholic adherent's religious experience is the eating and drinking of the bread and wine, whose essences were transformed during the Mass, according to Catholic belief, into the body and blood of Christ. The sense of hearing, aroused through the saying of prayers, the listening to sermons, the hearing of sacral music, and the ringing of bells, aids the believer in his or her spiritual quest. Using the sense of touch to caress the cross, stroke the sculpted image of a saint, take the communion wafer, or handle a string of rosary beads, the Catholic faithful is able to feel proximity to God, God's servants, and God's emissaries. Reliance upon the senses is so central to Catholicism that it is no wonder that the creation of works of art whose purpose is to elevate the soul has in it a religious significance. Unquestionably, Western art would not be the same had it not been supported and encouraged and, yes, sometimes also censored by the Catholic Church.

The World through Catholic Eyes

Just like a soccer fan might know the world through teams he or she admires, or a wine connoisseur through recognizing famous wine-producing regions, Catholics might also have a unique geographical perspective. The world for a committed Catholic is divided into dioceses, with cities and neighborhoods separated into parishes. The parish, or local congregation, is often named after the church at its center. At times, an entire neighborhood may be referred to by a parish church's name long after the church has ceased to play a major role in the community. At times the local church determines not only a neighborhood's name but also its daily routine. For generations, the sounding of the church bells marked the time of day for both public and private events, signaling to everyone festivities and disasters, hope and danger.

If Catholic geography is strongly influenced by the principles of the Church's structure, so is its demography. Not only is there a difference between Catholics and non-Catholics, but there are also many significant distinctions among Catholics themselves. A Church member can be a layperson or ordained, or belong to an Institute of Consecrated Life; the member may live in a bustling city or an isolated monastery. He or she can have tremendous authority and power or follow the orders of others as a way of life. For this reason, a Catholic might perceive another Catholic in a way that is entirely different from how an individual would from outside the Church, who is unaware of these finer points.

A Catholic knows that many of life's needs may be satisfied by institutions created by members of his or her Church: clinics and hospitals, kindergartens and schools, universities, community centers, nursing homes, and cemeteries. For Catholics, if they wish, being in a Catholic environment can extend well beyond the time spent in a church for worship.

Catholicism is a universal religion both idealistically and concretely. Catholics belong to almost every culture and language, and the Catholic religion does not see itself as bound by the borders that separate peoples and countries. Clearly, a Catholic can harbor strong nationalist feelings, especially if the opposing side is not Catholic, but eventually even the most nationalist of Catholics will come to realize that the borders of their religion are not equivalent to the borders of their country.

Church as Family

A strong communal feeling pervades the Catholic Church. Catholics can move from place to place, from country to country, and almost always find a church where, even if the language is unfamiliar, many would say they "feel at home." No matter where they happen to be, a Catholic can join the Lord's Supper and feel a part of a family. The prayers will be the same as those recited in their local church, even if they are spoken in another language. This applies also to readings from Scriptures: because Catholics the world over follow the same order of weekly readings, Catholic visitors to a church in a foreign country can always follow them in their own language and understand what is being read. At the same time, while Catholics may in some sense feel at home in any Catholic church in the world, they will also notice great differences. At times, especially because the visitors might not expect them, thinking that Catholicism is the same everywhere, these differences might surprise guests: after all, the sounds, visual art, dress, and behavior of the priest and community in a German, Brazilian, or Ghanan church are likely to be very different. This is also why Catholics are likely at the same time to feel a particularly strong bond to their own parish church. The parish is where one's children are baptized, where one participates in religious services, and also, perhaps, where one takes part in social activities. It might also be the place where one's ancestors are buried. The parish might be, for a Catholic, a microcosm of the universal Church, and the place where the fact of one's being a part of the world Church is made tangible.

Historical Sentiment

Many Catholics feel, understandably so, that they are part of a long and enduring history. Ancient traditions, some hundreds of years old or more, have been passed down in their Church from one generation to the next, and it is their duty to preserve the essence of these traditions and pass them on to the next generation. By doing this, they become part of a long Tradition. Catholics with a sense of knowledge about the Church's long history are likely also to be aware that belonging to such an ancient group brings a certain responsibility to apologize for some deeds of the past, improve the present, and build toward the future.

The Reality Beyond

For the believing Catholic, the notion of the afterlife is incontrovertible and has an effect on life in the here and now. The ability of the dead to assist those still alive is also irrefutable. Deceased family members, friends, and especially saints are with the faithful Catholic when he or she wants them to be. Of course, a great variety of attitudes exist on this point as well, ranging from those who think about such things daily, to those for whom it is an abstract idea of little impact on life. Among all those who are no longer in this earthly world, the Virgin Mary, mother of Jesus, mother of God, is the most important. It is to her that many Catholics turn in times of trouble and in times of joy, sometimes even more frequently than they would turn to her son.

For the Catholic, liturgical acts reflect the reality of, as well as form a bridge to, a world beyond this one. They are not symbols whose effectiveness is solely dependent upon the believer's sentiment; they carry mystical meaning and true power. The Catholic faith sees no conflict between this and its self-perception as a faith that attaches great importance to reason. Catholic theologians are likely to say that reason is meant to explain and assist faith in becoming a steadying and stabilizing force. Even if the average Catholic cannot explain all of his or her deeds or beliefs, he or she is likely to believe that the rational factor in his or her faith is particularly central; for example, in the fact that Catholics take into consideration the laws of nature and do not ascribe every occurrence to a direct divine interference. Obviously, outsiders to the faith might see things differently.

Hierarchy

Many religions have a hierarchical structure of some kind, but the Catholic one is particularly stable and old. This fact has great importance: not only does this time-tested stability make this structure seem obvious and natural for Catholics, but also it is thanks to this hierarchy, Catholics will say, that basic doctrinal stability, the "Deposit of Faith," has been continually upheld in the Church, despite currents that have tried to steer the Catholic boat in one direction or another. The pope stands at the head of this system, and the eyes of all Catholics turn to him. Whether they also listen to his words, however, is a different question.

Fractions and Diversity

The fact that the Catholic Church is so big and found in almost every place and culture brings with it a remarkable diversity of opinions, expectations, sensitivities, and assumptions. As with all human groups, when one watches carefully, one can find significant variations and disagreements between Catholics on issues such as doctrine, ideology, social outlook, liturgy, relation to the papacy, and many others. Some Catholics might fight fiercely, sometimes even mercilessly, over some of these topics because they feel they are crucial for their faith and religious life, or even because the alternative option might seem to them heretical. Our current tendency to bifurcate political actors and even entire populations between right and left, liberals (or progressives) and conservatives, seems to also be useful when discussing Catholicism. Though such a stark division is not perfect, and no doubt many objections and counter-examples can be raised against this model, it nevertheless contains some element of truth and is a useful tool for understanding such large and complex issues, as long as one remembers that it also has its limitations.

If we artificially divide Catholics into two groups, what should we call each of them? Many of those that others dub "Conservatives" do not appreciate the title. Some of those called "Liberals," likewise, do not embrace the label. Still, these terms seem to convey a certain ideological reality. Regardless of titles, two broad camps can easily be identified by, for example, the vocabulary they commonly share. Those commonly called "Conservatives" or "Traditionalists" will often speak about loyalty to the popes (more precisely, to popes such as Paul VI, John Paul II, and Benedict XVI, who were considered allies of conservative Catholics) and the higher hierarchy, the "Magisterium." They will often mention the Virgin Mary, The Holy Spirit, "family values," and what they see as "Catholic tradition." Those on the other side, the "Liberals" or "Progressives," might speak about "The Spirit of Vatican II," pope John XXIII, social action and justice, feminism, and the laity. Since the rise of pope Francis in 2013, they do something they did not do for decades: they align themselves again with the pope. These two groups, which can easily be subdivided into smaller groups themselves, have very different opinions on almost any topic at hand. Still, both will proudly define themselves as Catholic.

Unity

Even if bitter struggles arise between various Catholic groups—and they certainly do, as hinted above—these do not negate the basic unity that is at the heart of the Catholic mentality. No wonder, then, that the expression "Unity-in-diversity" is often used in the Church. It is extremely rare for a group of Catholics to leave the Church as a group and form another church (or Church). This, of course, does not mean that individuals do not leave the Church. In fact, the number of people worldwide who describe themselves as "ex-Catholics" is extremely high, and some of them join other Christian groups. And yet, splitting off and forming a new community that would no longer defer to the supreme hierarchy is not a possibility that the immense majority of Catholics would consider. For this very reason, a Catholic will never deny that within the Church there are and always have been sinners as well as saints, those with views they agree with and others with views they disagree with. The Church is big, and is not an exclusive club. The requirements for membership in it are minimal. Both the average Catholic and the professional theologian would probably say this is for the best.

Holy Days and Prayers

The daily life of a practicing Catholic is tied to a rather complex calendar. This calendar includes not only special feast days, but also longer periods that revolve around a specific event or theme. These may reflect sadness and penitence or joy and anticipation. The more one is involved in the life of the Church, the more special days there are to observe in the calendar year. If one were to mark every festival that the Church celebrates, the entire year would become a succession of days filled with religious significance of one kind or another.

A Catholic worshipper can conduct his or her prayers using texts that were composed hundreds and even thousands of years ago, such as the book of Psalms, which continues to be for many Christians and Jews a source of inspiration and prayer. Catholics also make use of prayers found in the New Testament and in early and later Christian sources. In many cases though, the texts used were arranged and sanctioned by the local or universal hierarchy. Catholics may also compose their own prayers and use them in personal or communal worship. In addition, Catholics occasionally venerate in silence. Any Catholic will argue that such a prayer is certainly not without power. Silent prayer is just one aspect, albeit an important one, of a larger system of mysticism that forms a key part of the Catholic faith.

Sin and Forgiveness

Though Catholics view the world and human nature as essentially good, they acknowledge that the world is far from perfection, and that humans are flawed. All humans, lay or clergy, saints or serial sinners, may sin: the only one who did not was Jesus himself (and according to many theologians, his mother as well). But not all sins are equal. Some are considered "Mortal Sins." Such a sin is, in Catholic eyes, a sin that separates the sinner from God and destroys the new life and grace that the person has received through baptism and other sacraments. It causes the sinner's soul to become mortal, and may prevent its eternal salvation after death. If a person dies having knowingly and intentionally committed a mortal sin that was not absolved sacramentally or by real repentance ("perfect contrition"), he or she might not be saved, but rather damned for eternity. Some of the sins that are considered mortal, or grave, are social in nature: for example, homicide. Others might have a more spiritual nature, for example, rejection of God. Still, the Catholic Church teaches that God is the final judge on the matter, and that God may treat even sinners with grace. "Venial Sins" are less grave sins. They will not prevent salvation, but they can distance the person from God, might be punishable in purgatory, and might lead the person to other more severe sins. One should therefore also repent for them. The Catholic list of the "Seven Deadly Sins"—pride, greed, envy, wrath, lust, gluttony, and sloth—is rather famous. These seven categories are supposed to help classify sins, and thus encourage one to repent and avoid repeating them. A sin that falls into one of these categories is not necessarily mortal.

Even though Catholics may worry about committing sins, Catholicism has in it a strong optimistic side, mainly due to the Church's belief in forgiveness. Even if prayer is not enough and evil inclination overpowers good, there is still hope. Sinning is not taken lightly; it requires remorse, atonement, and self-examination. But no sin is so great that it can cancel out a better future and salvation. Repentance is always possible, and if contrition is true and sincere, the sin can always be absolved.[4]

Law and Order

The Catholic Church, as any association uniting people, needs a system of laws. In the first decades after the crucifixion of Jesus, Jesus' followers were in need of rules regarding membership in the community, appointment of positions within it, and judgment of members who deviated from the prescribed path. Most of the laws in these first centuries were the result of local circumstances, formulated at gatherings of Church leaders. In the fifth and sixth centuries, various authors began assembling these laws along with relevant quotes from the writings of Church Fathers. These activities formed the basis of the Church's legal system, to which sections were added over the centuries, including laws promulgated by popes. From the eleventh century, Catholic Church law has been called "Canon Law," a term that is based on the combination of two Greek words: *kanon*, meaning measure, which accounted for the rules of the Church, and *nomos* meaning law, which indicated the secular laws. Together the words formed the Greek term *nomokanones*, or the Latin *iuris canonici*, from which the modern term is gleaned. The twelfth century is generally considered to be the time when Canon Law came into being as a specific area of intellectual pursuit and professional specialization. This was the period when "canonists," experts on Canon Law, began assembling commentaries on an organized systematic compilation of laws that had been published around 1140 in Bologna by a legal expert by the name of Gratian.[5] From then on, Canon Law continued to develop. The official version of the law in effect today was published in 1983 (the version of the law that was previously in use dates back to 1917). The official version is in Latin, but translations are available in many languages, including English. Although the expression "Canon Law" is used also by Orthodox and Anglican Christians, in this book it refers to Catholic Church law (even more specifically, to the law of the Latin, Occidental, Catholic Church).[6]

Catholics often have complex relations with their Canon Law. To begin with, most Catholics are not even aware of it and are oblivious to the fact that it is this law that regulates the rituals they participate in, the way their parish and diocese are run, the validity (or not) of their marriages, the selling of buildings that used to host their parish's school, or the acquisition of land where they can bury their dead. They might become aware of Canon Law only when problems arise: for example if they have a serious dispute with a parish priest, if they get divorced, or if financial acts of their bishop create an uproar in the diocese. Because of ancient and culturally ingrained Christian concepts that define "law" as the opposite of "spirit," most Catholics tend to find the very idea that their Church has a legal system disturbing. Experts of Canon Law have to continuously struggle with their own knowledge that without a clear legal system the enormous Catholic Church would not be able to function, and the fact that most Catholics do not think this law is important in their religious lives.

Salvation

The concept of Salvation exists in many religions, although its actual meaning might differ significantly. For Christians, salvation consists of being protected from sin and uniting with God, in very different ways, during one's lifetime and following one's death. In the Catholic understanding, salvation is a process, not an event. A person can never be assured of being saved or damned. A person can hope, though, that God will save him or her, and that his or her faith and deeds will play a part in this. For Catholics, salvation has also a communal aspect and ideally happens by being part of the Church. For this reason, discussions about individual salvation and the necessity of having a personal relation with Christ are not very common among Catholics. Catholics would also generally not say with certainty that one is going to be saved or damned.

Social Thought

Often, the ironic phrase "The Church's best-kept secret" is evoked when the Catholic Church's stances on social issues are mentioned. This joke highlights the fact that the Catholic Church has developed a comprehensive teaching on social justice but has been less successful in publicizing this issue, especially when compared to its success in asserting its position on issues such as contraception, gay marriage, and abortion. This situation is likely to change in the near future, especially with the 2013 election of a pope who sees social issues as the most important challenges for the Church and for humanity. It is likely that this core of teaching, which is based on earlier notions but which the Church began to systematically elaborate towards the end of the nineteenth century (and which was thoroughly developed in the following decades, including at the Second Council of the Vatican), will gain more prominence.[7] At the same time, it should be noted that even if many Catholics cannot systematically articulate all the ideas that are part of Catholic social thought, many of these ideas are nevertheless a part of Catholic mentality.

Among the main principles of Catholic social teaching, one can mention the importance of human dignity and equality and the value of life from conception to natural death. Humans have the right to associate and to have their associations, beginning with the family, recognized and respected. Humans should show solidarity with one another and give particular preference to the poor and powerless. Governments in particular should assist them. Humans have the right to decent working conditions and wages. They should work for the common good, and at the same time remember that they are only keepers of the world, not its owners: the planet should be protected. Humans should be given the power to decide their own fate, and no authority of any kind should interfere if worthwhile solutions can be found at the local level by those involved. Finally, except in the most extreme cases, wars are to be avoided.

Development of Doctrine

For Catholics, doctrines of many kinds,[8] traditionally held for generations, are of extreme importance. Something that has been believed or practiced for a long time should not be disregarded or discarded easily. Decisions regarding faith are made not only by the current generation of living Catholics, but also by all Catholics in all times. If a concept has been held for a long time, many would see this as a decision made by a majority of Catholics, including those who died in past centuries. As the dead are also members of the Church, their voice should not be ignored. And yet, Catholics accept the fact that doctrines may change. Indeed, any person with a basic historical understanding would have difficulties arguing otherwise. Even the most fundamental concepts in Christianity, such as the Trinity or the nature of Christ, received clear and accepted definitions centuries after the closure of the New Testament. The Church would argue, however, that doctrines are never "invented," but rather that, with time, the Church reaches a better understanding of the basic "Deposit of Faith" that was transmitted by the Apostles of the first century CE.

Notes

1. For a somewhat different way of looking at similar issues, see Andrew Greeley, *The Catholic Imagination* (Berkeley: University of California Press, 2000).
2. To be discussed further on, pp. 28–29.
3. See pp. 39 and 96.
4. This is considered true even regarding the sin of "Blasphemy against the Holy Spirit," said in various places in the New Testament (see Mark 3:28–30 and parallels) to be an unforgiveable "Eternal Sin."
5. On Gratian, the most important work in recent years is undoubtedly Anders Winroth, *The Making of Gratian's Decretum* (Cambridge: Cambridge University Press, 2000).
6. For a good review of Canon Law, see James A. Coriden, *An Introduction to Canon Law* (New York: Paulist Press, 1991).
7. The three most important papal documents on the matter are *Rerum Novarum*, published in 1891 by pope Leo XIII, *Quadragesimo Anno*, released, as its name hints, forty years later in 1931 by pope Pius XI, and *Pacem in Terris*, published by pope John XXIII in 1963. It is still early to judge, but it is possible that a more recent encyclical, *Evangelii Gaudium*, released in 2013 by pope Francis, will be considered a part of this list by future historians.
8. On the meaning of the term "doctrine" see p. 45.

CHAPTER 2

Catholic Belief

Catholic Christianity, like many religions, combines a way of life with principles of faith. While baptism in the Church is what normally defines someone as Catholic, there are certainly those who are Catholic "in name only": those who were baptized in the Catholic Church but do not embrace even the most basic of Catholicism's principles of faith. This chapter deals with the principles of faith that those who are more than just "nominal" Catholics are supposed to hold as true.

Belief in Christ and in the Holy Scriptures

Like several other religions, not only is the basic belief that God may be revealed to humans fundamental to Christian faith, but also that such a revelation has already happened, clearly and explicitly, in precise moments in history. Christian belief espouses the revelation of God as described in the Hebrew Bible: to the Patriarchs, to the Israelites in the desert through Moses and on Mount Sinai, and to their descendents, the Jews, through the prophets. Subsequently, God revealed himself in a new and bold manner through materialization in the flesh: the Son of God, Jesus, appeared. The Word of God, the Logos, was made now flesh: it became Incarnated.[1]

Belief in Jesus and his role as savior is the central pillar of Christian faith. Except for those who see themselves as part of what is often referred to as "Liberal Christianity," most Christians would say that in order to be counted a true Christian, one must believe that there is a fundamental and essential difference between Jesus and the rest of humankind. To say that Jesus was an especially moral person, or a brilliant philosopher, or a prophet possessing great courage, or a person of pure faith, or a social rebel, is not enough. To be counted as true Christian, they would claim, one must have faith in Jesus' divinity and his abiding presence, ideas we will return to later.

Alongside faith in Jesus, central also is a belief in or a major respect for the Holy Scriptures (the actual meaning of this belief or respect differs from one Christian to another and from one denomination to another). In fact, these two tenets depend upon each other: the Scriptures transmit the message of Jesus, while Jesus is the one who sanctions, for the believer, their truth. If Jesus is one aspect of the Divine revelation, then the Holy Scriptures, written under Divine inspiration, are another.

The Christian Bible includes the Old Testament and the New Testament. The Old Testament is a collection of texts that were written originally and almost exclusively in Hebrew, most of which are included in the Jewish Bible; the New Testament includes books that were originally written in Greek. They concern the life and ministry of Jesus and the faith that developed in the generation that followed him. For Catholics, seven books (Tobit, Judith, 1 Maccabees, 2 Maccabees, The Wisdom of Solomon, Baruch, and Sirach (or "Ecclesiasticus")), all stemming from Jewish authors but not defined by Jewish tradition as part of the Holy Scriptures, are also considered part of the Old Testament, along with additional chapters from the books of Esther and Daniel. Another short text, the "Letter of Jeremiah," has in the last centuries appeared in Catholic Bibles as part of the book of Baruch. Catholics traditionally divide the Old Testament into four parts: the Books of Law (the Five Books of Moses), the Historical Books, the Books of Wisdom, and the Prophetic Books (the seven books which are part of the "apocrypha" in Jewish tradition are integrated into the last three parts).[2] Not coincidentally, the New Testament is also divided into four parts, consisting of the Gospels, the Acts of the Apostles, The Epistles, and the Book of Revelation. The four Gospels are seemingly constructed as a biography of Jesus. The first three, which share many common elements, are known as the "Synoptic Gospels": the term synoptic is borrowed from the Greek, and means "those that can be seen together." The Acts of the Apostles deals with the formation of the first communities after the death and resurrection of Jesus. The Epistles include mostly directives handed down to individuals or to newly formed Christian communities, while the Book of Revelation, an apocalyptic text, deals with future events.

According to Catholic belief, God revealed himself to humans through the Holy Scriptures, which were written by authors under the inspiration of the Holy Spirit, delivering the plan for the redemption of the world.

The Old Testament paved the way for the advent of Christ, using hints and allusions to describe his coming. After his arrival, word of it and its meaning were spread openly by the disciples he sent out and through the writings of the New Testament. The Catholic Church recognizes the fact that the authors of all the books of the Old and New Testament used the writing style and methods of their time and place, and that this aspect of Scriptures must be taken into consideration in order to properly comprehend them. For decades already, the Catholic Church has accepted all modern forms of biblical scholarship, including those labeled "Bible Criticism," and encourages application of these methods.[3] It objects to a fundamentalist reading of Scriptures, which ignores the texts' historical and cultural context and sees them as containing an absolute, literal truth. This outlook is closely connected to the Catholic view that the Scriptures are just one part of the Church's tradition (or some might say, "Tradition"), transmitted in the Church, taught by the Magisterium, and cannot be comprehended without it. It is strongly related to the idea that the Church produced the Christian Bible, and not the other way around.[4] This is why the Church is the best interpreter of it. The Catholic faithful are encouraged to situate the Scriptures within their religious life and to draw continual inspiration from them through and outside of ritual worship.

The Most Ancient Proclamations of Faith

From the very beginning of the movement, believers in Jesus formulated various proclamations of faith. In the scholarly literature, a fundamental and primary proclamation such as this is termed *kerygma,* a Greek word meaning "proclamation" or "preaching."

Various passages in the New Testament bear out that a variety of versions of short proclamations of faith were in use in the earliest communities. In the Epistle to the Romans, for example, we find this: "For if you confess with your mouth that Jesus is the Lord and believe in your heart that God has raised him from the dead, you will be saved."[5] Similarly, Paul explains to the Corinthian community:

> Now I am reminding you, brothers, of the gospel I preached to you . . . Through it you are also being saved . . . that Christ died for our sins in accordance with the Scriptures; that he was buried; that he was raised on the third day in accordance with the Scriptures; that he appeared to Cephas and then to the twelve . . . so we preach and so you believed.[6]

Second-century sources contain more complex proclamations. Some explicitly include, among others things, the Christian principle of the Trinitarian nature of God.

The Nicene Creed

The more complex (and, often, also later-dated) proclamations are customarily called *Creeds*, from the Latin word *credo* ("I believe"), which appears at the start of many proclamations.[7] These statements of belief are very effective because of the fact that, on the one hand, they can be easily memorized, and on the other hand, they offer an orderly list of the principles of the faith. The list may encourage a systematic discussion of each of the principles in the creed, but also provides clear boundaries to such a discussion. The fact that it took centuries for these creeds to be formulated, and that they do not necessarily reflect the exact understanding of Christians in earlier centuries, is admitted in Catholicism, and is considered one of the classic examples of the idea of "development of doctrine."

Today, the Catholic Church mainly makes use of two creeds, the "Nicene-Constantinopolitan Creed," (also known simply as the Nicene Creed), and the Apostles' Creed. The Nicene version was developed by two Church councils convened in the fourth century in Nicaea (325) and in Constantinople (381), both in modern-day Turkey. This creed is used not only by the Catholic Church but also by the Orthodox Churches and many Protestant Churches. If implicit use is to be counted as well, one can say it is the core doctrinal text of almost all Christian groups.

The Apostles' Creed, so it seems, was composed in stages from the second to the eighth century. There are few today who will argue that this creed is a proclamation of faith that was actually written by the first-century apostles. The name is more commonly understood as asserting that the beliefs expressed in the text are those of the Apostles. This creed is not customarily used among Orthodox Christians, even though there is nothing in it that negates the principles of the Eastern Churches.

The Nicene-Constantinopolitan Creed[8]

I believe in one God,
the Father almighty,
maker of heaven and earth,
of all things, visible and invisible.

And in one Lord Jesus Christ
the Only Begotten Son of God,
born of the Father before all ages.

God from God, Light from Light,
true God from true God,
begotten not made,
consubstantial with the Father;
through him all things were made.

For us men and for our salvation,
he came down from heaven,
and by the Holy Spirit
was incarnate of the Virgin Mary,
and became Man.

For our sake
He was crucified under Pontius Pilate,
He suffered death[9] and was buried,
And rose again on the third day,
in accordance with the Scriptures.

He ascended into Heaven and is seated
at the right hand of the Father.

He will come again in glory
To judge the living and the dead
And his kingdom will have no end.

And in the Holy Spirit, the Lord,
The giver of life, who proceeds
from the Father and the Son
is adored and glorified,
who has spoken through the prophets.

And one, holy, catholic
and apostolic Church.

I confess one baptism
for the forgiveness of sins
and I look forward to the resurrection of the dead
and the life of the world to come. Amen.

In the ancient Greek text, the Nicene-Constantinopolitan proclamation of faith appears in the plural ("We believe"), and is recited thus in the plural in Eastern Churches. In the West, it was customary to recite it in the singular, thus making it similar to the Apostles' Creed, which is always recited in the singular. In recent decades, many Catholic communities and a number of other Western Churches have often opted to use the plural form, at least in certain contexts and ceremonies, a practice that gives the creed a clearer communal aspect. Nevertheless, in recent years authorities in the Vatican have objected to this practice. This and new editions of liturgical texts caused, for now at least, the discontinuation of this use of the plural in the Catholic world.

The source of this creed dates, apparently, to the third century, but its present format dates from the fourth century. In the first quarter of the fourth century, Arius, a priest from Alexandria, claimed, along with others, that the divinity of the Son is not the same as that of the Father. The Son has a different nature. Most importantly, he is not eternal: there was a time when the Son did not exist. Countering Arius were those who argued that the Father and the Son share an identical "substance," and that the Son is eternal as is the Father. The Emperor Constantine, who had transformed the central Christian faction into a legal and even favored religion a little more than a decade earlier, convened a council in order to discuss this issue. In the end, Arius's interpretation was rejected and the view of his opponents was adopted in the creed.

The opening line of the creed takes an anti-dualistic and anti-Gnostic position: there is only one God, the maker of all things. There is no good God and bad God, or one God that creates all visible things, and another that creates the invisible. Everything that exists was created by the one and only God. This God is called "The Father." This God has but one son, Jesus, who is called "The Lord." This Son was incarnated at a certain point in history, but his existence is not bound to a specific time. He is of the same essence as the Father, and is one with him. He is God. All of creation was carried out through him, but he is not a part of creation.

The Son, the only son of the Father, descended from heaven where he abided for eternity like the Father, for the sake of humankind and its salvation: "What he was, he remained, and what he was not, he assumed," summarizes an ancient liturgical formula.

Thus, the Eternal Son of God was born of the Virgin Mary with the aid of the Holy Spirit. In other words, as many theologians will explain, the Son has no earthly father. This event in Christian theology is called the "Incarnation": the spirit entered the corporeal world and became flesh.

Jesus, a real person, suffered, died, and was buried. The Creed's situating of his crucifixion in a precise moment in history, during the first-century reign of the Roman Prefect of Judaea Pontius Pilate (whose existence is confirmed by archaeological evidence) underscores, even if it does not prove, that Jesus was a historical human figure and not a mythological being that existed in the distant and mysterious past.

Three days after he died, the creed proclaims, Jesus rose from the dead. His resurrection had been predicted; it was foretold in the Scriptures, later called the Old Testament. After his resurrection, Jesus ascended to heaven, where he sits to the right of the Father. From there, he will return in all his glory to judge those who are alive and those who are already dead.

The creed does not include any additional information about the life of Jesus, his signs, miracles, or teachings, despite the fact that by the time the creed was produced, information about Jesus' deeds and teachings, whether historical or not, was widely available through the gospels, other texts of the New Testament, and texts not included in the canon. The most probable reason for this lack was that the early Church did not treat this information as essential for the faith.

Modern-day Catholics and Protestants, while quoting the Nicene Creed, say that the Holy Spirit comes not only from the Father but also from the Son. Despite this, it is important to bear in mind that the words "and the Son" in the Nicene Creed were only added to the Latin text in the sixth century. Western theologians supported this addition, for without it, in their view, the status of Father and Son was unequal. Eastern theologians, who held fast to the Greek version of the creed, did not accept this late addendum. It thus became the source for the so-called "Filioque" controversy between the Eastern and Western Churches (the name stemming from the Latin words *filius* meaning "son" and *que* meaning "and"). Those in support of the addition strove to emphasize the likeness between the three parts of the Trinity; those who objected sought to maintain the distinction between them, as well as to not tamper with the formula that was accepted several centuries earlier.

According to Western understanding, the idea that the Holy Spirit is equal in status to the Father and the Son is reemphasized in the declaration that the Holy Spirit is also adored and glorified. The creed identifies the presence of the Holy Spirit in history in the words of the prophets, who foretold, among other things, according to Christian belief, the coming of the Son. The word "catholic" at the end of the text means "universal" (and thus should be not capitalized). It was included in the creed long before this term became an adjective used to describe a specific Christian group. Some Protestant groups use instead one of the following words: "universal," "general" or "Christian," in their translations of the creed, while others leave the word "catholic" as in the original Greek.

The creed proclaims belief in the existence of a Church that is not only universal and holy but also unique, and that is the same Church of the Apostles. Following the declaration about forgiveness of sins through baptism, the creed ends with the evocation of the events that mark the end of earthly human life: belief in the afterlife and in the resurrection of the dead. With these utterances, the believer proclaims that while physical death is indeed a major step along a person's temporal journey, it is not the final one.

The Apostles' Creed[10]

> I believe in God, the Father almighty, Creator of heaven and earth,
> and in Jesus Christ, his only Son, our Lord,
> who was conceived by the Holy Spirit,
> born of the Virgin Mary,
> suffered under Pontius Pilate,
> was crucified, died and was buried;
> he descended into hell[11];
> on the third day he rose again from the dead;
> he ascended into heaven, and is seated at the right hand
> of God the Father almighty;
> from there he will come to judge the living and the dead.
>
> I believe in the Holy Spirit,
> the holy catholic Church,
> the communion of saints,
> the forgiveness of sins,
> the resurrection of the body,
> and life everlasting.
>
> Amen.

This much shorter creed contains, one may notice, the same fundamentals of faith as the one discussed previously. It is customary to explain the belief in the "communion of saints," mentioned here, but not in the Nicene Creed, as an expression of the notion that members of the community who have died continue to be in the company of God. As the Church is one body, its members comprise both the living and the deceased.

Though without a historical foundation, an enchanting early tradition divides the text of this proclamation into twelve lines, with each line relating to one of the twelve apostles of Jesus.

The Unique Elements of the Christian Faith

To someone unaccustomed to religious convictions, most of the proclamations in the Nicene-Constantinopolitan and Apostles' Creeds will seem unusual, if not peculiar. On the other hand, to someone comfortable with certain kinds of non-Christian religious traditions but not with Christianity, many of the statements in these texts may appear familiar, even if they are not necessarily accepted as truths. Obviously, many of those who are used to Christianity might not notice anything surprising in these texts.

It is reasonable that a passage about God being "maker of heaven and earth," or the notion of the hope of "life everlasting," would not shock adherents of many faiths. Other proclamations of a historic nature, such as that Jesus suffered, was crucified, died and was buried, would most probably also not cause much of a stir. But the creeds contain more than that. For someone who is not used to Christian concepts, some of the sentences are troubling, even shocking. There are at least five statements that would be quite disturbing for people who are not Christians: that the Divine has a tripartite nature; that Jesus is the son of God; that his crucifixion was for "our" sake; that three days after his very real death and burial, he rose from the dead; that he was born of a virgin. We will now set out to explain each of these claims, within the limited scope of this chapter.

The Trinity

The notion of the Trinity is at the heart of Christian faith, and is clearly expressed in the two creeds discussed above. According to Christian doctrine, it is possible to speak of one God, and at the same time of three separate entities that are manifest and concrete. Each entity, or *persona*, as they are referred to in Latin since the early third century, possesses specific characteristics, as well as fulfilling special roles. The Father, who was not born, is the creator. The Son, the savior, was born of the Father. The Holy Spirit, which is of the Father and of the Son (or "through the Son" as Eastern Christians will say), gives life. These entities are manifest and concrete, but no single entity is a third of the Divine whole. Rather, each one is God in its entirety. According to a popular image, the Godhead is like three circles placed one on top of the other. The Father comprises the Son, and is contained in him; the Son comprises, and is contained in, the Holy Spirit; the Holy Spirit comprises, and is contained in, the Father. Humankind is redeemed by the Father, through the Son, and by the power of the Holy Spirit.

This theological doctrine—meticulously formulated in the third and fourth centuries—does not appear explicitly in the Bible, although many Christians believe it is possible to find allusions to it there. Thus, for example, Christian tradition sees the use of the plural in God's utterance in Genesis, "Let us make man in our image, after our likeness,"[12] as perfectly clear. The Divine, in which plurality was implicit, had resolved to carry out the creation of man. The ending of the passage, "in our image, after our likeness," is also endowed with great meaning and clarity in Christian exegesis. The verses about the peculiar identity of Abraham's three guests are another example. His guests are described as three mysterious visitors in some verses, and in others as the Lord himself.[13] Another example is the three repetitions of the word "Holy" in a famous verse in the book of Isaiah,[14] which served Christian theologians and liturgists as an allusion to the three entities contained within the one God.[15]

Within the pages of the New Testament are still more verses traditionally believed to allude to the Trinity. Among the most well known are the opening verses of the Gospel of John, mentioned earlier:

> In the beginning was the Word, and the Word was with God, and the Word was God . . . And the Word became flesh and made his dwelling among us, and we saw his glory, the glory as of the Father's only Son, full of grace and truth.[16]

This text indeed appears to comment on the "Word" that became flesh; that resided with God; that was God himself. Even if there is no reference to the Trinity in these passages, there is room to speak, at the very least, of a dualism. In other places in the New Testament, Jesus speaks of God as his Father,[17] the Holy Spirit is described as a separate being,[18] and the three "entities," the Father, the Son and the Holy Spirit, are described as related to one another.[19] In a retrospective view, influenced by the formulation of the idea of the Trinity in the first centuries of the first millennium, Christians find the same three entities in passages like this, which describes the baptism of Jesus:

> After all the people had been baptized and Jesus also had been baptized and was praying, heaven was opened and the Holy Spirit descended upon him in bodily form like a dove. And a voice came from heaven, "You are my beloved Son; with you I am well pleased."[20]

Formulating, and then explaining, the concept of the Trinity has always been a serious challenge for Christian theologians. They had to be careful, on the one hand, not to tread into the realm of polytheism, which is condemned in no uncertain terms in the Old Testament. On the other hand, they did not want to abandon the distinctly Christian references to the Father, the Son, and the Holy Spirit, voiced many times over in the New Testament and in other later texts.

Many Christians today will underline the dynamic rather than the static quality that is the reality of the Trinity. The Father, the Son, and the Holy

Spirit exist in a communal relationship of love. Only thus can God not only love but also through the Trinity be love itself.[21] Only by understanding the interrelationship between these entities can one learn about God's love for the world, Christians would argue. Only through the plurality of the Godhead can the Divine affect and be fundamentally involved in the world.

Not every Christian is willing or able to attempt an explanation of the intricacies used by theologians regarding the Trinity. In fact, many theologians do not delve too deeply into it nowadays, being an issue that has already been discussed for many centuries. Those who cannot fully comprehend the idea, but would still like to, can take comfort in the fact that the Trinity is ultimately a mystery. Any attempt to definitively explain it will never succeed, due to the very fact of its being, according to Christian belief, above human grasp. One is not obliged to intellectually comprehend it, most will say: living it is what counts.

Other Christological Claims

The belief that Jesus is the son of God, human and divine at the same time, is difficult to understand for people used to other monotheistic traditions, such as Judaism and Islam. Nevertheless, it is not necessarily opposed to Hebrew Scriptures. Certain texts from what Christians call the Old Testament, texts which might be obscure and perplexing to Jewish readers, become comprehensible and rich in symbolism for Christians when read through this Christian belief.[22]

The Christian tradition regards Jesus' crucifixion as an act done "for our sake." Jesus took upon himself the sins of all humankind, and his willingness to die in exchange for and in expiation of humanity's sin of disobedience to God, for which all people deserved to die, was carried out according to the Holy Scriptures that heralded it.[23] Jesus on the cross, in a certain respect, embodied the situation of all humankind: sinners who believe that God had abandoned them. But while until then animals were offered as sacrificial offerings to atone for the sins of the people in the Temple in Jerusalem, the Christian tradition claims that in the crucifixion, Jesus himself became the sacrificial lamb, the Lamb of God, the absolute and ultimate sacrifice, after which there is no need for any additional sacrifices. The atonement of sins happened.

Christian belief in Jesus' resurrection from the dead, which could be seen as similar to other biblical miracles,[24] is considered unique by Christian theology, which views this resurrection as a cosmic event. Jesus lives again, but now he lives a different existence, one that is everlasting. This is not just a miracle; this is an unprecedented event, one without parallels.

Many modern theologians and scholars recognize that the belief in Jesus' return to lead and abide with his flock was formulated through the use of language and imagery typical for the first centuries: resurrection of the body, ascension to heaven, and the like. And yet, although their awareness of the possibility that in another historical context this idea might have been phrased differently, most theologians will avoid attempting to rephrase it using more "modern" terminology, due to the great centrality of this belief in the New Testament and Christian faith. Still, many of them will insist on the core meaning and implication of this belief, which is relevant in every culture and historical context: that Jesus, who died on the cross, returned, according to the Christian faith, to lead his disciples and followers. Jesus continues to be, in a real and tangible way, with his Church for eternity.

Mary's Virginity

Many contemporary Catholic theologians may assert that belief in Mary's virginity[25] is significant mainly in order to emphasize the divine nature and uniqueness of her son, and less so with regard to the question of the bio- logical possibility of such an occurrence or the purity of a birth that was not preceded by sexual relations. Mary's virginity offers another perspective on Jesus' being the Son of God. In answer to the question of whether a virgin may, in theory, give birth, many Christians will answer in the affirmative. Of course, this is not a common event. Maybe it happened only once. But if one believes in other assertions in the Bible, such as the assertion that God could create the world, cause Sarah to give birth to Isaac at the age of ninety, or part the sea and lead the Israelites through the parted waters, then there is no reason to reject the possibility that God may also make a virgin pregnant. Especially, they might add, when the event under consideration, the Incarnation, is analogous in magnitude and meaning to the creation of the world itself.

The Creeds: Conclusions

The beliefs discussed so far, describing Jesus as the Son of God, and as a mortal human who died for the sins of humankind and rose again from the dead, inevitably remain difficult to grasp. This is not surprising, nor is it a sign of a problem with the beliefs themselves, or a fault in those who find them impenetrable. After all, they comprise a part of the heart of the Chris- tian mysteries—those elements of the faith that are not comprehensible by reason alone. For almost two thousand years, Christian theological tradi- tion has been contending with their explication, availing itself of the latest methodological and intellectual tools, always bearing in mind the changing cultural environment. Amidst all the explanations, what remains fundamental is the notion of the limitlessness of divine grace, which is bestowed benevolently without expectation of reward. Wanting to redeem humanity from the endless cycle of sinning in which it found itself, God descended into its midst. By making himself human like them, by being punished for no personal wrongdoing, and by his dying, the Son bore the sins of humankind, offering himself to the Father as a sacrifice of atonement. His resurrection prepared a new way for humanity and victory over death, which was brought about through sin. In his resurrection he returned to being a living God, in whom faith, according to Christian doctrine, redeems.[26]

Doctrines and Dogmas

Apart from the main principles of faith in the two versions of the creed studied above, Christians of various denominations adhere to additional ones. Some of these beliefs—for example, that the canonical Holy Scriptures are the main source of knowledge about God and God's relationship to humanity—are accepted by almost all Christians; other beliefs, such as in the actual existence of angels, are accepted by some Christians.[27] Some other beliefs—for example the divinely accorded supreme authority of the Bishop of Rome—are accepted only by Catholics.

Catholic beliefs (some of which, as noted, are accepted by other Churches as well) can be divided into dogmas and doctrines. Doctrine is a codification of teachings concerning principles of faith that have been officially defined by authorized powers in the Church: ecumenical councils, popes, and, according to some, even gatherings of local bishops. Dogma, on the other hand, is an established doctrine that was declared as definitive, unchangeable,[28] and that, in its essence, cannot be wrong. It may be defined by an ecumenical council of all bishops, including the pope, or by the pope himself (though today, such a thing is likely to happen, if at all, only after the pope consults with bishops around the globe), in his role as head of the earthly Church. Every dogma is a doctrine, but not every doctrine is dogma.

Two doctrines became dogmas in the nineteenth and twentieth centuries.[29] Both of them are about Mary, and will be discussed in the following sections.

The "Immaculate Conception" and the "Assumption"

In 1854, with the claimed support of the majority of bishops, pope Pius IX defined the "Immaculate Conception" as dogma. This was not a new principle, but rather the permanent anchoring of an age-old belief that had been acknowledged for generations by many theologians. Defining this doctrine as dogma brought hundreds of years of liturgical and theological arguments in favor of and against it to an end.

The dogma declares that Mary's soul was preserved from the stain of original sin. In contrast to the rest of humankind, who are in need of Christian baptism in order to remove the stain that has marred all of humanity from the time of Adam and Eve's disobedience of God's command, Mary had no need for the stain to be removed: her soul had never been blemished by it. This privilege, which no other human being had been given before her, with the exception of Adam and Eve, was owing to her being the new "Eve," the future mother of Jesus.[30]

In 1950, pope Pius XII, again supposedly with the support of the vast majority of bishops, defined a second dogma related to Mary. This dogma of the "Assumption" fixed firmly a belief that had been held since at least the sixth century (and was often depicted in Christian art): that Mary was bodily taken up into Heaven at the end of her earthly life. The dogma did not, however, unequivocally define whether Mary was already dead, or whether she was taken up while still alive, or where and when this miracle took place. A universal feast day marking Mary's Assumption, was established on the 15th of August, a date on which various events in the life of Mary have traditionally been commemorated since the Middle Ages. Among the various reasons that led initially to the creation of this belief was probably the view that it would be unthinkable that the body that had given birth to the Son of God would perish in a grave, together with the idea that the son of God, already in Heaven, would certainly have taken care of his mother.

Other Dogmas

The line separating dogmas and doctrines is not always clear, and to formulate a list of dogmas that would be agreed upon by all members of the Church, or even by all bishops or theologians, is unfeasible. Though outright rejection of accepted dogma would be considered heretical, a dogma can sometimes be reinterpreted. Such an act would usually be justified by the claim that the original formulation was imperfect, and that the newer wording positions the dogma closer to the truth. The belief that Christ eternally guides the course of the Church is fundamental in the Catholic faith, and therefore many Catholics are able to view such changes of dogma as accepted and legitimate: Christ assists every generation to understand the mystery of faith in its own way and language.

Not every Church rule or practice is a doctrine that must be believed. Many customs are considered matters of ecclesiastical "discipline." The

Church recognizes that such rules and practices are subject to change, without necessarily the need for doctrinal revolution. Thus, for example, the obligation of a priest in the Western, "Latin" part of the Catholic Church to promise to remain celibate, or the ban on eating meat on Friday (which was lifted a few decades ago), are connected to the Church's disciplines and not to its doctrines. A Catholic is not compelled to believe in the eternal correctness of these principles, but he or she must accept them in practice if the Church demands it.

All the articles in the creeds are dogmas. The following list includes examples of additional key Catholic dogmas, although many Catholics might say they are not all on the same level of importance: the list of the books included in Scriptures; the idea that the bishops are the successors of the apostles; the view that the Bishop of Rome, the occupier of the Chair of Peter, holds greater authority than the other bishops; the belief in the uniqueness and power of the seven sacraments; the belief in the essential transformation[31] of the bread and the wine during the Mass into the body and blood of Christ; the belief in the power of the Church to absolve sins; the belief in the special status of those ordained to the priesthood; the belief in the special status of the Virgin Mary, mother of Jesus, among the communion of saints; and the view that the superior hierarchy may define additional dogmas.

The Reality: What Do Catholics Believe?

Though the dogmas listed above (and others not mentioned) are considered fundamental precepts of belief by the Church, not all are viewed in the same way by the Catholic public. As already stated, dogma is doctrine that is deemed essential by the supreme hierarchy of the Church. Segments of the public may relate to these same doctrines differently. Thus, for example, it is no secret that a significant portion of Catholics have difficulty accepting the dogma that the essence of the bread and wine turns into the body and blood of Christ during Mass.[32] For many others, the idea of the resurrection of the dead is unreasonable, and for others the discussions of the place of original sin in the life of Mary are of little importance. The gap between the precise, academic, theological definitions of the "True Faith" by the hierarchy and professional theologians and what the average Catholic believes in can be at times very large.

In order to teach the "correct" faith, the Catholic Church (as probably almost all other religious groups) uses both frontal teaching, generally for young children and teenagers, as well as books that can guide the teachers, young people, and other Catholic (or Catholic-to-be) adults about the faith.

In many Christian denominations, including in Catholicism, these courses and books are called "Catechism," a word whose Greek origin means to teach orally. Several official books of Catechism, from different times and for different audiences, were produced by the hierarchy, and countless have been produced by local churches and individuals. In 1997 (after an initial version in 1992), the Vatican published an official book of Catechism, *The Catechism of the Catholic Church (CCC)*. As this book is rather voluminous, a shorter version, *The Compendium of the Catechism of the Catholic Church* was issued in 2005.[33] These two books are the official sources in which Catholics are supposed to find answers to questions they might have about the faith of the Church.

Despite all this, sociological studies show over and over again that within a single, local church, on one bench, one may find people for whom all the precepts of faith mentioned in this chapter, as well as many others, are absolute truths and need to be understood as precisely as possible following formal definitions, and other Catholics who do not even believe in the existence of God, or who believe in concepts that will make most theologians shriek. Most Catholics sit somewhere between these two extremes.

Notes

1. From *Carnis,* "Flesh" in Latin. The most important New Testament text to present this idea is the beginning of the Gospel of John, particularly verses 1:1 and 1:14.
2. In modern editions intended for use by Catholics as well as Protestants ("Ecumenical editions") these books usually appear as a separate section between the Old and the New Testaments. Included for Catholic readers, they do not interfere with Protestant readers' use.
3. Three documents published, not incidentally, over fifty year spans, should be cited among the official documents of the Catholic Church dealing with this subject: *Providentissimus Deus,* published in 1893 by pope Leo XIII, *Divino Afflante Spiritu* published by pope Pius XII in 1943, and the highly regarded *The Interpretation of the Bible in the Church,* published in April 1993 by the Pontifical Biblical Commission. One should add to these works another crucial text, the "Dogmatic Constitution on Divine Revelation," commonly referred to as *Dei Verbum,* one of the most important documents of the Second Council of the Vatican, promulgated in 1965.
4. If by the word "Church" at the beginning of this sentence one understands "Christians," or "Believers in Christ," then this statement is in fact not only theologically important but also historically correct.
5. Romans 10:9. This Epistle was written around 50 CE.
6. 1 Corinthians 15:1–11.
7. The word "credit" comes from the same root and has to do with the relationship of trust that exists between buyer and seller.
8. Since November 27, 2011, this English translation is the official version used by Catholics in the U.S. People who have a Catholic background but who have not frequented churches in recent years, and who are thus unfamiliar with this new version, might find it awkward.
9. In some ancient versions, the word "death" does not explicitly appear.

10. The translation follows, yet again, the Missal of 2011.
11. In the Middle Ages, discussions were held around the question of Jesus' descent into Hell, with a typical response being that he redeemed the souls of the Just that had died before him. It is more likely, however, that when the line was originally written, its intention was to strengthen the fact of Jesus' real death: like every departed, he passed over to the afterlife. This line was not always part of the Apostles' Creed, but was included in the final version codified in the eighth century.
12. Genesis 1:26.
13. Genesis 18.
14. Isaiah 6:3.
15. It should be noted that both modern biblical criticism and traditional Jewish interpretations see very different things in these texts. The Christian interpretations mentioned here are unquestionably possible, but they are certainly not the only valid and convincing interpretations ever suggested to these verses.
16. John 1:1 and 1:14.
17. For example, Matthew 10:32–33; Matthew 18:10.
18. 1 Corinthians 12:1–11.
19. Matthew 18:19; John 15:26; 2 Corinthians 13:14.
20. Luke 3:21–22. See also Matthew 3:13–17; Mark 1:9–11.
21. See for example 1 John 4.
22. See for example Genesis 49:10; Exodus 4:22–26; Numbers 24:17; Isaiah 7:14; Isaiah 9:5–7; Isaiah 40–42; Isaiah 52–53; Jeremiah 31:30–33; Psalm 22; Psalm 72; Psalm 110:1–4; Daniel 7:13–14, and others.
23. One of the main chapters in the Old Testament read in this way by Christians is Isaiah 53. One should remember though that the Jewish tradition (and most Bible scholars, regardless of their religious or non-religious affiliation) see this chapter as having nothing to do with Jesus.
24. See for example the story of the resurrection of the boy by Elijah in 1 Kings 17, and two stories involving his disciple Elisha in 2 Kings 4 and 2 Kings 13. Accounts of resurrections are also found in the Gospels. See for example Luke 7:11–17; Mark 5:21–43 and parallels; John 11.
25. Although the Creed is vague on the matter, according to Catholic (and Orthodox and early Protestantism) doctrine, already common in the first centuries, Mary was not only a virgin before Jesus' conception and birth, but remained virginal during the birth and beyond. This is the doctrine known as "The Perpetual Virginity of Mary," and the reason for the common referral to Mary in liturgical texts as the "Ever Virgin." Today, many Protestant Churches reject the idea that Mary remained a virgin during Jesus' birth and following it, considering it an unnecessary belief, one that not only is hard to accept rationally but that also contradicts verses in the New Testament that refer to some people as brothers of Jesus. The Churches that adhere to this doctrine answer by saying that these people were children of Joseph in a previous marriage, or only "spiritual" brothers of Jesus.
26. Those looking for examples of lengthier discussions of the creeds, particularly as some contemporary Catholic theologians see them, can consult Luke Timothy Johnson, *The Creed: What Christians Believe and Why it Matters* (New York: Doubleday, 2003), and Berard L. Marthaler, *The Creed: The Apostolic Faith in Contemporary Theology (Third Edition)*, (New London: Twenty Third Publications, 2008).
27. For an almost classic work on angels, see Jean Danielou, *The Angels and Their Mission According to the Fathers of the Church*, trans. David Heimann (1953; reprint, Notre Dame: Ave Maria Press, 1996).
28. As a matter of fact, and most certainly from the perspective of an outsider observer, dogmas can also be "changed," but the Church will say this is not a change, but rather a

new and better explanation of the existing, unchangeable truth that the dogma attempts to describe.

29. Some might say that the decision of the First Council of the Vatican in 1870 regarding papal infallibility is a dogma, therefore should be included as a third. We will address this later in the discussion about the pope, pp. 73–74.

30. Despite the convictions of many, another earlier idea stating that the sexual relations in which Mary herself was conceived were untainted by original sin (unlike "regular" sexual relations), is not part of the dogma. It should also be noted that many Catholics conflate various ideas and believe that the dogma on the "Immaculate Conception" refers to Jesus' conception and not to his mother's.

31. It is worth remembering that even in Catholic belief there is no transformation in the chemical makeup of the bread and wine; the bread remains bread and the wine remains wine. The transformation has to do with the spiritual "essence" of the bread and the wine. On this, see p. 111.

32. An example of senior Church officials' acknowledgment of and attempt to change the situation is the text "The Real Presence of Jesus Christ in the Sacrament of the Eucharist: Basic Questions and Answers," published in 2001 by the United States Conference of Catholic Bishops.

33. Both works are available online and for free at the Vatican's website.

CHAPTER 3

The Catholic Church

Ecclesiology

"Ecclesiology," the study of the Church, the *Ecclesia,* is a branch of Christian theology concerned with the visible and invisible structure of the Church. Catholic scholars engaged in ecclesiology consider such questions as, what is the Church? Is it a global establishment, similar to many human organizations, or is it mystical, with its representation in the temporal world limited or partial at best? Do Christians (and non-Christians) who do not identify themselves as belonging to the Catholic Church still belong to the "Church of Christ"? Who founded the Church? What is the role of the Holy Spirit in the Church? Is the performance of various religious acts fundamental to the Church's structure? Is the existing Church hierarchy essential or merely practical? Are those with official positions in the Church filling administrative or authoritative roles, or is their aim to serve the members of the Church, perhaps even as "servants of the servants"? Are they emissaries? If so, are they emissaries of God or of humankind? Are members of the Church only those who are alive, or also the deceased? Is the pope the head of the Church or is Christ?[1]

The People of God, the Body of Christ, the Temple of the Spirit

Many Catholic ecclesiologists today will state at the outset that the Church is the "People of God," the "Body of Christ," and the "Temple of the Holy Spirit." In this, they will link the Trinitarian idea of God the Father, Christ the Son, and the Holy Spirit to the very structure of the Church. Christ himself is at its head, and the Church, generally referred to as a "she," is the People of God and the dwelling place of the Spirit. A fundamental document of the Second Council of the Vatican, *Lumen Gentium,* defined the Church as a Mystery, an instrument (the document used the key term "Sacrament"), connecting God and humanity, providing humans with divine grace. All these concepts hint to a fundamental ecclesiological concept in Catholicism: the Church's structure is essential and divinely instituted.[2]

But what happens in the tangible world? Where in this picture does the pope fit, for example? Is the Church like a pyramid constructed out of layers, one on top of another, or it is more like a body with various members, each assigned a different role, with one not necessarily dependent upon another? If the Church is the People of God, what is the status of those who do not count themselves among its members? What is the essence of their connection to God? Is the Spirit found only in the Church?

Theologians are able to describe the Church in various ways based on diverse theological and ecclesiological images.[3] These descriptions, at times resembling no more than intellectual games, can in fact offer clear aims for Church members, and history shows they often lead to quite noticeable outcomes and transformations in and of the Church.

This chapter does not pretend to answer most of the questions posed above, due to their complexity as well as to the multiple and even conflicting responses that might be given by different ecclesiologists. Nevertheless, the ensuing discussion may indirectly suggest some possible answers.

For Catholics, two parts—one earthly and one heavenly—make up the entire Church. This chapter will deal mainly with the human, everyday aspects of the earthly Church's structure, its hierarchy and organization. Following this, the heavenly Church, which includes, among others, angels, saints, and other deceased members, will briefly be addressed.

The Laity

Lay people make up 99.9 percent of the Church: Catholics that have never been ordained as clergy or joined an Institute of Consecrated Life.[4] Due to this group's size, as well as its heterogeneous character, any generalizations about it will naturally be deficient. There are those among the laity who spend every available moment performing some religious act or contemplating the religious significance of their every deed, and there are those who cannot remember the last time they crossed the threshold of a church or thought about Catholic doctrine. There are laypersons who work full-time for Catholic organizations, which are dedicated to the bettering of society by aiding immigrants, feeding the poor, or healing the sick, and there are others for whom the most basic support for these organizations will suffice, or who are even opposed to some of these organizations' activities. Some lay people are members of various Catholic groups, such as student associations or organizations like "The Knights of Malta," while others distance themselves from them. Some laypersons believe that every word uttered by the pope of their time is holy, and there are others who openly and vehemently criticize him. There are laypeople (in the broadest sense of the term) that live in monastic communities, and others who know next to nothing about this way of life.

In recent decades, a significant "theology of the laity" has developed, defining the positive place of the laity in the Church and stressing the importance and necessity of lay life for it.[5] Theologically speaking, the core of this thinking is a Catholic notion which had been reinforced over and again since the Second Council of the Vatican. It emphasized an ancient idea that all members of the Church (there are those who would say, all those who have been baptized) are, in a certain way, "priests." According to this inclusive concept, all are accounted for in the biblical saying, "And you shall be unto me a kingdom of priests, and a holy nation."[6] Their "rite of ordination" to this "priesthood" is baptism, followed by confirmation. Their "priestly acts" include partaking in communion,[7] receiving other sacraments, and meticulously following a Christian life. This includes performing charitable acts, aiding the Church, leading an untarnished married or chaste life, bearing and educating (if applicable) children to become the next generation of the Church, and so forth. They are all called to a life of holiness, as expected of priests.

Many would say that the laity can be divided by levels of activity: while the majority of lay people are passive with regard to most matters touching the Church, an important minority is actively involved in the life of the Church. This division certainly has many practical advantages, but some object to it, saying that at least part of the less-active laity have withdrawn not because of indifference but because of disagreement or disillusion with the current hierarchy. Their removal from the life of the Church is therefore an act by itself, not necessarily a sign of apathy or passivity.

Among both active and non-active members, one can find progressive/liberal-minded people and conservative/traditional ones. If there are consistent differences between the passivity or activity of members of these camps, they can be observed only by using sophisticated studies, taking into account factors such as socio-economic level, gender, nationality, age, and more. In a similar way, all shades and variants of opinions are to be found both among the active lay people and among the low and high hierarchy. Here also, a binary division stating that one group (i.e., "passive lay people," "priests," etc.) is more liberal or conservative than another is, most often, mistaken.

Institutes of Consecrated Life

A significant group within the Church are those men and women who have chosen to devote their lives to what they consider to be service to God and humankind, through activity within the framework of "Institutes of Consecrated Life."[8]

Members of these "Institutes" share a number of commonalities. Almost all view their choice of lifestyle as a divine calling. Daily prayers at appointed hours are of primary importance for them, as is a desire to shape their lives and deeds to resemble specific aspects of the way of life advocated and practiced, according to belief, by Jesus and his disciples. They believe that for them it is likewise beneficial to choose to give up things that form significant aspects of most other people's lives. This "sacrifice" helps them, they believe, to come closer to the love of God and salvation by providing them freedom, time, and energy, which they can channel in other directions. All members of such institutes are in principle committed to the three "Evangelical Counsels," which view positively a life of poverty (refraining from acquiring significant personal wealth, and, often, being part of a group that lives modestly), chastity, and obedience to one's legitimate superiors. Above all, the vast majority of them seek to be part of a group having a clear and defined orientation, purpose, and ideology within the Church. Many of them devote their lives to a specific cause that they see as aiding one or another human group.

Religious and Secular Institutes

Men and women who took or plan to take vows of commitment to the three Evangelical Counsels "in public," meaning, in the presence of a senior legitimate Church official who is authorized to accept their vows in the name of the Church, are considered to belong to "religious" Institutes of Consecrated Life.[9] Those taking these vows generally join the monastic orders that developed in the early and later Middle Ages or orders and communities that were later offshoots. Though members may not always go about dressed in them, the orders dating back to the Middle Ages have prescribed types of clothing. The group to which a member belongs will provide for his or her livelihood, and if a member has an outside income it will be transferred to the group. In principle, the members lead communal lives that are cut off to some degree from secular public life. Due to this separation from the "secular," the Church calls their way of life "religious," and members refer to themselves in this way. The words "brother" and "sister" are also used to describe them.

In other Institutes of Consecrated Life, members profess their vows before God, but without the vows being received by an official of the Church. Even if the ceremony takes place in a church in the presence of members of the group, relatives, and friends, these vows are termed "private." In other groups there are no vows, not even private ones; instead, members promise in various words to uphold a certain version of the three Evangelical Counsels. Institutes in which there are no "public" vows are called "secular." The members of these groups are considered closer to secular life. Many of their members are interested mainly in activity in and not detachment from the outside world. They do not have a special dress or habit, and thus it is often difficult to tell them apart from the general public. Affiliates of these groups might live together, but, as opposed to their "religious" counterparts, they are not obligated to do so. For the most part they live on their own while maintaining close contact with fellow members, meeting for prayer as well as for spiritual and communal activities. They are responsible for their own livelihoods. These groups, in general, are newer than most of their "religious" equivalents; many having arisen for various reasons in the nineteenth and early part of the twentieth century.

The hierarchy within the Institutes of Consecrated Life is complex and depends upon the group's character, its association (or not) with a large order, etc. Often, each local community is headed by a member (man or woman) who has been in many instances chosen for this position by fellow members. In many monasteries—the most "classic" form of an Institute of Consecrated Life—that person is referred to either as the Abbot or Abbess. In some other cases, that person is referred to as the Superior. Besides this figure, and in accordance with the group's character, there may also be another leader in the organization, wielding regional and at times even global authority.

Monks and Nuns

The monastic system is probably the most well known of the "religious" Institutes of Consecrated Life, though its specifics may be unfamiliar to many. Among the reasons for the broad interest in the monastic way of life are its antiquity, the dissimilarity between monastic life and the lives of most people, the special dress worn by those living by it, and its unique architectural structures. No wonder, therefore, that monasteries are a rather common motif in many mystery films.

Monks and nuns (or *moniales*) belong to "religious" groups. They often live in monasteries, which enable them to live together while remaining at a distance from the outside world; at the very least, their living areas and additional living spaces are closed to the public. A monastery might be a large complex dating from medieval times, but even a modest apartment in a bustling modern city can, in certain instances, serve the same purpose for a small group. In the vast majority of cases, the group is made of men or women, but mixed groups exist as well. Usually a number of monasteries are connected to a particular monastic order that follows a specific ideology or set of regulations. The communality between monasteries belonging to the same order may vary, depending upon the order's character and homogeneity.

The exact types of vows taken by monks and nuns may differ among the various orders and monasteries. In some monastic orders, the monks and nuns take vows to the three already mentioned "Evangelical Counsels": chastity, poverty, and obedience. In other monasteries these vows may be slightly different, with adherents vowing fidelity to the monastic way of life, which includes chastity and poverty, a vow of stability, meaning a commitment to remain in the same monastery for life (barring, of course, special circumstances), and, lastly, a vow of obedience to the head of the monastery or the group's rules.

Monastic Life

Almost all monastic orders that are resolute about maintaining a stable lifestyle within a particular monastery have, at some point in their history, adopted the sixth-century "Regula," or Rule, of Saint Benedict.[10] Stricter and more lax interpretations of the Rule, or the forming of new movements based on the charismatic leadership of one person or another, have nevertheless guaranteed that even among these groups one may find many variations.

Many of the monks and, even more so, nuns almost never leave their monastery. Visitors are not permitted within designated private areas, which may encompass large or small parts of the monastic complex. The routine of a monastic's day is determined by the schedule of prayer, from which stems the system known as "The Liturgy of the Hours."[11] There are nuns and monks who dedicate much of their time to prayers. Others are likely to engage in various kinds of work on the monastery grounds in between prayer times, either out of necessity or for ideological reasons. Most monks and nuns who live in monasteries are called "contemplatives," as the main part of their lives is devoted to contemplation, prayer, and introspection. Their physical labor is often connected with food and agriculture: growing fruits and vegetables, producing cheese, honey, wine, liquor, and more. It may also encompass skilled handiwork that demands many hours, such as carpentry and embroidery.

Members of other monastic orders—for example, those belonging to the "mendicant" orders (who were known to collect charity from the public—once permitted by the Church, this practice has long since been revoked)—leave the monastery frequently and are sometimes even compelled to live entirely outside of the monastic setting. These monks and nuns, having taken upon themselves a worldly mission, like the first apostles, to serve beyond the physical confines of the monastery, are called "apostolic" and are generally less connected to a specific monastery. They often live in urban communities, and their activity is commonly performed outside of their living quarters. They might be academics, medical professionals, educators, social workers, journalists, parish priests, or involved in other occupations. Their work not only provides them with a livelihood but, in most cases, is also connected to their group's aims, which often involves assisting those with special needs, such as the poor, the sick, or youth. The most famous of these mendicant orders are the Franciscans ("The Order of the Friars Minor") and the Dominicans ("The Order of Preachers"), two groups founded in the thirteenth century.

The Habits of Members of Religious Institutes

Many people are familiar with the special clothing worn by some of the members of the religious orders, which essentially preserve a type of medieval robe-like garb. The Franciscans, for example, are recognizable for their brown robes, and the Dominicans for their black and white ones. The Jesuits, a later group formed in the sixteenth century, and which differs in many ways from the other two groups mentioned, wear black robes that preserve their tradition of priestly dress. Today, the traditional dress of the members of religious Institutes is often used during liturgical ceremonies but not necessarily worn outside of such events. In general, "contemplative" monks and nuns more frequently hold on to their traditional dress than do members of other "Institutes of Consecrated Life." According to the custom in their group and surrounding society, many members of these groups may don their traditional dress only on special occasions, and otherwise wear ordinary clothes.

Joining and Leaving a Group

Joining a religious Institute of Consecrated Life takes several years. Generally after a period lasting several months, during which the candidate lives alongside but not with the community, his or her candidacy is considered. Often the candidate will decide that this is not, in fact, his or her true calling. If the candidate has been accepted, a trial period will commence. The first part of the training in most groups lasts from one to two years, during which time the "novice," as he or she is now called, will familiarize him or herself with the group, its ethos, and its customs. At the end of this period, the suitability of the novice will again be considered. If both the novice and the members of the community decide that this trial was positive, the novice will take temporary vows—usually for a period of three years—from which time, he or she is considered a full member of the group. If at the end of the three years the person wishes to bind him or herself to the group, he or she will take permanent vows. It is possible at times to delay the taking of permanent vows and extend the period of temporary vows for an additional three years.

Should a member wish to leave the Institute—not an uncommon occurrence—he or she must submit a request to his or her superior. The process of release often corresponds to the stage at which the person making the request finds him or herself (still a novice, after taking temporary vows, after taking permanent vows): the earlier the release is requested, the simpler and faster the process. But even permanent vows may be annulled by those with the proper Church authority, if this   e member's wish. Needless to say, a member of an Institute of Consec.   d Life may also leave without permission. Today, the Institutes rarely desire or have the ability to force someone to stay against their will, although this does not mean they might not try to convince him or her to stay, attempts that at times might be hard to deal with for some. It is obvious also that leaving an Institute of Consecrated Life is often not an easy step, just as leaving any closed community requires a period of acclimation to new financial, social, and spiritual realities.

Secular Institutes of Consecrated Life

"Secular" Institutes of Consecrated Life, of which there are many, are in principle characterized as having a deeper involvement in the secular world than do the religious Institutes. As a matter of fact, it is not always easy to find much difference between secular and religious-apostolic groups.

Members of secular groups generally do not live together, and each is responsible for his or her own livelihood. They do not have a distinguishing type of dress, and the casual observer might not be able to recognize them, especially if their work is not clearly connected to the religious and social ideology of their group. Despite these differences, religious and secular groups do have many similarities, among them several aspects of the processes of joining and being released from an Institute, the adherence to an intense prayer schedule throughout the day, and frequent attendance at Mass.

Some Contemporary Aspects of Institutes of Consecrated Life

Many more women than men are members of Institutes of Consecrated Life, with women numbering about 700,000 and men about 200,000.[12] Of this last figure, almost three quarters are ordained to the priesthood, making the disparity in numbers among men and women who have chosen to join Institutes of Consecrated Life but who do not serve as clergy (in other words, remain in the "lay state") even greater.

One of the clearest trends of the last decades among these groups is the creation of small communities. While large communities can still be found in some places, with some numbering tens and even hundreds of monks or nuns, this is a rare phenomenon. Communities with significantly smaller numbers of members, often less than five, are much more common. The view that this is a normal or even ideal situation, as opposed to a failure, is slowly taking hold. These last decades have also seen the creation and blossoming of new Church movements, which draw from various facets of Institutes of Consecrated Life such as communal living, working with the sick and the poor, and obedience. Members of these movements, many of whom are laypeople and some of whom are married, want to devote their lives to the Church or to a specific goal supported by it, but prefer to remain outside of the Institutes' framework. Often, one can find among the members of these movements also clergy and members of the "classic" orders. It could be said that these groups are moving a step closer to the "secular" world. They have varied social aims, but one of their clearest characteristics is the desire to work mainly among and with the laity. Among the numerous groups of this type, one may note many that are considered, often with reason, to be on the conservative side of the Church. Three examples are the Neocatechumenal Way, Opus Dei, and Communion and Liberation. Other groups, such as Focolare, are somehow harder to define. There are, however, groups that are more closely identified with the progressive side, for example, Dignity, We Are Church, and Call to Action. They do not always enjoy the same official status as some of the more conservative ones, but in practice their functioning is often not radically different.

The number of such groups as well as the range of "secular" Institutes of Consecrated Life is vast. Attempting to find the right balance between allowing new groups to establish themselves according to their own path and desiring that those hoping to join an Institute of Consecrated Life find their calling among the existing groups still remains a challenge for the Church hierarchy.

Last, but not least: the Institutes of Consecrated Life, in one or another of their variants, hold, since the very beginning of the monastic movement, and certainly since the creation of the great medieval orders, a special place in the Church. Their members are different in many ways from the vast majority of lay people by being heavily involved in the life of the Church, but they are, at the same time, not part of the hierarchy (even those among them who are ordained do not report generally to a bishop). Some would say they fulfill, in a way, the role of Biblical prophets. This gives them a certain liberty and possibility to try new ideas, whether they are theological, pastoral, spiritual, or otherwise. By doing this, they provide the Church with an experimental laboratory, out of which sometimes emerge successful developments that can influence the Church at large. This role continues today, and watching these communities can, at times, provide the careful observer with insights into the future of the Church.

Ordained Members of the Church

Notwithstanding the importance of the idea that all members of the Church are "priests," the Catholic Church believes that there is an inherent difference between those who have received the sacrament of Ordination (or "Holy Orders") and those who have not, whether they are the non-ordained members of Institutes of Consecrated Life or simply non-ordained laity. Those who have been ordained, while of course part of "the People of God," are placed apart as bishops, priests, or deacons. It should be noted that about a third of them belong to an "Institute of Consecrated Life."[13]

The ordained members of the Church will be the focus of the following pages. They will be discussed in the order of their ranking, beginning with the most senior level, the bishops. This order of presentation is also the one used by the Second Vatican Council, and is, as we shall see, theologically significant. One should remember, though, that the Council was almost entirely made of bishops. It would be naïve to assume that this did not affect their choice to place bishops as the core element of the hierarchy.

The Apostles and Their Successors

In theological terms, all ordained members of the Church derive their strength, in a certain respect, from the Apostles, the first disciples of Jesus. According to various sources in the New Testament, while Jesus walked the earth, he appointed twelve disciples, sending them to heal the sick, drive out demons, spread the Gospel, and baptize more disciples.[14] As Christianity took hold and spread, every community near and far was in need of individuals who could instruct, sanctify, and lead them. Recent research suggests that up until about the middle of the second century, leadership was often not entrusted to a single person, but was placed in the hands of a local council of "elders." At a certain point, however, there was a shift towards one-man leadership. This individual was now considered the successor, as well as the substitute, of the apostle to whom the founding of the community was attributed. The holder of this position was commonly referred to, in Greek-speaking communities, as *episcopos*, "overseer" or "supervisor."[15] The word "bishop," as well as the adjective "episcopal," derive from this Greek term.

Bishops

In Catholic theology, the bishops of each generation (and today there are about 5,200 of them), are considered the successors of the Apostles. They are, theoretically and theologically (and in popular conception, historically as well), the last in an unbroken chain of succession that extends directly from Jesus' first disciples. For Catholics, a crucial element in this "succession" is the belief that each bishop can trace a chain of ordination going from the person who ordained him, up to the Apostles.[16] Many other Christian Churches are not interested in such claims, or outwardly deny them, saying that other factors, such as teaching the same faith the apostles taught or performing the essential tasks they did, are what make their leaders successors of the apostles. Other denominations do not see the entire issue as significant.

From the fourth century, following the Roman example, the Church divided the known world into dioceses (or "bishoprics"), which are determined, ideally, by geographic size, political factors, historical importance, and demography. A bishop is generally responsible for each one of these dioceses.

The Bishop's Roles

A bishop living in an area for which he is responsible is called a "Diocesan Bishop" or "Regular Bishop." Today, most bishops, about 3,000 of them, are diocesan bishops. Such a bishop is the head of a local Church: his seat is in the cathedral, the main church of the diocese, where his "chair," his *cathedra,* is located. He is the spiritual leader of all members of the Church in that area, and the person to whom all priests active in the diocese, not belonging to religious orders, must be obedient. Borrowing a term from the secular world, he is their "employer."

Traditionally, a bishop has three duties: to teach, sanctify, and govern. A bishop will compose and deliver sermons in fulfillment of his duty to teach. He will sometimes write a missive to members of the congregation to be published in the diocese newspaper (and today, website) and sometimes to be read aloud. Sanctifying the community is carried out first and foremost by the celebration of sacraments in general, and those sacraments reserved for him in particular. It is also done by the delegation of his authority to priests and by supervising and ensuring that sacraments are celebrated properly in the diocese. Governing his diocese entails the establishing of rules, jurisdiction over priests, and, in unusual instances, imposing sanctions on transgressors.

A breakdown of these roles into individual elements reveals the bishop's numerous duties. Besides the daily liturgical acts that are similar to the priest's, a bishop must render decisions that affect the entire diocese. He must be in contact with the priests in his diocese, and may be asked to help solve problems that might arise in his diocese. On Easter, he is charged with the baptizing of adults, and at various times during the year he dispenses the sacrament of confirmation. The bishop is responsible for accepting new candidates for the priesthood, following their progress, and ordaining them. He is responsible for educational programs, the orderly running of the diocese, including its finances, overseeing documents that are either received by or sent from the diocese, implementing changes, communicating with Rome and with other bishops, and managing relations with secular authorities.

Each bishop is required to travel to Rome at least once every five years for what is entitled *Ad limina apostolorum* ("to the threshold of the apostles"). During his stay he celebrates Mass in the two churches erected over the assumed burial places of the apostles Peter and Paul and meets with the pope. At this time, he must present a report on the state of his diocese or the area in his care. Today, a number of bishops from one country or region usually travel together to Rome and hold a joint meeting with the pope about the condition of their Churches. The visit usually includes meetings with other members of and offices in the Roman curia as well.

Bishops Who Are Not Heads of Diocese

Some bishops are not in charge of an actual functioning diocese; some hold administrative roles in the Vatican or serve as diplomats representing the pope and his state. Others, although in charge of at least certain aspects or parts of a diocese, do not stand at its head: they are "Auxiliary Bishops," helping the "Diocesan Bishop." Since according to the Catholic tradition every bishop must head a diocese, each bishop of this kind (unless he is a "Bishop Emeritus" of a diocese he formerly headed, or becomes a "coadjutor bishop,"[17] or is in some other rare case, such as a bishop of armed forces) is granted "virtual" authority over a diocese that may have existed in the past but is no longer extant, becoming, effectively, its "Titular Bishop." Many such "ghost" dioceses are to be found in Africa, in areas in which there is no longer a significant Christian population or which were historic dioceses that were abandoned or integrated into others. Still others are real dioceses but are actively administrated, although not headed, by another bishop.

Archbishops

An archbishop is usually a bishop standing at the head of a major diocese at the center of an ecclesiastical province, a region that contains a number of dioceses. There are also archbishops who hold senior positions in the Vatican and do not stand at the head of a province. The title of archbishop is mainly honorary and generally does not grant additional judicial authority to the bearer. An archbishop is not permitted to interfere in the functioning of other dioceses in his province, his "Suffragans," and is not a "super-Bishop." In unusual instances, where the archbishop becomes aware of a serious problem in the functioning of a diocese in his province, he is duty bound to inform the pope. The latter, carrying global authority, may intervene.

Patriarchs

Patriarchs are bishops who preside over one of the "autonomous" Churches that comprise the one universal Catholic Church. The Western Church is made up of only one "autonomous" Church, the Church of Rome (in which, one should remember, about 98 percent of worldwide Catholics are members). The bishop at the head of the Church of Rome—the pope— was also known, therefore, at certain times, as the Patriarch of Rome, even if this term is rarely used in recent centuries.[18] In addition, a number of Eastern Catholic Churches are headed by patriarchs.[19] In fact, when the term "Patriarch" is used in a Catholic context, the intent is generally to one of the patriarchs of the Eastern Catholic Churches.[20] These patriarchs usually have their seats in the main city after which they are named. All the bishops belonging to a Church presided over by a Patriarch are under his jurisdiction. Patriarchs are elected by the council of bishops of the specific Church to which they belong. Immediately following their election, they formally declare their allegiance to the pope and communion with the other patriarchs. In the ranking of Church hierarchy, patriarchs are placed above all other bishops and below cardinals (unless they are cardinals themselves).

Personal Dioceses

In addition to "geographic" dioceses (and most dioceses are of this type), there are dioceses where geography and demography combined create the diocese, or where belonging to a diocese is not a function of being in a prescribed area. Thus, for example, a bishop might be in charge of all the Catholics following the Greek-Byzantine rite living in Australia; his authority is built upon the confluence of geographic area with a cultural factor. Another bishop might be in charge of all Catholic soldiers serving in the US army and their families. Their physical location is irrelevant, as this bishop's diocese is not dependent upon a specific geographic place.

Coadjutor Bishop, Bishop Emeritus

In cases where a serious problem arises with regard to the bishop's ability to perform his duties (for example, in the case of grave illness), the pope may appoint a "coadjutor bishop" for the diocese. This bishop shares the position with the existing bishop and, therefore, is not the "titular bishop" of another diocese. The coadjutor bishop will automatically assume the role of diocesan bishop upon the death or retirement of the bishop he is assisting.

Every bishop—with the exception of the bishop of Rome, the pope—must resign from his post upon reaching seventy-five years of age. The pope will usually accept a bishop's resignation, however, in exceptional circumstances he may request the bishop to remain in his post. A bishop may retire earlier than age seventy-five for reasons of health, in order to relocate somewhere else, or if decided by him or the pope that this is the right thing to do for any other reason.[21] A retired bishop is still a bishop, but as "Bishop Emeritus" he would have no administrative authority over a diocese.

The Bishop's Dress

A bishop may not always be identifiable by his dress. When not in liturgical garb, he might wear a large crucifix around his neck, a purple skullcap, or both, but he might also choose not to always wear these identifying symbols. A Western bishop will regularly wear a special "Episcopal Ring." A bishop can be easily recognized when in full liturgical dress: besides the other liturgical attires, he will wear a special hat, the "miter,"[22] and carry a "Pastoral Staff," known also as a crosier. The characteristic color of the bishop's dress and skullcap is purple. It is important to keep in mind though that the use of certain colors in the Church depends on many factors, among them the date on the liturgical calendar, the type of event, the person's role in the event, etc.

Appointment of a Bishop

Throughout the history of the Church, bishops have been appointed in a number of ways. Because a bishop's appointment had both political as well as economic consequences, it became a major point of conflict among various authorities in the Middle Ages, a conflict often referred to as the "Investiture Controversy."[23] In the first centuries of Christianity a bishop was appointed often by his community. In later periods a bishop might have been appointed by the secular authorities, by other bishops, and sometimes by the pope. With today's understanding of a bishop's role, his ordination by other bishops (which might include the bishop of Rome) is the only valid method of appointment. Since the nineteenth century an important element was added to this rule: although the actual ordination of a new bishop is usually the privilege of the other local bishops, it can be celebrated only following an explicit papal order to do so.

Today in the Western Catholic Church, when the need arises to appoint a bishop to a diocese, the other bishops in the region decide together on a list of possible candidates and forward it to the pope's representative in that country (the "Apostolic Nuncio," or "Ambassador"). The Apostolic Nuncio then conducts his own research into these candidates, consults discretely with various local authorities, and forwards a final list of three candidates to the Vatican, along with recommendations and relevant information about the diocese. These candidates are then discussed at one of several "Congregations" in charge of bishops in Rome.[24] The Congregation advises the pope about the most appropriate candidate, but the final decision whether to accept the proposal (which is usually the case) or to appoint another person instead rests with the pope. The candidate is then discretely asked whether he would be willing to accept the position, and if he answers in the affirmative the Vatican will shortly thereafter release a formal announcement. Appointment of an auxiliary bishop is less complicated, and is generally done using a list of possible candidates compiled by the diocesan bishop himself, a list that is then sent to Rome. In both instances, if the candidate that has been chosen is not yet a bishop, he will generally be ordained within a few months in an impressive ceremony, at the climax of which three bishops (sometimes more, or in exceptional circumstances, less) will lay their hands on him. The new bishop will assume his position a short time after his ordination.

The process described above is done only in the Western Church. In the Eastern Catholic Churches, appointment of a bishop is carried out by the local council of bishops of that Church, though the appointment only becomes valid after approval by the pope.

The pope's complete control in the appointment of bishops to the Western Church is, in many ways, the core of the centralization of the Catholic Church since the nineteenth century. Because appointments must be done very frequently (about twenty per month in the last few years), the pope cannot in all practicality choose only bishops who agree absolutely with his overall attitude and approach. Nonetheless, it is reasonable to assume that most of the appointees do not disagree with his ways.

Many members of the Church are critical of this method of appointment and would like to see the return of a certain level of active involvement on the part of the local churches in the appointment process of their bishops. In their opinion, it is perfectly reasonable to demand that a person who is supposed to lead a community of laypeople, as well as a group of priests, be chosen by them or, at the very least, that they be consulted. Discontent usually surfaces when a bishop fails miserably at his post, or when a serious difference of opinion arises between a bishop and the majority of the members of his diocese, lay or clergy or both. It seems unlikely that in the foreseen future a pope will relinquish control over the appointment process, as it provides him with most of his universal authority over the Church. It is possible, though, that at some point the current pope or a later one will decide to broaden the type of consultants in the appointment of bishops and to include in the process more people from the relevant diocese. Popes, after all, have been bishops themselves and are aware of the importance of having good relations between bishops and those they are in charge of.

Ordination of a Bishop without the Approval of the Pope

Ordaining a bishop without the approval of the pope is, from the standpoint of the Church, a threat to its unity. The Church considers the celebration of such an action a sign of revolt against the authority of the pope, as well as an attack on the collegiality of bishops. Such an ordination, although against the Church's discipline and law, is nevertheless valid. This creates an often realistic fear that the new bishop may later ordain new valid, though illegitimate, bishops, potentially creating a schism, in which entire communities are not, in a certain sense, duty bound to Rome. Thus, in such instances, the necessity for immediate intervention of the Roman hierarchy is understandable. Canon Law declares that a bishop who celebrates such an ordination, and any person who has been ordained as bishop in such a manner, is automatically excommunicated, even without an official declaration.[25] True, there are cases where the Vatican hierarchy ignores such incidents if it is determined that excommunication of these same bishops will do more harm than not excommunicating them.[26] But in other instances, such as the famous case of French archbishop Marcel Lefebvre, the Vatican has reacted. In 1988, Lefebvre, an ultra-conservative bishop who objected to many of the decisions of the Second Vatican Council, ordained without permission four new bishops who were to carry on his legacy. In order to dismiss any doubts, the Roman authorities declared openly that the automatic excommunications were valid.[27] However, the excommunications were lifted in 2009,[28] probably due to the desire of the pope at the time, pope Benedict XVI, to stop this schism from becoming permanent.[29]

Cardinals

The status of cardinals today is the fruit of an evolution that began in the first centuries of the first millennium, when special titles of "Cardinals" ("Chiefs," "Principals") were granted for various reasons to three categories of clergy in and around Rome: to deacons who were responsible for aiding Rome's poor, to priests who were in charge of various communities in the city, and to bishops who presided over several neighboring dioceses. The number of cardinals was never constant; at times there were only seven, at other times around twenty-four, and at still other times they numbered seventy and even up to around two hundred in recent years. Over time, bishops, priests, deacons, and even laypersons who did not belong to the hierarchy of the Church in the region of Rome were declared cardinals. Cardinals enjoyed many special rights and privileges and were considered the "Princes of the Church," positioned below the pope and above all the other bishops.

In the sixteenth century, the Council of Trent, fighting corruption, decreed that cardinals who are in charge of actual dioceses must reside in them, not in Rome, unless their duties required it.[30] At about the same time, their power was limited in various ways, in order to fight the intrigues that all too often accompanied the role of cardinals in the selection of new popes. Though some could, on an individual basis, preside over various Roman institutions, or hold other positions on behalf of the pope, their ability to wield daily influence on the papacy was significantly reduced. What remained was their main task: to elect a new pope when the papal seat was vacant (*sede vacante*). Since 1971, only cardinals who are under the age of eighty on the day a pope dies can be among the electors of his successor. At such a moment, the "College of Cardinals" is a unique body in the Catholic Church: when it is assembled to elect a new pope, it is a truly a democratic body (leaving aside, of course, aspects of charisma and influence that exist in any democratic system), comprised of members with equal rights.

According to the current Catholic Canon Law, a cardinal must be before his election "at least in the order of priesthood." If not a bishop already (an extremely rare case), he must be ordained as such. At the same time, because the rank of cardinal is not part of the hierarchy that the Church believes to be divinely ordained, but rather a late historic creation, and because the pope, who freely selects the cardinals, is the supreme legislator in the Church and thus not bound by Canon Law, ignoring these rules is not impossible. In other words, although in most cases the instructions in Canon Law are followed, a pope can appoint to the position whoever he wants, including, in theory, a woman.

In recent decades, the advisory role of the cardinals as a group, the so-called "College of Cardinals," has been on some level revived. Air travel enabling a cardinal residing in a distant diocese to reach the Vatican quickly has certainly contributed to the resurgence of this duty. In practical terms, it seems some of the recent popes mostly used their joint meetings with cardinals to disseminate their decisions to them and the public, but it is reasonable to believe that the current pope, pope Francis, will often act differently.

Cardinals who are in charge of active dioceses—about three-fourths of the non-retired cardinals today—come to the Vatican only for special events or meetings. Due to the advanced age of many of the cardinals, the pope must appoint new ones every few years, an act that is done during a "consistory": a formal meeting of the pope with the current cardinals and those to be elevated to the status.

The demographic constitution of the College of Cardinals does not reflect the reality of Catholicism today, and certainly not of Catholicism of the future decades. True, the fact that Italian cardinals constitute the biggest group from a single country has some theological justification, considering that the cardinals are supposed to be, in a way, from the diocese of Rome. And yet, the lack of correlation between the size of the Catholic population in many countries and the number of cardinals appointed from these countries does not seem just. European and North American countries are by far better represented than countries from other parts of the world. Although each pope's possibility to appoint new cardinals depends on the health and age of current cardinals and on long-standing traditions that bishops of certain dioceses normally become cardinals, it is likely that pope Francis and future popes will try to slowly fix this imbalance.

The color red dominates the cardinals' various types of official dress, and is also the color of their skullcaps.

The Pope

The direct contact of most Catholics with their Church's hierarchy happens through priests. Although they might see the bishop of their diocese, or the auxiliary bishop(s), at special events, in most instances, regular churchgoers will not have any personal dealings with them. Very few have ever seen the pope, the Bishop of Rome, the leader of the entire Catholic Church, without the aid of the media. Nevertheless, many Catholics closely follow him.

The Supremacy of Peter

According to the New Testament, Simon Peter, *Kepha* in Aramaic, a fisherman by trade, was one of the first of Jesus' disciples. As recounted in some of the Gospels, while the two were in the area of Caesarea Philippi, about twenty-five miles north of the Sea of Galilee, Jesus proclaimed Peter to be the "rock" upon which he would build his earthly "Assembly," *Ekklesia,* "Church," and one who would have great authority on earth and in heaven. This proclamation uses certain wordplay, relating *Petros,* Simon's name in Greek (*Petrus* in Latin), to the Greek word *Petra,* meaning stone (which is also the meaning of *Kepha* in Aramaic, thus not impossible for Jesus himself to make in his own language):

> You are Peter, and upon this rock, I will build my church, and the gates of the netherworld shall not prevail against it. I will give you the keys to the kingdom of heaven. Whatever you bind on earth shall be bound in heaven; and whatever you loose on earth shall be loosed in heaven.[31]

Some interpret this statement as coming after Peter's earlier recognition of Jesus as the Messiah, and according to one of the versions, the "son of the living God." The Catholic tradition infers from this passage that Peter was granted supremacy over the other disciples. It is difficult to reject this interpretation out of hand: although in some texts Peter (or "Simon-Peter") is opposed by other disciples,[32] in several passages in the Gospels he does seem to enjoy special status as the first and most senior of the disciples, both before and after Jesus' death and supposed resurrection.[33]

Early Roman Christianity

During the first three centuries of the first millennium, Rome was the cultural and economic center of an empire that, at the time, controlled vast regions around the Mediterranean basin. It is, therefore, not surprising that this city attracted many newcomers, among them some of the first adherents of the Christian faith. The fact that Rome also boasted a sizeable Jewish community may also have been a significant draw for these first Christians, especially those of them who were themselves Jewish. According to the final chapter of the New Testament's book Acts of the Apostles, Paul (or *Saul* in Hebrew), who had not been among Jesus' first disciples but who became a believer in him some years after Jesus' death, was under house arrest in Rome. Early Christian traditions also attest the apostle Peter's presence in Rome, as well as the execution in Rome of both Peter and Paul.[34] It is possible these claims have a historical basis.

Western Christianity also holds that not only did Peter remain in Rome for some twenty years, but also that up until his death he served as the first leader of its Christian community.[35] This claim, however, is somewhat more difficult to prove. It is more likely that up until the middle of the second century there was no single known leader of the Christian community in Rome, but, rather, that the community was led by a group of elders. Only from the last decades of the second century can scholars discern a clear succession of single leaders in Rome.

By the third century, leaders of the Roman community considered themselves responsible for the proper functioning of other churches, even distant ones. They believed that theirs were the customs according to which all Christians must live. As inhabitants of the capital of the Empire, they saw themselves entitled to legislative rights similar to those of the secular authorities. Slowly, they indeed succeeded in implementing their leadership, at least partially. More and more small communities recognized the Church of Rome as the one to approach with questions and problems regarding custom, doctrine, and even matters of internal politics. The efficient mail system that serviced the Empire's capital also helped the Christian community there to remain involved in the affairs of the outlying churches. Later, when the secular authorities of Rome collapsed with the Empire, the Bishops of Rome successfully seized the opportunity to fill in the power vacuum and gain authority. In later times, a forged document known as "The Donation of Constantine," which declares that Emperor Constantine of the fourth century gave the Church lands, and power to rule over the western part of the Roman Empire, was used by popes and their supporters to give credit to their political claims.[36]

Alongside these practical reasons, the Roman community's emergent theological traditions offered further justification for its rising status. These traditions were neither simple nor obvious. Even a presumption that Peter did indeed found the community in Rome does not necessarily sanction this community's supremacy. To achieve this status, a complex system of logic was designed in the fifth century. The interpretation noted above, regarding Peter's preeminence, formed the basis of this theory of supremacy, with additional corroboration coming from two further claims: the first asserts that Peter's authority was not exclusive and restricted to his lifetime, but is passed on to his successors. The second claim, based on the first, defines it in practical terms: the bishops of Rome are the successors of Peter; they carry the authority that was first given to him. Though not directly descended from a continuous lineage of ordination that begins with him, all bishops who occupy the seat that Peter first held are his spiritual descendants. His supremacy is now theirs. The Church of Rome is considered supreme because it was founded by Peter; the bishops of Rome are considered Peter's successors and hold the same authority he was given by Jesus, because they are the leaders of the community that he established.[37]

The Pope's Various Titles

In the first centuries, many Church leaders were referred to by the honorifics *Pappas* and *Papa,* the Greek and Latin words for father. This title began to be associated in particular with the head of the Church in Rome around the eighth century, and became exclusively associated with this position in the Western Church, from the eleventh century on. Other official titles for this position include "Supreme Pontiff" (a term originating from an ancient Roman title for religious or secular leaders), "Holy Father," "Servant of the Servants of God," and others. Some titles that were customary in the past are no longer in frequent use today; for example, most theologians avoid referring to the pope as the "Vicar of Christ" or "Head of the Church," though some do use such terms. Even if the title of pope and other corresponding titles in various languages are legitimate and accepted, the expression "Holy Father" is considered the most deferential form of addressing the bishop of Rome.[38]

The Role of the Pope Today

Several Christian communities, mostly from the eastern Mediterranean and western Asia, have never considered the bishop of Rome their leader. Other groups, which at one time or another acknowledged his leadership, have not been part of his flock for hundreds of years. The pope today stands at the head of only one faction of world Christianity, and his temporal power is very limited. His faction, however, is Christianity's largest: more than half of the world's Christians see him as their spiritual leader. Moreover, due to the fact that other Christian denominations do not have, for a variety of reasons, leaders of the prestige and authority of the pope, some, especially non-Christians, consider the pope the representative of all Christians.

As the bishop of Rome, the pope is in principle responsible for the everyday functioning of the diocese; his role is identical to that of other diocesan bishops. In point of fact, the involvement of many recent popes in the everyday concerns of the community of Rome was and still is limited: a number of auxiliary bishops are responsible for the actual administration of the diocese, and above them stands the "Cardinal Vicar." The role of that cardinal is analogous to that of any "Vicar General" in any diocese: a person (most often, a priest) who functions as the closest aid to the bishop. Still, considering that the bishop of Rome is occupied with so many other things, the Cardinal Vicar is in practice the diocesan bishop of Rome.

The pope's status as bishop of Rome grants him his authority. This fact is well illustrated in the rules regulating the election of a new pope: not only are his electors the cardinals, who are considered, even if they reside elsewhere, "The Elders of Rome," but also following his appointment as Bishop of Rome, no other ceremony is necessary for his investiture as pope (assuming that he has already been ordained a bishop). His standing as head of the community of Rome automatically invests him with the role of leader of the universal Church.

As leader of the universal Church and as the successor of Peter, the bishop of Rome is considered by Catholics to be the ultimate authoritative expositor of the faith tradition that originated with Jesus. In addition to his importance as a symbol of the unity of the Church, his main role is to be the spiritual leader of the Church in the current, ever-changing world. Commanding total, immediate, and supreme authority over the entire Church, the entire world, in a sense, is his diocese. The pope may preside in judgment over all members of the Church, and all Church members may appeal to him for his judgment. This does not mean, of course, that the pope necessarily deals personally with every local issue that arises, but, should he be willing, he can intervene in any matter, great or small.

The pope wields special authority on matters of instruction and teaching. Only he has the authority to grant sainthood, approve the creation of Catholic universities, or permit the founding of a new religious order. He is also the supreme authority in all doctrinal and legal matters. As noted earlier, the pope appoints all other bishops of the Western Church, and every bishop is obligated to meet with him every few years in order to report about his diocese. The pope may also call for various types of assemblies, as well as request meetings with specific individuals.

Because the pope is first and foremost the bishop of Rome, his dress is essentially an elaborate version of bishop's robes. Like other bishops, he also carries a crosier. In the last decades it has become customary for the pope's crosier to feature a crucifix. For the last few centuries, white has been the color of the pope's robes and *zucchetto,* the skullcap that is also worn at times by other members of the Catholic hierarchy.

Is the Pope Fallible?

The Catholic principle of papal infallibility is often met with criticism and ridicule from outside the Church and, at times, even from within. Some of this criticism is based on misconceptions. Every modern pope would admit that the pope is liable to err. The real application of the dogma of the infallibility of the pope, which was defined in 1870, is limited to very specific situations regarding matters of faith or moral, and in which the statement from the outset is declared to be of such authority:

> We teach and define that it is a Dogma[39] Divinely revealed that the Roman Pontiff when he speaks *ex-cathedra*—that is when in discharge of the office of pastor and doctor of all Christians, by virtue of his supreme Apostolic authority, he defines a doctrine regarding faith and morals to be held by the universal Church, by the Divine assistance promised to him by the Blessed Peter—[he] is possessed of that infallibility with which the Divine Redeemer willed that his Church should be endowed.[40]

As this declaration makes clear, use of this power may only be made in fundamental matters of faith and moral. Since being defined—in what at the time was a problematic process—this power has been invoked only once, when in 1950 pope Pius XII defined the Assumption of Mary as dogma.[41] It should be noted that the dogma of infallibility does not assert the pope's unique brilliance, as those who wish to ridicule it often infer. It does not even say in a positive way that the pope will reveal truth. What it states is that God preserves the pope from the possibility of error (and through him, preserves the entire Church) concerning the issue at hand and for that particular moment.

Despite this stipulation, the dogma of papal infallibility indeed seems opposed to contemporary sensibilities. It comes as no surprise that not one of the last six popes since Pius XII has made use of this power, nor have any of these popes ever openly proclaimed that any declaration of theirs was infallible.[42] Popes and their advisors are perfectly aware that use of this dogma will inspire anger as well as contempt both from within and outside the Church, and that the damage from the explicit use of this power today would probably be much greater than any benefits that might be reaped from it.

Papal and Curial Statements

Popes routinely issue numerous documents. The authority, audience, and purpose of these texts vary greatly from one to the next. Contrary to some public perceptions, Catholics do not deem everything the pope utters to be "the word of God" (or even close to it). What he says is certainly important, and for some Catholics, objection to or even passing thoughts about the pope's statements might be considered disrespectful and even heretical (as long as the pope's ideas are, of course, in line with theirs), but from a theological and doctrinal standpoint, most papal statements carry no such weight. Experts on the Vatican and Canon law are able to differentiate between various categories of papal declarations: a weekly sermon is very different from an encyclical sent to the world's bishops, and a statement made to a visiting guest at the Vatican is obviously not the same as a public declaration of an article of faith. Among the documents popes tend to publish, one can find, for example, encyclicals, constitutions, letters, and exhortations. The difference between them has to do with their content, purpose, reason for publication, and the degree of authority given to them. Thus, for example, an apostolic letter carries much less authority than does an apostolic constitution, and an encyclical is generally intended for a larger audience than is an exhortation. Another type of document, the *Bull*—named after the lead "bulla" or seal attached to it—is the most solemn of papal communiqués, but not necessarily the most important. Today Bulls are mostly used for the announcement of an appointment of a new bishop.

Some of the recent popes used less traditional methods for spreading their ideas, such as books and interviews, and in recent years also Facebook and Twitter. Although from a doctrinal perspective these methods carry little weight, it seems very reasonable that these ways of communicating with Catholics and with the entire world will become more and more significant, and will, in practice, become an important way for the popes to have an impact on Church and world affairs.

Many documents released by the Vatican are not generated by the pope. There are significant differences among them as well. Thus, for example, a document published by the "Congregation for the Doctrine of the Faith," will receive much more attention than one published by the "Pontifical

Council for Health Pastoral Care," and a communiqué with an apostolic letter attached will receive more notice than one without such a letter. Some apostolic letters affixed to other documents may grant papal approval of the document, but the document's authority remains dependent upon the body that issued it, while other letters may grant papal patronage as well as authority.

The Election of a New Pope

According to current Canon Law, a pope cannot be unseated. He may retire, and this indeed happened in 2013 when pope Benedict XVI suddenly did exactly that. But unless his resignation starts a new trend (which is not impossible to imagine), we may still say that a pope's reign generally ends with his death.

The period between the moment the seat of the pope is vacant and the start of the process for appointing a successor, a period that today can take between about ten to twenty days, is an especially intense one for the cardinals. All cardinals not permanently residing in Rome (usually the majority) and who are under eighty years of age must immediately make their way to Rome to fulfill the main function of their rank.

The process of electing a new pope has changed much over time, from election by a cheering crowd to secret ballots cast by cardinals. The procedure followed today was formulated in an Apostolic Constitution issued by pope John Paul II in 1996, with some changes made by pope Benedict XVI in 2007 and 2013.[43]

The "Conclave," the process for choosing a new pope, commences between the fifteenth and twentieth day after a pope's death. The term, deriving from the Latin expression *cum clave,* "with a key," dates to the year 1271, when, after nearly three years without a pope, the secular authorities in Rome put the cardinals under lock and key so that they would choose a pope without further delay. This method, which has since become the standard routine, was originally intended to speed up the decision-making process by virtually incarcerating the cardinals and depriving them of food and other necessities. Later, the practice was kept to ensure the secrecy of the voting process. All cardinals under the age of eighty at the time of the pope's death (and whose number should not exceed, according to the regulations, one hundred and twenty) gather together in the Sistine Chapel, adjacent to the Basilica of Saint Peter in the Vatican. Then they begin voting on a candidate to fill this supreme office, all the while remaining isolated from the rest of the world. All discussions, campaigning, and closet agreements are carried out elsewhere, before and in between the voting rounds. Luckily for them, the cardinals do not have to endure harsh sleeping conditions in the Sistine Chapel or in the papal palace, as in times past. Following instructions made by pope John Paul II, they are now transferred under tight security to a modern guesthouse, the *Domus Sanctae Marthae,* located inside the Vatican.

Theoretically, every male, even one still unbaptized, may be elected pope. In practice, the list of candidates is infinitely smaller. One clause in the constitution issued by John Paul II calls for the cardinals to choose a worthy candidate, even if the person chosen is not a cardinal, but the overall supposition, whether plainly or indirectly stated, is that the one chosen will be from among their ranks. As a matter of fact, the last time a non-cardinal was elected to this high office was in the fourteenth century.

Even among the cardinals, the list of realistic candidates is generally quite limited. Many of the cardinals would not wish to be chosen for this demanding position. Over the last decades, several popes have stated that they did not wish to be chosen, and there is no reason to doubt their claims. Among the many factors used to evaluate a particular candidate, his command of languages, status in the Vatican, ethnic and national origin, positions on doctrinal matters, and age seem to be of special importance. Most cardinals do not know one another on a personal level; not infrequently, the first time they meet as a group is during the days preceding the conclave itself. In elections of this kind, the impression a cardinal makes during those days and the importance of a few prominent and charismatic participants who can convince others to vote for specific candidates cannot be overestimated. Still, taking all these factors into account, one must note that the final outcome of conclaves, even if one does not take into consideration the impact of the Holy Spirit, which, according to Catholic faith, is present with the cardinals during the entire process, often surprises even the experts, and is generally unpredictable.

Voting in the conclave is done using paper ballots. At the end of each voting session, which may include one or possibly two rounds of voting, the ballots are burned. A chemical agent is added to the fire to ensure that black smoke rises from the chimney,[44] signaling to the waiting crowd that a decision has not yet been reached. When the necessary two-thirds vote is reached, the cardinal most senior in age asks the chosen candidate if he is willing to accept the nomination. Should the candidate consent (which is likely, otherwise he would have probably raised his objection earlier), he becomes the bishop of Rome, in other words the pope, at that very instant. He is then asked to select a papal name. It is customary that the pope's chosen name expresses a special connection between him and his predecessors, or with a particular saint, or one that symbolizes his worldview.

Thus, for example, pope John XXIII chose to be named after his father John; John Paul I combined the names of his two predecessors, John (XXIII) and Paul (VI), in order to signal his intention of continuing in their path; and Francis chose to associate himself with the medieval Saint Francis and his care for the poor. The number that accompanies the pope's new name is of course "serial," and simply signifies how many popes have previously held that same name.[45] The popes generally choose from a list of traditional names, but they can adopt a name that has never been used, such as with pope Francis. There is one name that has never been chosen: no pope has ever dared to call himself pope Peter II.

The paper ballots used in the final vote are also burned, but now white smoke is released from the chimney, signaling to the outside world that a new pope has been elected and will shortly be presented from the balcony above St. Peter's Square.

The Vatican

The pope has secular duties in addition to his religious ones. He is the head of a state, albeit a tiny one. In spite of its size, it maintains diplomatic relations with most of the countries of the world and is certainly not powerless. It is no surprise that in order to fulfill these duties and many others the pope makes use of a complex system of assistants and administrative staff, which operates out of the Vatican hill, located in the western part of Rome.

Contrary to common conception, even if the name dates back to antiquity, Vatican hill has been the seat of the papacy for a relatively short period of time, in terms of Christian history. In the first century CE, the hill was the site of various sports complexes, among them a hippodrome. The site also contained a cemetery, where, according to tradition, the apostle Peter, who is believed to have been executed in Rome between the years 64–68 CE, was buried.[46] At the end of the second century, a red-colored wall and a small marble monument were built on the spot to mark Peter's burial place, and in the fourth century the Emperor Constantine constructed a church on the site. Most probably, this was the first church built over the supposed tomb of a Christian martyr.

The bishops of Rome did not live on the Vatican hill during the larger part of Catholic history. They resided in proximity to their cathedral, known as the Basilica of Saint John Lateran, located at the southeastern part of Rome, where it was built on land granted to the bishop of Rome by the Emperor Constantine.[47] Popes resided in an adjacent complex, known as the Lateran Palace, from the fourth through the fourteenth century. Beginning in the eleventh century, a number of popes also lived, for part of the time, in a palace built on Vatican hill, but the Lateran Palace remained their official residence. In 1377,[48] after the return of the papal court from a self-imposed seventy-year exile in Avignon (today, in France), the Vatican became the popes' official residence, though some of them still spent considerable time in other locations (for example, during the summers, in another palace on Rome's Quirinal hill).

In 1870, the papacy was dispossessed of its control over Rome as well as vast regions of Italy that it had ruled, more or less, since the eighth century. The pope of the time, Pius IX, maintained control of the Vatican, which was by then a fortified area with defined boundaries. Nearly sixty years later, in 1929, during the reign of pope Pius XI, his Secretary of State, Cardinal Pietro Gasparri, and the then Italian Prime Minister Benito Mussolini signed a "Concordat," a treaty of mutual agreement, which granted the popes territorial and political authority over the Vatican compound. Since then, the "Vatican City State" is considered a separate, sovereign, and neutral state. The expression "The Holy See," used mainly in a diplomatic context, designates the non-territorial power of the pope, and emphasizes that the standing of this entity is not solely based on the physical existence of the Vatican, but rather (certainly, from the Church's perspective) on its religious authority.

The Vatican City State

The Vatican is approximately 110 acres in size. An additional fourteen buildings outside of the city-state's borders enjoy the same political status as those inside. Close to one thousand people live in Vatican City, and about four thousand people work there and in the buildings connected with it. The Vatican has its own postal service, clinic, pharmacy, supermarket, library, museum, bank, police, military guard, and many other apparatuses necessary for the smooth running of a city-state such as this. The body responsible for the diplomatic relations of the Holy See is the Secretariat of State. Given that most countries in the world post an ambassador to the Holy See, the Secretary of State, a cardinal, is one of the most senior positions in the Vatican apparatus.

The Roman Curia

The Roman Curia (in the sense of "court") is made up of various "work groups" that are responsible, both individually and collectively, for the management of various aspects of the universal Catholic Church. Other administrative bodies that are housed in the Vatican, but which deal with the diocese of Rome or with the State of Vatican City, are not considered part of the curia.

The curia includes three tribunals, nine "Congregations," and twelve "Councils." Of the tribunals, two deal with mostly very rare issues of excommunications declared by the pope and appeals regarding decisions made by lower ecclesiastic tribunals. The third tribunal, the "Roman Rota," is much busier: today, it deals mostly with matters concerning annulments of marriages.

The "Congregations" and the "Councils" are similar in structure. Each is headed by a President (in the congregations, a "Prefect") and a Secretary. In addition, a congregation or council is made up of permanent members, usually a few dozen, as well as a permanent staff that assists the head of each congregation or council. Each council or congregation has a more or less defined scope. Its members make decisions, advise the pope, carry out his instructions, or try to promote a certain agenda. The main differences between congregations and councils are seniority (most of the councils are newer), prestige (congregations are considered more prestigious), makeup of its members (the percentage of cardinals, participation of laypersons, etc.), location of the offices, and executive power.

As stated previously, there are currently nine congregations: The Congregation for the Doctrine of the Faith, The Congregation for the Oriental Churches, The Congregation for Divine Worship and the Discipline of the Sacraments, The Congregation for the Causes of Saints, The Congregation of Bishops, The Congregation for the Evangelization of Peoples, The Sacred Congregation for the Clergy, The Congregation for Institutes of Consecrated Life and Societies of Apostolic Life, and the Congregation for Catholic Education. The roles of many of the councils, as their names suggest, lie more in the area of pastoral care, or they operate as "think tanks" on specific issues: Council for the Laity, Council for Promoting Christian Unity, Council for the Family, Council for Justice and Peace, Council Cor Unum ("one heart," deals with matters of charity and material aid to the needy), Council for the Care of Migrants and Itinerants, Council for Health Pastoral Care, Council for Legislative Texts, Council for Interreligious Dialogue, Council for Culture, Council for Social Communications, and Council for New Evangelization.

A short time after the election of pope Francis in 2013, he declared his intention to reconsider the structure of the Curia. He also appointed a group of cardinals whose role is to advise him on the matter. At the time of this writing, no significant changes have yet been made, but it is very possible that in the coming months or years pope Francis will indeed reform and reshape the structure described here.

The Vatican: Image and Reality

The institutions described above make do with a very limited staff. Despite its bureaucratic image, the Vatican does not have a large administrative system. Besides the many art treasures and some very elaborate buildings, which cannot be converted into ready capital and for which the cost of maintenance is very high,[49] the Vatican is not wealthy. The Roman curia employs about 2,600 men and women, of which about three-quarters work in administrative and service positions (secretarial and postal work, drivers, etc.).[50] Compared with the variety of activities expected of the Vatican, the number of persons able to make decisions is very small. In financial terms, the Vatican's image is quite different from its reality: the Vatican's annual budget is around three hundred million dollars, certainly not a high number for such an enterprise. Surprisingly, some claim that the Vatican's administration should receive the title of "world's most efficient bureaucracy" because, on a very limited budget,[51] a small number of people are able to manage an enormous number of issues in many languages.[52]

The Holy See's International Status

The international role of the Holy See is dependent in many ways upon the international status of each pope. Though the pope commands neither armies nor legions, in the eyes of many, even among non-Catholics, he is held up as a moral authority who must be taken seriously. Many leaders who have a significant Catholic population in their constituency consider a photo op with the pope a wise act. One should remember, nevertheless, that such a status is not automatically guaranteed to the man occupying the Seat of Peter: in recent decades, some of the popes were international celebrities, and some were, to say it politely, not.

In official diplomatic terms, it is the "Holy See," not the geographic city-state of the Vatican, that is awarded international status. In the United Nations, the Holy See currently has the status of "non-member permanent observer state." This position, higher than "permanent observer" (the present status of the European Union for example) and below member states, enables a representative of the Holy See to propose resolutions, take part in discussions, address the General Assembly, and demand that its comments be included in official resolutions. Some believe that the Vatican could have also been granted full rights, including voting rights, but chose to abstain from this request. In addition to the United Nations, the Holy See is represented in many other international organizations.[53]

The Importance of the Pope Today

Despite all that was said above, the religious lives of most Catholics are barely affected by the status of the Vatican, the election process for a new pope, the pope's personal views, or even by how the pope fulfills one or another of his functions. This is not a new phenomenon, to say the least. The question of the importance and authority of the pope with regard to the actual functioning of local Churches has always been a controversial topic in the Church. Often the term "ultramontanists" is used to describe those who support the strong involvement of Rome, that place "beyond the mountains," while "gallicanists" (a term of French origin: those who are from and for Gaul, the ancient name of France) are those who believe the local and national customs and authority should prevail.

In the past, there were many periods and places in which the majority of Catholics, laity, priests, and bishops alike could not have cared less about what the pope said or wanted. At times, some even seriously imagined the possibility of a Catholic Church functioning permanently without a pope. The Church went through many periods, as short as a few hours and as long as centuries, without having a significant and powerful figure sitting in Rome. One can hardly speak about these periods as particularly bad for the Church's growth and persistence. But today, with a much more centralized power, such attitudes are considered unacceptable in the Church. Given the current state of affairs in the universal Church, ultramontanism unquestionably has the upper hand. This does not mean that lay Catholics today necessarily follow the pope's statements no matter who he is. But their bishops and most of their priests, with a few exceptions, do.

Since the election of pope Francis in 2013, an almost unprecedented interest in what the pope says and does has been felt in the Catholic Church: another example to the fact that the personality of the pope has tremendous effect on his status. Only time will tell what the impact of this situation will be. What is obvious though, and what will continue to be true no matter who is pope, is the idea that papacy symbolizes Church unity and makes this unity visible. The pope makes many Catholics feel they have a special direct link to Jesus through his most important apostle, Peter. The Church believes that through the pope, the prayer of Jesus that those who believe in him "may all be one"[54] can be fulfilled. The pope thus symbolizes the unity of the Church of the present with the Church of the past and with the Church in Heaven.

Priests

Naturally, the pope, the cardinals, and the bishops cannot care for the immediate daily needs of the faithful. Even if some dioceses count only a few thousand members, the laity in many dioceses number in the hundreds of thousands or even millions. The members of the hierarchy that are in more direct contact with the laity are generally the priests.

Already in the first centuries, men, and in some times and places women as well,[55] were appointed in order to help bishops carry out their duties. In later periods, with the rise of the monastic orders and monasteries, some of their members were appointed to do similar tasks under the supervision of their superiors. Of the many types of such assisting positions, only four are still extant in the universal Church. Two positions, "Lector" and "Acolyte," which in times past belonged to what was known as the "minor orders," associated with providing service during the celebration of the Mass, are filled generally by lay people. Those who fill them are not ordained and do not become part of the Church hierarchy. In practice, both men and women fill them, but canonically women who accomplish these roles, and many of the men who do so as well, do not hold the formal permanent title of "Lector" and "Acolyte" given through a special rite. The two other roles require ordination. They also can presently be received, according to the Magisterium's teaching, by men only. The more familiar to the non-Catholic public, and the higher in status, is that of priest. The other is the deacon. We will address first the role of the priest, and later the role of the deacon.

The historical process of the creation of the priest's role is not entirely clear. According to the traditional Catholic outlook, it was created in order to assist the bishop in the celebration of the Mass. With the growth and spread of Christian communities, these assistants were slowly awarded greater authority in various areas of communal life, the most important being the authority to celebrate the Mass even without the physical presence of the bishop, provided that they were carrying it out under his spiritual authority.

Some scholars cast doubt on this depiction, suggesting that it was more likely that the role of priest came into being during the years when the councils of elders (in Greek, *Presbyteroi*), which had led many of the communities up until the middle or end of the second century, were disbanded. When a single leader, now taking the place of the council, assumed the role of bishop, other council members who had not received the leadership role became known as priests. In any case, and regardless of its exact evolution, by the end of the second and certainly by the third century, the role of priest was a distinct one in many churches.[56]

The priest is in most instances responsible for the liturgical needs of the community, whether it is a community of consecrated life or a local community of laypersons. Such a local community, a parish, constitutes the cornerstone of the diocese and of the entire universal Church. At times, a few priests can serve a single parish. In this case, one will be responsible for the parish and the others will assist him, with their relationship similar to that of a diocesan bishop and his auxiliary bishop(s).

A priest's main function is the celebration of the Mass, although, in accordance with the type of community under his auspices or to which he belongs, he may celebrate many other rituals, such as baptisms, funerals, marriages, anointing of the sick, or the hearing of confessions. The priest is also responsible for the orderly running of the parish, including its finances, the registering of births, deaths, and marriages, the organizing of prayer or study groups, chairing several committees and/or appointing their members, etc. On the parish level, the priest is the public face of the Catholic Church hierarchy and the one person who has to deal with the laity's expectations from the Church on a daily basis.

The Status of Priests Today

The status of the priest in the theology that came out of, or at least is associated with, the Second Vatican Council and its aftermath is complex. One might say that the priest's status suffered a double diminution in this theology, being squeezed from two directions. On the one hand, the Council emphasized the importance of the bishops, and the fact that only their ordination, and not that of deacons or priests, provides the "fullness" of that sacrament. Where, then, in this worldview, is the priest? On the other hand, the Council reinforced the idea that all members of the Church are "priests." If everyone is a priest, what meaning is there to the priest's priesthood? How is his status higher than that of a layperson's?

Some view these changes in perception as positive. In their opinion, the formal gap that existed in the past between laypersons and priests resulted in the difficulty priests sometimes had in relating to and understanding the real needs of the laity they are supposed to serve. For them, narrowing this gap between priests and the laity is a positive, corrective change. Others view it as a negative one, and indeed a number of studies show that among young priests over the last decades, there has been an upward trend in the desire for establishing clear boundaries between themselves and the laity.

The Priest's Vestments

A priest's outward appearance when not performing ceremonial duties is very much dependent upon local culture. The traditional and generally black robe, the "Cassock," that some might associate with priests, is worn today mostly among conservative groups or by priests living in areas that are considered, correctly or not, more conservative. In some places, a Catholic priest might wear the characteristic white "roman" collar;[57] in others, only a small metal cross on his chest may hint at his status. During the celebration of the liturgy, a priest dons a number of characteristic vestments, the most familiar being the chasuble, a colorful, wide, sleeveless robe, which the priest generally wears over his regular clothing.

Deacons

In addition to the role of a bishop or a priest, there is a third role in the Catholic Church that also requires ordination. The deacon, whose name stems from the Greek word *diakonos* ("servant"), helps the priest and bishop in their work.[58]

The first appointment of deacons is recorded in the New Testament and occurs following complaints about the aid given to the needy:

> So the Twelve called together the community of the disciples and said, "It is not right for us to neglect the word of God and serve (*diakonein*) at table. Brothers, select from among you seven reputable men, filled with the Spirit and wisdom, whom we shall appoint to this task, whereas we shall devote ourselves to prayer and to the ministry of the word." The proposal was acceptable to the whole community, so they chose Stephen . . . also Philip . . . they presented these men to the apostles who prayed and laid hands on them.[59]

It seems from the context of this story that the task of those chosen was first and foremost to assist in charity work in the community. And indeed, for generations, deacons were appointed mainly to care for the needs of the community's poor. Later, functions such as assisting the priest in his responsibilities were added, particularly the celebration of certain rituals in which the priest's presence was not essential. Deacons became responsible, for example, for recitation of passages from Scriptures, and for distribution of the Host during the Mass. In fact, already in the New Testament it seems some of these assistants were taking an active part in communal proceedings.[60]

Following the decisions of the Second Vatican Council, a thorough revision was made with regard to the various assisting roles in the Church. As noted earlier, on the one hand, those that were called "minor orders" were abolished; on the other hand, the status of deacon was maintained and even expanded.

For several centuries, a deacon was generally a temporary status for the ordained on the way to priesthood. Following the Council, the status of a "permanent deacon" was redefined to denote a deacon who is not seeking later ordination to the priesthood. The Council decided that if the pope allows it—and in 1968, pope Paul VI did—a married man may also be ordained a permanent deacon. For the Eastern Catholic Churches, where priests could be married, this was not a major innovation. But for the 98 percent of the world's Catholics following the Roman, Western Rite, this was nothing short of a conceptual revolution: a married man, possibly the father of children, could now be considered part of the Catholic hierarchy, able to celebrate some of the sacraments and sacramentals that are often associated with a priest, and able to deliver a homily during Mass.

The position of "transitional" (temporary) deacon is still, needless to say, in effect: every candidate for the priesthood, after completing or nearly completing his studies and after being deemed worthy of the priesthood, is first ordained as a deacon. Only about a year later will he be ordained as a priest.

Deacons Today

Transitional deacons assist the priests in their duties and fulfill various liturgical roles. In many respects, this period of service can be considered a continuation of their training and preparation for the priesthood. Even if they are serving the Church well in this manner, it is clear that it is only an intermediary stage in their ordination to the priesthood.

The significance of a permanent deacon is very different. There are more than forty thousand permanent deacons in the universal Catholic Church at the time of publication. Since the beginning of the twenty-first century, their number increased by about 50 percent (as a comparison, the number of priests increased during the same period by about 3 percent). About 95 percent of the permanent deacons are or were married. Their geographic distribution varies throughout the Church: the majority, more than two-thirds of all permanent deacons, live in either the United States or Europe, even though only about one third of the world's Catholics live in these two areas. Their numbers are so small in many countries (and in some they do not exist at all, for either fundamental or circumstantial reasons) that it is difficult to attribute to them any real power or influence. However, in the places where they do exist, permanent deacons are often considered an important element in the preservation of the parish, especially in areas where there is severe a shortage of priests. The constant dramatic growth in their numbers in recent years almost ensures that they will become a group with considerable impact on the Church.

Many permanent deacons are ordained at a rather advanced age. In terms of Canon Law, thirty-five is the minimum age for a married deacon; in practice, however, many permanent deacons are ordained at much later ages. Despite the problems that may arise from this, the fact of their being established and recognized in their community may help give the parish a certain stability that a priest, who is generally replaced every few years, may not be able to provide.

The Deacon's Vestments

In liturgical ceremonies, a deacon may be recognized by the type of vestment he wears, called a dalmatic, which is a sleeved robe (the priest's robe is sleeveless and wider) and a wide fabric band, a stole, worn along a diagonal. This same kind of band is draped over the two shoulders when worn by priests and bishops.

The Earthly and Heavenly Church

Following this certainly limited survey of the lay as well as ordained members of the Catholic Church, this chapter will conclude with a discussion of the Church's celestial members. For the believing Catholic, the earthly Church constitutes just one part of the Church, which includes, according to the Catholic faith, those members who departed from this world and those who were never humans: angels. Appreciation of this fact is essential for a true understanding of Catholic mentality, not just in relation to questions having to do with the meaning of life, reward, and punishment, or the relationship between the living and the dead, but also in order to understand the Church's very structure.

According to Catholic belief, a person's fate is sealed at the moment of his or her death. Those who lived righteously and died in grace and without sin are worthy of entering Heaven, where they will be forever in God's presence. Those who lived a generally righteous life, but at the moment of their death were not entirely free of sin, are also promised entry into Heaven, but must first undergo a process of purification through the "purgatory." While the Church authorities today do not attempt to determine who is worthy of being confined to hell (many past leaders did so in the past, and more than once) and even declare praying that no person ever be condemned to that fate, the Church does believe that those who were guilty of particularly grave sins will be sent there. An everlasting separation from God will be their punishment.[61]

The celestial Church includes those already in Heaven, where they abide in the shadow of God the Father, along with Jesus, Mary, the angels, and the saints. The hierarchy in heaven is not at all like the earthly hierarchy: a person's place in heaven is based upon that person's deeds on earth, not upon money or power. The saints, headed by Mary, stand high in this celestial hierarchy.

The Saints

Many theologians will point out that there have always been more sinners than saints in the Church. Nevertheless, it has also always included saints. According to the current doctrine, a saint is a person who was declared by the Church, after a thorough investigation, as someone who is now in Heaven, someone who had perfect faith and impeccable deeds, and who is a model to follow. It must also be concluded that a miracle happened to individuals who specifically invoked this person's help. In practice, many early saints attained their saintly status as a result of popular veneration (with the hierarchy's approval coming only later), or by going through martyrdom, the quasi-automatic ticket to sainthood.

In the past, the processes that led to the canonization of an individual were quite complex and often varied. Events leading up to such a declaration often started at the grass roots, with the public's veneration at a local level of a deceased person. Often this included ceremonies being held at the person's grave, attributing to him or her special healing powers, etc. The Church often viewed these ritual activities as a threat to its authority over the religious needs of the community, a fear that was indeed in many cases well justified. In order to emphasize its control and primacy, the Church admitted some of those venerated into its ranks of saints and rejected others.

The Catholic Church commands a long list of saints, estimated by some to number around 10,000. Many lived in the first centuries of the first millennium, during the time when Christians were persecuted.[62] Their death for their faith made them, by this very fact, saints. Other saints have been added throughout the Church's history. There have been also some rare instances of de-canonization of saints, or at least removing their name from the Church's list, when it was discovered that the reasons for their canonization had not been well enough established, or that the historical proofs for the very existence of the saint are seriously lacking: Saint Christopher is one the most famous saints who suffered this humiliating fate.

For centuries the canonization process took on the characteristics of a legal proceeding, during which two Church-appointed delegates—titled "Promoter of the Cause" and "Promoter of the Faith" (or "Devil's advocate")—would respectively argue for and against canonization, with the latter trying to find deficiencies in the candidate. Today, the process is different. The role of the "Devil's advocate" does not exist anymore, and the process resembles more a scholarly preparation of a well-annotated biography than a legal trial.

Once a request for canonization of a specific individual is made (usually not less than five years after the person's death, although permission to begin the process earlier may be granted by the pope), the diocesan bishop where the candidate resided opens an investigation, at the end of which he prepares a report containing all possible information about the proposed candidate: his or her virtues, belief, works of charity, etc. Where applicable, this information must be confirmed by witnesses who had contact with the individual. Should the candidate have left any writings, the bishop must also study them, aided in this by experts on the matter and a legal council appointed by him. The bishop must also collect any information about miracles that may have taken place through this person's intercession. All this information is then passed on to the "Congregation for the Causes of Saints" in the Vatican, which oversees the process of canonization. This office might recommend declaring the person "Venerable," thus encouraging people to pray that he or she will perform miracles. Meanwhile, various experts, among them historians, psychologists, and theologians, are asked to study the various aspects of the case. If miracles involving healing are attributed to the candidate, physicians may be asked for their opinion. Once all the information is gathered, it will be presented to the congregation, whose members will vote on it. The results of the vote will be passed on to the pope, who will render the final decision. Following an affirmative decision, the candidate is declared beatified or "Blessed." After a number of years and normally only after another miracle (which has taken place after the declaration of beatification) has been verified will the candidate be canonized and declared a saint, who may then be invoked by all members of the universal Church.

The Presence of Saints in the Church

In ancient times, relics of saints were interred beneath every altar, the furnishing similar to a table, often made entirely or partially of stone, on which the ritual of the Mass is celebrated.[63] Sometimes the altar was built atop remains that were believed to be previously in that location. In recent centuries, small relics have often been placed within a special space embedded in the altar's top. Following the Second Vatican Council, the earlier practice has once again been taken up. Thus, when a local church constructs and consecrates a new permanent fixed altar, relics of saints (often, parts of bones)—which in many instances are received from a special office in the Vatican—are buried beneath the altar in a ceremony overseen by the bishop. The name of the church is often associated with the identity of the specific saint.

It is reasonable to assume that the placement of the relics of saints in churches originates from the early Christian practice in Rome and other locations of praying and celebrating the Mass at the gravesites of deceased and venerated members of the Church. That custom, as well as the present practice of consecrating a new altar with the relic of a saint, carries great theological significance: it demonstrates the role saints play in spatial and in spiritual terms in the Church. Saints are thus part of the universal Church and the local one in a very tangible way, having their remains placed where the faithful gather. The "communion of saints," mentioned in the Apostles' Creed, is given a physical presence: the saints are present in body and in spirit with the members of the Church on earth.[64]

Mary

Any discussion of the saints in particular and of the Church in general would not be complete without touching upon the place of the most revered person among all the saints: the Virgin Mary, the mother of Jesus, the Mother of God. Her exceptional status has made her the focus of a special branch of theology known as Mariology.

According to Christian faith, Mary was chosen by God from among all women (and from among all humankind, some might say) to be the mother of his son. Many Catholic theologians will argue that this proves Mary's exceptional status. Moreover, her unhesitating assent to this holy mission, uttered to the angel Gabriel at the Annunciation, "Behold, I am the handmaid of the Lord. May it be done to me according to your word,"[65] have made her a model and exemplar of the believer who acquiesces to the will of God. Other passages in the New Testament, such as Jesus' words to his "beloved disciple" at the crucifixion, "Behold, your mother,"[66] while pointing to Mary, have been interpreted as Jesus' declaration of his mother as the mother of all his present and future disciples.

Mary enjoyed a special standing in many early Christian communities, but in doctrinal terms the turning point in establishing her status came in the year 431 at the Council of Ephesus. That Council decreed that Mary was worthy of the title *Theotokos*, ("birth-giver of God"), for she is not only the birth-giver of Jesus the man, as those who objected to this title had argued, she is also the birth-giver of God incarnated in human flesh.[67]

The veneration of Mary continued through the centuries, with many rituals associated with her, countless churches built in her honor, and famous prayers addressed to her. Though in recent decades several Church documents insisted that the veneration of Mary should not cause the absolute centrality of Jesus to be sidelined, Mary continues to be of the utmost significance for the Church and for the Catholic faith, counting among her admirers both simple lay people and popes. Mary, along with the other saints, continues to be a light to which, and a compass by which, the Catholic believers in Jesus march.

Notes

1. For a good introduction to the field of Christian ecclesiology, see Veli-Matti Kärkkäinen, *An Introduction to Ecclesiology: Ecumenical, Historical & Global Perspectives* (Downers Grove: InterVarsity Press, 2002).
2. Professional theologians would call such ecclesiology "High Ecclesiology," to distinguish it from "Low Ecclesiology," typical to some other Christian Churches, who do not consider their own structure as essential for redemption or divinely instituted.
3. Among the most important works on Catholic ecclesiology in English in recent decades, one must mention Avery Dulles, *Models of the Church*, expanded edition (New York: Doubleday, 2002); Richard P. McBrien, *The Church: The Evolution of Catholicism* (New York: Harper One, 2008).
4. For more on such "Institutes," many of which are known also as "Orders," see pp. 54–60. In fact, even non-ordained members of the Church who are members in an Institute of Consecrated Life are "laypersons," but for reasons of clarity, they will not be part of the present discussion.
5. See for example Paul Lakeland, *The Liberation of the Laity: In Search of an Accountable Church* (New York: Continuum, 2004).
6. Exodus 19:6.
7. One needs to bear in mind that ancient Christian traditions connect the Eucharist with the showbread in the Temple in Jerusalem, which was only eaten by the priests. For this reason, the partaking of the consecrated bread is a definite "priestly" act. See Leviticus 24:5–9; 1 Samuel 21:1–7; Matthew 12:1–8.
8. The word "Institute" here refers to a social organization, not to a physical brick and mortar structure.
9. To simplify the discussion, I will occasionally use the word "group" as a simple ersatz of the more clumsy expression "Institutes of Consecrated Life."
10. For a scholarly edition of this extremely important text, see Benedict of Nursia, *The Rule of Saint Benedict*, ed. and trans. Bruce L. Venarde (Cambridge: Harvard University Press, 2011).
11. On these prayers, see pp. 144–145.
12. A wonderful exploration of the very varied life of different nuns today appears in Mary Gordon's "Women of God," *The Atlantic Monthly* (January 2002): 57–91.

13. At the time of publication, the pope himself, pope Francis, is a member of such a group, being a Jesuit.
14. Matthew 10, and parallels; Matthew 28:16–20, and parallels.
15. For a good overview of the issue, see Francis A. Sullivan, *From Apostles to Bishops: The Development of the Episcopacy in the Early Church* (New York: Newman Press, 2001); Claudia Rapp, *Holy Bishops in Late Antiquity: The Nature of Christian Leadership in an Age of Transition* (Berkeley: University of California Press, 2005).
16. In reality, almost all current bishops of the Roman Catholic Church can trace their lineage up to one Italian cardinal in the sixteenth century, Scipione Rebiba. There is no reliable documentation about who ordained Rebiba, and through which line of succession.
17. On this function, see further on in the chapter.
18. Although a number of Western bishops, such as the bishop of Venice or the Latin bishop of Jerusalem are also called "Patriarchs," they are not "real" patriarchs. Their title is only an honorific one. Unlike the patriarchs we discuss here, they do not stand at the head of a Church with a particular liturgical tradition. For various reasons, pope Benedict XVI decided in 2006 to discontinue the use of the title "Patriarch of the West" that was used in the past to refer to the pope. Some saw this as a sign of humility. Others, including some Orthodox theologians, suspected that the opposite is true, and that this dropping of the title hinted that Benedict thinks the pope should be considered the universal patriarch, and not only the one heading the West.
19. Some Eastern Catholic Churches are headed by "Major Archbishops." Although a less prestigious title, the function of the Major Archbishop is relatively similar to that of a Patriarch.
20. On these Churches, see the relevant appendix, pp. 229–232.
21. In recent years, in some high profile cases, bishops resigned or were forced to resign due to accusations related to the improper handling of priest child-abuse cases, or even for being personally guilty of such acts.
22. The shape of this conical hat has changed over the years since its appearance in the eleventh century. The color of the miter changes according to the liturgical calendar. The headdress of bishops in the Eastern Churches is different. Some have on them either a standing or flat-lying cross.
23. For a useful exploration of the issue see Maureen C. Miller, *Power and the Holy in the Age of the Investiture Conflict: A Brief History with Documents* (New York: Bedford/ St. Martin's, 2005).
24. On these Congregations, see further on in this chapter.
25. Code of Canon Law, c. 1382.
26. For example, this is how Rome treats ordinations in the official Chinese Catholic Church, which is under the close scrutiny of the Chinese authorities and is not supposed to recognize the authority of Rome. Though this Church is considered a "schismatic" Church, one that has relinquished its ties to the universal Church, the sacraments celebrated by its clergy are considered valid, as the line of succession of its bishops is legitimate. It is reasonable to imagine that a solution to this complex situation, and to the very nature of the relations between the Holy See and China, will be reached in the coming years.
27. *Motu Proprio Ecclesia Dei* of pope John Paul II, July 2, 1988. This ordination took the Vatican by surprise because it was done while Cardinal Ratzinger, then head of the Congregation for the Doctrine of the Faith, was engaged in finding an acceptable formula for appeasement with Lefebvre.
28. In August 2005, Ratzinger, by then pope Benedict XVI, met with the most senior of the four bishops. The meeting was described as both warm and positive. A number of years went by, and in January 2009 he declared the annulment of the excommunication. Only

later did he learn that one of the four, in addition to his other controversial views, was also a Holocaust denier. Benedict XVI apologized for his lack of awareness of this fact, but the excommunication was not restored.

29. On the Catholic tendency to try to avoid schisms of all kinds, see also pp. 26–27.
30. Council of Trent, 23rd Session, Decree on Reformation, par. 1.
31. See Matthew 16:13–20 and parallels.
32. See, for example, James as the final adjudicator in the Acts of the Apostles 15:12–21, or the attack of Paul against him in Galatians 2.
33. Matthew 4:18–20, and parallels; Matthew 10:1–4, and parallels; Matthew 14:22–33, and parallels; John 21:15–17, and parallels; and more.
34. See for example the end of chapter 5 in the First Epistle of Peter. The word "Babylon" is undoubtedly a reference to Rome. The prophecy regarding Peter's death, put in Jesus' mouth by the author of the relatively late Gospel according to John (see John 21:18–19), might be yet another hint to the circumstances of Peter's death. More information about these events appears in the late first- or very early second-century "Epistle to the Corinthians" by Clement of Rome.
35. Orthodox Christianity claims that Peter was the founder of the Church of Antioch (today's Antakya, in southern Turkey, close to the Syrian border). It does not object, though, to the shared early tradition that he eventually arrived in Rome and was executed there. Most Protestants, originating from the Western Church, accept the idea that Peter had special role in Rome, but do not attribute to this possibly historical fact a major theological significance.
36. Doubts were raised already in the Middle Ages regarding the authenticity of the document, but not until the fifteenth century was it demonstrated irrefutably to be a forgery. Most scholars believe the text was drafted in the eighth or ninth century.
37. For discussions on the issue from both historical and theological perspectives, see Walter Kasper, ed., *The Petrine Ministry: Catholics and Orthodox in Dialogue* (New York: Newman Press, 2006).
38. The repetitive use of the word "sir" by former American President George W. Bush during his meeting with pope Paul John II in 2001 is often considered as the classic example of how one should not address the pope. It is possible, however, that this neutral, secular term was used by President Bush in order to avoid an honorific that would have been at odds with his own religious beliefs and those of many of his most vocal supporters.
39. On the meaning of the term "dogma" see p. 45.
40. Vatican I, *Pastor Aeternus* (1870), ch. 4. This declaration was the culmination of centuries of theological debates about the issue.
41. See p. 46. The fact that this dogma is a product of the nineteenth century should not, however, lead one to believe that the concept of papal infallibility is a recent one. In fact, the definition of the dogma followed debates on the issue that lasted for centuries. On the origins of this idea see Brian Tierney, *Origins of Papal Infallibility, 1150–1350; A Study on the Concepts of Infallibility, Sovereignty and Tradition in the Middle Ages* (Leiden: E. J. Brill, 1972).
42. The closest a modern pope came to a declaration that neared a supposedly infallible teaching was probably *Ordinatio Sacerdotalis*, a statement about the impossibility of ordaining women to the priesthood, released by pope John Paul II in 1994. Even there, though, the precise terms that should have been used were not included, leaving the possibility for many progressive Catholics to claim it was not an infallible declaration. See more on this document on p. 196.
43. *Universi Dominici Gregis* from February 22, 1996, and *De Aliquibus Mutationibus in Normis De Electione Romani Pontificis* from June 11, 2007. Pope Benedict XVI made some

final changes in February 2013, several days before the end of his papacy, in particular in order to adapt it to the unusual case of a retiring pope.

44. In reality, today there are two furnaces servicing the cardinals: one is used to burn the ballots, while another releases black or white smoke.

45. At times the number is of greater significance (or might even be erroneous). Thus, for example, the fact that pope John XXIII, elected in 1959, was "23rd" and not "24th" was based on the conviction that the fifteenth-century "pope John XXIII" was illegitimate, an "anti-pope." In the succession of the "Johns" there was even a mistake: the John that followed John XIX called himself, for various reasons, John XXI. There was never, therefore, a John XX.

46. In 1941, archeological excavations uncovered a first century CE cemetery underneath the Basilica of St. Peter in the Vatican. One of the graves there was attributed to Peter. In 1968, pope Paul VI published a declaration asserting that in his opinion, and based on expert opinion, the likelihood that this grave and the bones found inside it belong to Peter is very high. A sarcophagus with the remains is housed in the Basilica of St. Peter. There is historical evidence of the existence of a monument to Saint Peter in the area, and it is likely that there was also a grave. In regard to the question of whose bones were found, it is difficult to give a definite answer. At the end of 2013, the bones were shown to the public for the first time. Needless to say, this did not help resolve the question about their authenticity.

47. This local act by Constantine should not be confused with the forged document known as "The Donation of Constantine," which I mentioned earlier on p. 70.

48. Though people claiming the papal throne continued to live in Avignon until 1414, there was also a pope in Rome from 1377. During this period, known as the "Great Schism," there were two or even three simultaneous claimants to the papacy.

49. Like other leading museums in the world, the Vatican has not considered selling any of its art treasures during periods of financial crisis. It views its collections as an important part of humankind's cultural and spiritual patrimony. It feels that dividing up the collection and selling it would not only cause grave financial damage to the Vatican Museum, to which millions of visitors come every year, but would also fail to bring any long-term solutions. The selling of a number of artworks during the reign of pope Paul VI is viewed as exceptional, and it seems there is no current intention to repeat it.

50. The State of Vatican City, an administrative-geographical unit separate from the curia, employs about 1,500 men and women. This number includes staff of the museum, the library, maintenance services, the police, medical professionals, postal workers, supermarket employees, and the like.

51. Needless to say, the fact that many of the Vatican's employees are priests and nuns who receive a very modest salary, and often even that from other sources such as their original diocese or order, helps.

52. In 2001 the National Geographic Society produced a worthwhile film on the Vatican, entitled "Inside the Vatican." It is freely and legally available on YouTube. A book with a similar name, Thomas J. Reese, *Inside the Vatican* (Cambridge: Harvard University Press, 2003), remains an outstanding scholarly piece on the functioning of that institution.

53. On various aspects of the international political involvement of the Holy See, see Eric O. Hanson, *The Catholic Church in World Politics* (Princeton: Princeton University Press, 1987).

54. John 17:21.

55. For an excellent collection of sources on the matter, see Kevin Madigan and Carolyn Osiek, *Ordained Women in the Early Church: A Documentary History* (Baltimore: Johns Hopkins University Press, 2005).

56. For a good summary of some aspects of this history, see Aidan Nichols, *Holy Order: The Apostolic Ministry from the New Testament to the Second Vatican Council* (Dublin: Veritas Publications, 1990).

57. The same or very similar white collar and black cassock are also used at times by male and female clergy of other Christian denominations. Thus, not all those who wear them are necessarily Catholic priests.

58. At times, Catholic theologians have explained this role as similar to the Levites in the Temple in Jerusalem, who assisted the priests that worked under the supervision of the High Priest (which they compare to the Bishop).

59. Acts 6:1–6. Another important text dealing with this issue appears in 1 Timothy 3:8–13. This text also will be discussed in the context of ordination of women; see p. 197.

60. See for example Acts 6:8. For an exploration of many historical, theological, and sociological aspects of the roles of deacons, see James Keating, ed., *The Deacon Reader* (Mahwah: Paulist Press, 2006).

61. For an interesting discussion of various opinions on the matter expressed by Catholic theologians in recent decades, see Avery Dulles, "The Population of Hell," *First Things* (May 2003): 36–41.

62. As said earlier, the actual magnitude of persecutions was probably smaller than claimed. See this on p. 12.

63. In the United States, an altar made of solid and high quality wood is also valid today.

64. For another discussion regarding saints in the Catholic Church, see pp. 150-153.

65. Luke 1:38.

66. John 19:27.

67. For a comprehensive work on the history of Mary, see Miri Rubin, *Mother of God: A History of the Virgin Mary* (New Haven: Yale University Press, 2009).

CHAPTER **4**

Catholic Rituals

The vast majority of religions have acts that are done repeatedly, following a prescribed manner, and which have important meaning for the community. These rituals are related in various ways to the beliefs of the group, and both express and shape them. Generally, they are performed in a formal way and are often supposed to be the exact replication of the way the ritual has been performed in the past. The analysis of such rituals is considered by many scholars of religions to be one of the best ways to understand the religious group in question.

The Catholic Church also has its own rituals. In fact, it has countless of them. Understanding these rituals is a crucial part in our attempt to understand Catholicism. We cannot explore all Catholic rituals here, but we can investigate the most important of them. Therefore, the greater part of this chapter will be devoted to the sacraments, the central rituals of the Catholic Church. The last part of the chapter will discuss additional Catholic ritual acts, many of which are referred to as sacramentals.

Sacraments: Connection between Humans and God

According to the Catholic faith, sacraments are central elements in God's mysterious plan for the redemption of humankind. In fact, in the early Christian era the Latin *sacramentum* carried the same meaning as the Greek *mysterion*, from which the English word "mystery" is derived. One common definition for sacrament is a means through which God's grace is transmitted to humans. Augustine, the famous Church Father of the late fourth and early fifth centuries, explained that the sacraments are "a visible sign of an invisible reality."[1] Though this definition is still helpful, one should remember that Augustine considered acts such as prayer and statements of faith to also be sacraments. Unlike him, the definition accepted by the Catholic Church for the last seven hundred years refers to seven, and only seven, very distinct rituals. These rituals produce a "grace," a kind of divine gift that the faithful who "receives" them enjoys. For Catholics, the fact that the performance of many of the sacraments requires material elements such as water, oil, bread, or wine, and that there is the inclusion of visible gestures and actions in all of them, is another aspect of God's incarnation in the world. The sacraments are an important way to emphasize it.

The Seven Sacraments

The majority of the seven sacraments are either overtly or covertly connected to what anthropologists term "rites of passage:" rituals that mark a person's progress from one status in life to another.[2] While many Catholic theologians may not deem this to be the reason that these particular rituals and not others are considered sacraments, they are unlikely to claim that such a correlation is irrelevant. Other elements of Church ritual, such as liturgical reading from Scriptures or prayer, if not performed in connection with one of the seven sacraments, are not defined as sacraments.

Today, the most common names for the seven Catholic sacraments are these (alternative names in parenthesis): Baptism, Confirmation, Eucharist (Communion, Mass), Reconciliation (Penance, Confession), Matrimony (Marriage), Holy Orders (Ordination), and Anointing of the Sick.

The Church also recognizes and accepts the existence of many "sacramentals," additional religious acts performed by Catholics both individually and communally. The variety of sacramentals is very large: among them one can mention the making of the sign of the cross, wearing specific medals, using holy water, going on pilgrimage, lighting candles, reciting personal prayers, making processions, conducting and participating in funerals, and many more. I will return to the sacramentals later in the chapter, following our survey of the seven sacraments, which are, in the eyes of the Catholic Church, above and beyond any other ritual act in terms of their importance and spiritual power.

Baptism

Baptism, a ritualized act that includes bodily contact with water and is related in some way to an individual's joining of the community of believers in Jesus, exists in almost all groups that consider themselves Christian. Some Christians will even say that a community that does not have such a ritual cannot actually be called Christian.[3] A part of them might also hold the opinion that a person who has not undergone such a ritual is not a Christian in the fullest sense of the word. A significant segment of those Christians who fully espouse the ritual of baptism, Catholics among them, consider baptism to be the "First Sacrament" and the gateway through which one enters the Christian community.

Baptism in the New Testament

Baptism is mentioned many times in the New Testament. John the Baptist, mentioned in the Gospels as the herald of Jesus, seems to have viewed baptism as part of an atonement and/or purification process, associated with preparations for the end of days.[4] In this, he was not significantly different from other Jews of his time: many Jewish groups used ritual immersion in water for a variety of purposes. Among them were those who emphasized the importance of immersion in water for the purification of the body; others saw it as an act that purifies the spirit, while many others viewed baptism as a kind of merging of the two. The synoptic gospels assert that Jesus was baptized by John[5] and that following baptism (or in the Gospel of John, perhaps without it) the Holy Spirit descended upon Jesus, and a voice proclaimed: "You are my beloved Son; with you I am well pleased." According to the synoptic tradition, this baptism signaled the beginning of Jesus' public ministry. Later on, it is asserted that Jesus desired that his disciples be baptized and baptize others. Concluding the Gospel of Matthew is one of the most well known declarations attributed to Jesus regarding this:

> Go therefore, and make disciples of all nations, baptizing them in the name of the Father, and of the Son, and of the Holy Spirit.[6]

Baptism in Theological Thought

Many Christian thinkers have compared baptism to various human experiences and biblical events. It is common to view baptism, or more precisely the emerging from the baptismal water, as a rebirth, similar to emerging from the womb. Entering and then emerging from the water also symbolizes death and resurrection. Like the Israelites leaving Egypt and crossing the Red Sea on their way,[7] one who is newly baptized passes from slavery to freedom. Like the Israelites crossing the Jordan River,[8] the newly baptized leaves the desert and enters the Promised Land.

According to Catholic belief, baptism absolves the newly baptized from the original sin of Adam and Eve[9] and from his or her own sins committed up to that moment. It also invites the Holy Spirit to descend upon him or her, turning the newly baptized into one of the disciples of Jesus and a member of his Church.

Celebrating the Rite of Baptism

Baptism is normally celebrated in one of two ways: either by immersing the entire body in water or by pouring water on the person's head. Baptizing oneself is not possible: it must be done by someone else (who need not necessarily be a Christian). The ceremony is accompanied by declarations invoking elements of the Trinity. In its ideal form, the ceremony begins with questions of faith, based on the Creed, addressed to the person to be baptized: "Do you believe in God, the Father Almighty . . .?" The person responds, "I do believe." "Do you believe in Jesus Christ, His only Son . . .?" "I do believe." "Do you also believe in the Holy Spirit . . .?" "I do believe." Following the respondent's replies, the person celebrating the ritual recites the following passage during the immersion: "N., I baptize you in the name of the Father, and of the Son, and of the Holy Spirit." This declaration is based on the verse at the end of Matthew noted above, detailing Jesus' instructions to his disciples. In the Western Catholic Church, baptism is usually administered through the pouring of a small amount of water over the head of the baptized three times, each time invoking another persona of the Trinity (invoking first the Trinity and then pouring the water only once over the head of the baptized is also possible). In Eastern Catholic Churches, the candidate for baptism stands facing east, and the person who baptizes him or her says, "The Servant of God, N., is baptized in the name of the Father, and of the Son, and of the Holy Spirit." The baptism is performed generally by a triple immersion.

The formula for invoking the Trinity during the baptism is important: many Christian Churches will consider a baptism invalid if done without referencing the Trinity, even if the verse, "I baptize you in the name of Jesus Christ," which has a scriptural basis,[10] and which is customary in some Churches, is used. Following the baptism, a certificate confirming the ceremony is issued, and the event is also registered in a special registry kept by the local parish. Space is left for registering any future changes in the ecclesiastical status of the newly baptized, such as confirmation, marriage, ordination, or the joining of an Institute of Consecrated Life.

Baptism in water, while the most desirable, is not regarded as the only option by many Churches, including the Catholic Church. A person is considered as having undergone "Baptism of Blood" if killed because of his or her Christian beliefs, but before he or she has been baptized. When a person desiring to be baptized dies not as a result of his or her faith, but still before he or she succeeded in undergoing it, he or she is said to have undergone a "Baptism of Desire."[11]

Catholic, Orthodox, and many Protestant Churches consider baptism a once-in-a-lifetime act that leaves a permanent spiritual mark (or "character") on the baptized. Some of God's grace might be withdrawn should the person sin, but should he or she return to the right path, the sacrament need not be celebrated a second time. Repeating this ritual is not only invalid, it is forbidden.

From Baptism of Adults to Baptism of Infants

From the description above, it is clear that from the beginning, baptism was intended to be performed on adults able to express their wish for it. Despite this, baptism of infants was not unheard of in many of the early Christian churches, as can be deduced, for example, from a text that was composed probably between the second and the fourth century:

> The children shall be baptized first. All of the children who can answer for themselves, let them answer. If there are any children who cannot answer for themselves, let their parents answer for them, or someone else from their family.[12]

During the Middle Ages, when fear was rampant that a dead, unbaptized child would not be granted salvation,[13] and with an extremely high level of child mortality, the custom of baptizing infants became more common. In places where the conversion of the adult population to Christianity was completed, infants were the only ones still being baptized. Adult baptism became a rare event. Since that time and up to today, the majority of Catholics are baptized while still infants.[14]

The Modern-Day Baptism Ceremony

The ritual of baptism has undergone a number of changes in the modern-day Catholic Church. Already in the seventeenth century, the formula used during the baptism ritual of infants was shortened, as it became clear that posing certain questions to an about-to-be-baptized infant made little sense. Nevertheless, it was still evident that the baptism ceremony was geared towards adults, and the parents of the infant continued to answer the questions posed. Another important stage in the adaptation of the baptism ritual involved the revival of the Easter Vigil (the night preceding Easter Day) Mass after it was phased out in the Middle Ages.[15] In earlier centuries, adults who joined the faith were baptized with great pomp on that night, after having undergone a long period of preparation and indoctrination. All those present at the ceremony participated at least partially by declaring their faith along with those being baptized. When the public and festive celebration of Easter Vigil was renewed in the modern period, adult baptism once again penetrated Catholic consciousness, and with it the recognition that baptism is a meaningful act, and not just a *pro-forma* ceremony connected to the birth of a child.

The ritual in use in the Catholic Church today was ratified by pope Paul VI following the Second Vatican Council, and is divided into two distinct types: baptism of infants and children, and baptism of adults.

Baptizing Infants and Children

Baptism of infants is generally celebrated within a few weeks or months of birth, and, if possible, in the local parish church. Only in unusual circumstances is a baptism celebrated in a private home or hospital. Contrary to past practice, where the mother was often excluded from participating in the ceremony—being considered impure after the birth or too physically weak to attend (baptism was usually celebrated during the first week of the child's life)—today, circumstances permitting, both parents should be present, as essential parts of the ceremony are reserved for them. Sunday and Saturday are generally considered the most appropriate time for celebrating the ceremony and, if possible, a number of infants should be baptized at once. These two elements are intended to emphasize the communal aspect of baptism and ideally arouse in those present at the baptism awareness of the importance of their own baptisms. The Church considers it desirable that the expecting parents participate in a number of sessions before the birth, where the significance of the baptism as well as the Church's position on the importance of the religious education of their children is explained.

The ceremony begins with the presentation of the child by his or her parents and godparents, who today in many cases are two of the parents' close friends. They will also be the child's "spiritual guardians," and in theory are responsible with assisting in the child's religious education (they usually also commit to care for the child in the event of the parents' death). In some places, this role is reserved for the grandparents; in others, the role of godparent is reserved strictly for persons other than family members. In the latter case, the godparent becomes an adjunct family member, to whom the godchild may turn in a time of need (and also from whom the child is entitled to expect gifts).

After the child is presented, the celebrant (generally a priest) greets the parents and godparents with a blessing, welcoming them into the church. He will follow it by asking the name with which they would like to name their child. After receiving the parents' response, the priest asks what they ask of the Church for their child, to which they customarily reply: "baptism." Parents may also reply "faith," "eternal life," "Christ's mercy," "acceptance into the Church," and so forth. The priest then asks the parents if they are aware of the importance of their child's spiritual education, in order that he or she keep God's commandments, love God, and love humankind. After their response, the priest asks the godparents if they agree to help in this endeavor, to which they answer, "Yes." Then, while reciting formulas that include the child's name, his or her acceptance into the community, and being marked with the sign of Christ, the priest makes the sign of the cross over the child's forehead with Chrism, consecrated anointing oil. The parents and sometimes the godparents also make the sign of the cross on the child's forehead.

The parents and children continue in a procession to the middle of the church, with the congregation commonly accompanying them in the singing of appropriate verses from Scriptures. When the procession comes to a halt, verses about baptism are read out loud and the priest delivers a sermon. In some places, after the sermon a number of additional prayers are said, in which the Church asks the saints to pray for the child, his or her parents, and the entire Church.

At this point in the ceremony, the celebrant begs God to free the baptized from the power of Satan and from original sin. In some places, he also rubs the chests of each of the baptized infants with "oil of catechumens," intended for those beginning their journey in the Church. Then he lays his hands upon the child's head for a few moments in silence.

Following this, the water used in the baptism is sanctified. In his prayers, the celebrant recalls various biblical events connected with water, and while touching the water with his fingertips summons the Holy Spirit to descend upon the water. The ceremony now reaches its climax around the sanctified water. The parents and godparents are asked to recall their own baptism and to reject original sin and Satan. If appropriate, the celebrant may add a few sentences enjoining the parents to abstain from the use of and faith in local beliefs that the Church considers "superstitious": the well-being of the child is to be looked for in Christ, not in other forces. Following the parents' affirmation, they are asked about their belief in the Trinity and the other articles of faith that appear in the creed. This part of the ceremony is conducted in a responsive dialogue between celebrant and parents. After concluding this dialogue, other family members might be asked to approach the baptismal font. The celebrant asks the parents and godparents, "Is it your will that N. should be baptized in the faith of the Church, which we have all professed with you?" Once they have given their consent, the baptism is celebrated. The celebrant declares: "I baptize you, N., in the name of the Father," whereupon he immediately immerses the child in the water or sprinkles water on his or her forehead, and then continues, "and of the Son," and again either immerses them in or sprinkles them with water, and finally says, "and of the Holy Spirit," repeating the ablution for the third time. It is customary for either the parents or godparents to hold the child during baptism if the celebrant sprinkles the child with water, or to take the child from the water after the immersion: a symbolic act of supporting the child in his or her new life chapter. At this point it is also customary for those attending the service to begin singing appropriate hymns.

After the baptism ritual, the celebrant recites the following blessing to each child: "God the Father of our Lord Jesus Christ has freed you from sin, given you a new birth by water and the Holy Spirit, and welcomed you into his holy people." Following local customs, he might again anoint the top of each of the infants' heads with Chrism. The child is dressed in white clothes and one of those accompanying the child holds a candle that has been lit from the flame of the Easter candle, a large candle kindled at the start of Easter Mass every year.

In some places an additional short ceremony is performed: the "Ephphatha." The name of this ancient ceremony stems from an Aramaic word in the New Testament meaning "be opened."[16] The person presiding over the ceremony touches the mouth and ears of the child while declaring: "The Lord Jesus made the deaf hear and the dumb speak. May he soon touch your ears to receive his word, and your mouth to proclaim his faith, to the praise and glory of God the Father."

If not in the context of a Mass, the ceremony concludes with a procession of the parents and children toward the altar, the reciting of the "Our Father" prayer,[17] and the blessing of the parents of the children and the entire congregation.

Central Aspects of the Current Ritual

The rite of baptism practiced today is much different from the one practiced prior to the Second Vatican Council. The custom of questioning the child about his or her faith, with the adult responding for the child, has been done away with. The ceremony's "exorcism" component has also been altered. Today, the celebrant makes only short reference to the freeing of the baptized from the power of Satan, whereas prior to Vatican II, the exorcism made up a very significant portion of the rite. It was customary for the priest to place a grain of consecrated salt in the infant's mouth, which, according to belief, aided in protecting and bestowing wisdom upon the child. These components of the ritual have been dispensed with—firstly so that the participants will not be distracted from the act of the baptism itself, which is, after all, the main part of the ceremony, and secondly because highly placed liturgists considered this ceremony to be discordant with the modern outlook.

Another change is the fact that the consecration of the baptismal water has become a part of the baptism ceremony. Until the Second Vatican Council, it was customary to use water that had been consecrated on the previous Holy Saturday, before Easter. Various reasons, among them hygiene, may account for this new practice, but the fact that the water is consecrated as a separate act, with formulas similar to those recited during the celebration of Mass, adds much splendor to the baptism ceremony. More than all these, it is important to note the fundamental and prominent invoking of the Holy Spirit during and after the baptism. This third persona of the Trinity had, in many respects, been marginalized prior to Vatican II. Today the Holy Spirit is invoked repeatedly in this ceremony and in many others.

Adult Baptism

The ceremony of baptism for adults is similar to the one described above, although in it, needless to say, the person being baptized recites the statements of faith and holds the ritual candle. Adult baptism, generally celebrated during the Easter Vigil ceremony, is the culmination of a process of preparation (catechumenate, or as it is known today, "Rite of Christian Initiation of Adults" or RCIA), which generally lasts several months and includes studying about the Church and its doctrines, spiritual guidance, and various rites of passage. The baptized is usually accompanied only by his or her godparents, who in many cases would also have supported him or her throughout the process. The reason for the usual lack of parents' involvement in the ceremony is clear: even if the adult's parents are alive, they are probably not Catholic; otherwise, generally, he or she would have been baptized in infancy.

Immediately following the baptism, the newly baptized receives the sacrament of confirmation, which we will discuss shortly, and may then take part in the Mass and receive communion as a full member of the congregation.

Recognizing Baptism Celebrated in Other Churches

Because baptism is considered by most Christian Churches as a ritual act celebrated only once, it is important for them to know whether a person has been validly baptized or not. One implication is if he or she should be considered a "Christian" or not, both for theological considerations and for practical issues such as if he or she would like to marry a Christian of another denomination. Another practical significance of this issue may come up should the person decide to leave one Church and join another. In a statement by the famous Church Father Augustine of the fourth and fifth centuries, the secondary role of the person who effectively performs the baptism appears to offer an answer to such cases:

> Peter may baptize, but this is He [Christ] that baptizes; Paul may baptize, yet this is He that baptizes; Judas may baptize, still this is He that baptizes.[18]

And indeed, the immensely important sixteenth-century Council of Trent ruled decisively that a baptism done by a heretic (referring to Protestants in the context of that period) in the name of the Father, and of the Son, and of the Holy Spirit, with the intention of "doing what the Church does," is valid.[19]

In accordance with this weighty theological principle, the Catholic, Orthodox, Anglican, and majority of "mainline" Protestant Churches reached an agreement in 1982 to mutually recognize the other Churches' baptism ritual. This agreement was possible because all these Churches use water in the ritual, invoke the Trinity, and have similar intent in the act of baptism. This decision carries practical implications: if a person wishes to join a different Church than the one he or she was baptized in, that person does not undergo another baptism, not even a "conditional" baptism, which had been customary before the agreement was reached. Moreover, members of other Churches are considered Christian by members of all the signing Churches. This last point is particularly important, for example, in marriage ceremonies involving members of two different Churches, as well as in the giving of sacraments, in special cases, to members of different Churches. Some say that this is one of the ecumenical movement's greatest successes so far.[20] Many see powerful symbolism in the fact that baptism served as a somewhat uniting factor for the Christian world.

Confirmation

Confirmation[21] is not an obvious sacrament from a theological perspective. Its inclusion in the Western Church as an independent sacrament separate from baptism stems more from a complex historical development than from clear theological logic. Despite this, Catholic theologians were able to accommodate it and have situated it clearly among the seven sacraments.

In the West, this sacrament is ordinarily administered by a bishop. For centuries it has encompassed a few basic elements (which are not necessarily of equal importance): laying of hands over the head of the recipient, a prayer invoking the Holy Spirit, the making of the sign of the cross on his or her forehead with scented consecrated oil, and an additional prayer asking the Holy Spirit to dwell in him or her. This sacrament is considered one of the three rites of "Christian initiation": baptism allows a person to be reborn, confirmation strengthens him or her, and the Eucharist continues to provide him or her with spiritual nourishment. An effort to emphasize this is evident in the way the confirmation is celebrated today.

Like the other sacraments, confirmation may only be administered to a person who has already received the first sacrament, namely baptism. Like baptism and ordination, confirmation is a sacrament one can receive only once. According to Catholic doctrine, like these two other sacraments, confirmation leaves a mark of heavenly grace upon the one who receives it.

The History of Confirmation

According to Catholic teaching, confirmation, like the other sacraments, was established (either explicitly or implicitly) by Jesus. However, unlike the sacraments of baptism and the Eucharist, serious theologians would not insist upon pinpointing and detailing the moment of its foundation, nor claim that there is a clear scriptural basis for it. Still, a number of New Testament passages have traditionally been associated with this sacrament. In many passages in the New Testament, Jesus proclaims that the Holy Spirit will dwell among believers in him and assist them.[22] How does one receive this spirit? For the Church, an answer to this is given in the New Testament book Acts of the Apostles, where the following episode is presented:

> Now when the apostles in Jerusalem heard that Samaria had accepted the word of God, they sent them Peter and John, who went down and prayed for them, that they might receive the Holy Spirit, for it had not yet fallen upon any of them; they had only been baptized in the name of the Lord Jesus. Then they laid hands on them and received the Holy Spirit.[23]

This text seems to imply the notion that after baptism, which was performed without the actual involvement of the apostles (and one should note also, without evoking "The Father" or "The Holy Spirit"), their intermediation through prayer and the laying on of hands was necessary in order for the newly baptized to receive the Holy Spirit.[24]

In early periods of Christianity[25] following this text, immediately after a person was baptized the celebrant would anoint the head of the baptized with oil and pray for the Holy Spirit to descend upon him or her. In some times and places, prior to the anointing the celebrant would lay his hands on the head of the newly baptized. As the Church grew and the baptism ritual was celebrated by priests (or even by members of the laity) and not bishops, who, according to Catholic belief, are the true successors of the apostles, the Western Church's stance regarding the necessity of setting aside the ceremony of receiving the Holy Spirit specifically for the bishop gained in strength. At an even later phase, when baptism became a sacrament administered mostly to infants, the view that a ceremony of the laying on of hands and anointing with oil, celebrated by the bishop and separate from baptism, became even more resolutely grounded.[26]

The Sacrament of Confirmation Today

The sacrament of confirmation today is generally celebrated separately from baptism. In the Western Church it happens together with baptism only in cases of adult baptism, which in most communities is still comparatively rare.

The current confirmation ritual comprises a number of features, which emphasize its link to both baptism and the Eucharist, the sacrament we will discuss later. Thus, if in the past the candidate for confirmation was accompanied by persons other than his or her baptismal godparents, today the ritual calls for the candidate to be escorted, if possible, by the same persons. This element helps to emphasize the intrinsic link between these two rituals. Many will also point to the fact that in the Western Church confirmation is conferred upon youths who, by receiving it, implicitly declare their acceptance of the baptism that they underwent as infants. In most instances, the confirmation ceremony is celebrated within the framework of a Mass, thus also making clear the connection between confirmation and the Eucharist.

After the "Liturgy of the Word,"[27] during which portions from Scriptures are read aloud, the candidates are called up by name to receive the sacrament. They stand at the front of the church, facing the bishop (if necessary, a priest appointed by the bishop may also officiate at this ceremony). After the bishop's sermon, the candidates declare their faith through questions and answers based on the creed. Only then, the bishop, and priests if they are asked to assist, spread their hands over the heads of the recipients[28] and ask God the Father to impart his spirit over them. After this, each candidate and the person accompanying them approach the bishop. The accompanying person places his or her right hand on the shoulder of the candidate and introduces him or her by name to the bishop. The bishop dips his thumb in the consecrated scented oil, the Chrism, makes the sign of the cross with the oil on the candidate's forehead, and says: "N., be sealed with the gift of the Holy Spirit," to which the recipient responds, "Amen." The bishop and the recipient bless one another with a handshake, hug, or another sign of peace.

After the anointing with oil and the blessing of peace, the congregation recites a prayer asking God for blessings and assistance for the newly con-firmed, their families, and those who have accompanied them. An especially festive celebration of the Eucharist, which is the second part of the Mass, then begins.

Confirmation as an Act for Joining the Catholic Church

Christians desirous of joining the Catholic Church but who belong to non-Orthodox Churches whose ritual of baptism is recognized by the Catholic Church as valid (as is the case for most Protestant Churches) are generally accepted into the Catholic Church by receiving the sacrament of confir-mation.[29] This practice is not done for those who come from Orthodox Churches because their sacrament of confirmation ("chrismation") is gen-erally celebrated as part of the baptism ceremony and is considered valid (thus, non-repeatable) by Catholic standards. For them, participating in the sacrament of the Eucharist and a declaration of faith will suffice.

Eucharist (Mass)

The sacrament of the Eucharist, also known as Mass,[30] is considered today, as it has been during many periods in the history of the Church, the cer-emony at the center of Catholic life. The second Vatican Council continu-ally emphasized its being "the source and summit of Christian life." For this reason, but also because of its complexity and due to the fact that it is the Catholic ceremony that a non-Catholic is most likely to witness, our discussion of this sacrament will be more comprehensive and detailed than the other six.

The Last Supper

All four gospels contain an account of a meal Jesus held with his disciples before he was put to death, but only the three synoptic gospels and the First Epistle of Paul to the Corinthians describe mysterious acts Jesus performed with the bread and the wine.[31] There are important differences among these four versions, but all four state that Jesus asked his disciples to partake of the bread and the wine, and that he indicated that the bread was his flesh and the wine was his blood (or "in" his blood[32]). In two versions it is stated that Jesus commanded that they perform this act in his memory in the future. In the Gospel of John similar statements by Jesus are recorded, but they are part of a sermon that the redactor of the gospel sets at Capernaum in the Galilee,[33] not during the fateful meal in Jerusalem. The *Didache,* an early Christian treatise composed probably in the later part of the first century recalls a ceremony that combines the eating and drinking of bread and wine, but without any mention of an analogy between bread and wine and flesh and blood.[34]

The complex relationship between these sources is a matter of controversy, and it is difficult to assess the exact historical value of these various testimonies. Did Jesus indeed share a meal with his disciples shortly before his death? If he did, what, in fact, transpired at that meal? Even the time of the meal, if it indeed did take place, remains uncertain. The four gospels agree that Jesus was crucified on Friday and that an evening meal with his disciples took place at some point before that. According to the three synoptic gospels, it seems that the meal took place on the night between Thursday and Friday, and that Friday was the first day of the Jewish holy day of Passover. Thus the meal took place on the night in which, when the Temple existed in Jerusalem, it was customary to eat from the paschal lamb, sacrificed a few hours earlier, in the afternoon.[35] According to John, the execution of Jesus took place on the eve of the Passover festival, at the same time the paschal lambs were sacrificed in the Temple. Following this tradition, the meal obviously could not have taken place on the night when the paschal lamb would have been eaten, but on a night preceding it.

Most scholars today are more or less convinced that Jesus shared a meal with his disciples shortly before his death. The exact content of his actions and sayings, their meaning, and whether Jesus commanded that his actions be repeated at a future time, as well as whether this custom stems from the first generation of his disciples, are less certain. Many scholars today support the following views: John's dating is historically correct. The meal took place one or a number of days before the Passover sacrifice in the Temple. It is possible that this was not a Passover meal at all, or it could be that

Jesus followed a calendar different from the one followed by the Temple priests. Jesus perhaps commanded his disciples to eat from the bread and told them that it was "his flesh" or "body." There is more disagreement with regard to the use of wine. Some scholars believe Jesus also said the wine was his blood, while others hypothesize that this was a later addition, coming from a non-Jewish milieu. Mainstream scholars today do not generally support the claim, which was somewhat common some decades ago, that Paul contrived the entire event or at the very least the link between the bread and the body.

By the year 57 CE, when, in all likelihood, Paul composed his ("First") Letter to the Corinthians, various communities were already performing a ritual enacting such a meal. It was thus celebrated by early generations of believers in Jesus, who had died less than three decades before.

Names of the Ritual

Up until the Second Vatican Council, this ceremony was generally known in the Catholic Church as "Mass." This title has its origin in a Latin sentence that concludes the ceremony, "Ite, missa est," which might be translated as "go, it is sent" (as related to the conclusion of the ceremony, or the distribution of the communion bread).

In the texts promulgated by the Second Vatican Council, the use of the term "Eucharist" for this ceremony is significantly more common than the term "Mass." The word Eucharist derives from the Greek verb *Eukharisteo,* "to give thanks." Until Vatican II, this term was used mostly to mark the moment which, at least according to popular perception, was the climax of the Mass: the ritual during which the priest or bishop recreates the actions of Jesus, who presented the bread and wine and gave thanks for them to God, the Father.[36] Today, both terms are generally used interchangeably in public as well as in official documents. The term "the Lord's Supper" is also sometimes used in a Catholic context, but is used much more consistently in Protestant Churches.

Eucharistic Bread and Wine

The bread used during the Mass must be made from wheat, and in the Western Church, as opposed to the Eastern Churches, without yeast. In order to avoid creating crumbs during the cutting of the bread after it has been blessed, when its essence, according to the Catholic belief, is the "Flesh of Christ," the Western Catholic Church generally uses round white wafers and not "real" bread. These wafers, which may come in a variety of sizes, are made especially for this purpose, often in women's monasteries. These wafers are often called "Host" from the Latin *Hostia,* "Sacrifice."

The wine used during the Mass must be made from grapes and ideally contain no additional additives. To prevent it from fermenting, it generally has high alcohol content. Its color is not important: it can be white, red, or any other shade.[37]

The Structure of the Mass

Since very early in Christian history, the liturgy of the Mass seems to have consisted of two parts: the liturgy of the Word and the liturgy of the Eucharist. The first revolves around the reading of various passages from Scriptures; the second around the bread and wine.[38] Though the influence of customs of other ancient religious groups may have been equally significant in the historical development of the ceremony, it can be still seen as combining two major Jewish customs: synagogue prayer (specifically on the mornings of the Sabbath and some holy days), at the center of which is the reading from the Torah, and a family meal (specifically, the Passover meal), which includes festive blessings over the bread (regular, or if on Passover, an unleavened bread known as *Matzah*), and the wine.

The Theological Significance of the Mass

Any one-dimensional explanation of the Eucharist (for example, using the historical roots of it as explained above) will be deficient. This ceremony was perceived in multiple ways by many Christian groups in different periods. For the Catholic Church, only a combination of these many ways of looking at the Eucharist will enable a spectator or participant to better understand and appreciate it. And yet, combining various outlooks does not translate into an amalgam of them. Different theologians, even if they may be in agreement that various insights regarding the Eucharist are important and valid, might place more emphasis on one notion rather than on another. This may lead them to quite varied theologies regarding this central Catholic ritual.

For many, this ceremony is first and foremost a meal—the "Lord's Supper." Participants partake of a meal with Christ, a symbolic preparation for the meal to be eaten with him at the end of time. Viewed in this way, the ceremony is seen as a joyous event, a social occasion that unites the community. A theology that emphasizes this way of understanding the Eucharist will be commonly characterized by certain features, which may include the use of the terms "Lord's table," for the surface on which the Eucharist is celebrated, and the "Lord's supper," for the ceremony itself. This theology will more easily recognize the use of plain bread (and not specially prepared wafers) in the ceremony and will encourage the congregation to partake of the wine and not only the bread. Also typical of this theology is calling the bread "bread of life" and the wine "spiritual drink."[39] Viewing this ceremony as a meal is, as some readers might suspect, quite close to various Protestant understandings of it. In many Protestant groups, this ritual is known as the "Lord's supper" or "holy communion," terms that emphasize the participation of the congregation in the meal. Catholics eager to build bridges between the Catholic and Protestant worlds view this as a positive fact. On the other hand, Catholics believing Protestantism to be a grave mistake, or worse, a dangerous heresy, may suspect that stressing the aspect of the meal in the Eucharist is a renunciation of Catholic uniqueness or even a "Protestantization" of the Catholic Church.

Most authors from early Christian churches seem to have understood the Eucharist ceremony in the way described above. It was connected to the *agape,* an ancient religious type of communal meal, and was similar to feasts held by certain Jewish and non-Jewish groups in the ancient world.[40]

The Eucharist as a meal may be emphasized by some theologians, while other theologians may stress the notion of the Mass as a sacrifice. According to this perspective, every Mass is a reminiscence, some might say a "reenactment," of the historical crucifixion of Jesus, who was sacrificed in order to atone for the sins of humankind. Like a Jewish person at the ritual Passover meal, who, according to the Jewish tradition, must imagine himself or herself as if being personally liberated from the servitude in Egypt, so must a Christian person at the Eucharist imagine at that moment, in front of his or her eyes, Jesus being crucified and the world being redeemed. While implicit in this kind of evocation is a certain element of reenactment, the intention is not an actual returning to the historical moment of the crucifixion. Then it was a violent sacrifice. After that cosmic event, what is needed is a bloodless sacrifice. This approach puts a particular emphasis on the notion of the transformation in the essence of the bread and wine during the recitation of the Eucharistic prayers into the flesh and blood of Christ. This is the famous Catholic dogma of "transubstantiation," declaring that even though the taste, smell, appearance, and chemical composition of the bread and wine have not changed, their essence is no longer that of bread and wine but rather of the body and blood of Christ. His "real presence" is brought about through these agents, resulting in Christ being really and tangibly present with his Church.[41] The wine, whose essence has become blood, and the bread, whose essence is now flesh, are placed on the altar. This is an offering of thanks to the Father, through the Son, and with the power of the Holy

Spirit. The sacrifices in the Temple in Jerusalem ended with the sacrifice of the Son to the Father, but the acts performed in each and every church continue to evoke this same sacrifice: "I have no pleasure in you, says the Lord of Hosts; neither will I accept any sacrifice from your hands," proclaims the anonymous prophet from the book called Malachi, with regard to the Temple in Jerusalem. But substitutions, he adds, are welcome: "For from the rising of the sun, even to its setting, my name is great among the nations; And everywhere they bring sacrifice to my name and a pure offering; For Great is my name among the nations says the Lord of hosts."[42]

This sacrificial theology has a number of characteristic traits. The surface on which the ritual is celebrated is always referred to as the "altar." The ceremony is dramatic and even to some extent tragic, for it reenacts Jesus' death. Even though here too there is a duty for the priest and a recommendation for the community to partake of the host, this act does not make up the core of the ceremony, for the offering is to God: it is valid even without the worshippers eating of it. For this same reason, those who support this theology will not necessarily react negatively to a Mass that is celebrated by a priest without the presence of a congregation, for in their view what is at issue is first and foremost a sacrifice to God and not a social event.[43]

According to historical scholarship, the perception of the Mass ceremony as analogous to a sacrificial offering was mostly developed in the Middle Ages, reaching its climax in the sixteenth century in the theology upheld by the Council of Trent.[44]

For most theologians and for the general Catholic public as well, these two approaches are not mutually exclusive. And yet, a greater emphasis on the first or the second reflects different theological or social views and might influence how the Mass is described, how it is celebrated, the various roles of those involved in it, and the spiritual connection of the believer to it.

The New Order of the Mass and the Tridentine Mass

Unrelated to the above two views regarding the Mass,[45] there are two accepted versions of the Mass in practice today in the Catholic Church. The "New Order of the Mass" (*Novus Ordo Missae*), as it is referred to specifically by those who oppose it (supporters refer to it simply as the "Order of the Mass" or *Ordo Missae*), is the version familiar to most Catholics. It is generally viewed as based on principles promulgated by the Second Vatican Council. Its (very few but vocal) critics refer to it as the "Mass of Paul VI" because of its having been revised in 1969 under that pope's leadership. Even though Latin is the official language of the Mass in the Western Catholic Church and although the most authoritative version of this "New

Order of the Mass" is also in Latin, it is almost always celebrated in the local vernacular. This version is simpler and more concise than the earlier one, and the congregation's participation during the celebration is of much greater significance.

The "Tridentine" Mass had been the standard prior to the appearance of the newer version. Despite having been altered periodically over the last centuries, this version is based on one ratified by pope Pius V in 1570, a few years after the conclusion of the deliberations of the Council of Trent. Its name thus derives from the Latin name for the city of Trent, *Tridentum*. The two versions overlapped for a short period of time after the new version of the Mass appeared in 1969, but the older version was quickly prohibited.[46] It was permitted anew in stages beginning in 1984. Since 2000, the Tridentine Mass has been permissible even in the basilica of Saint Peter in the Vatican, although not at the main altar.

Over the last decades of the twentieth century, there has been widespread suspicion of those wanting to celebrate the Latin Tridentine Mass. When it involved those who generally celebrate the new Mass, and would only occasionally celebrate the Tridentine Mass, the hierarchy has been more tolerant; some have even been supportive of such initiatives. On the other hand, when it involved those wishing to celebrate the Tridentine Mass exclusively, the suspicion that this was indicative of their objection to the entire tradition of Vatican II was not entirely baseless.

It is possible that the first decades of the twenty-first century will witness the resurgence of the Latin Tridentine Mass among some conservatively inclined congregations. Pope Benedict XVI, who has never hidden his fondness for this Mass, or his objection to the emendation and forcing of the "New Mass" by Paul VI, published procedures in 2007[47] that eased the way for priests and congregations wishing to celebrate the Latin Mass. At this point, it is estimated that about 1 percent of Western Catholics celebrate Mass in Latin on a regular basis. Whether their numbers grow or shrink now that pope Benedict XVI's reign has ended and while pope Francis, who is not a particular supporter of the Latin mass, is in charge, is hard to say.

A Detailed Description of the Structure of the Mass

In the following pages, we will take a closer look at the structure of the common "new" rite of the Mass established by Paul VI, which is almost always celebrated in the local language. The description provided below is of a general nature. In certain instances, specific parts may be omitted and others may be enlarged upon.

The Mass is composed of various sections. Some might divide it into two principal units; others may separate it into many small components. I will take the middle ground, splitting the entire ritual into five major sections, each of which is made of multiple components.

Section I: Opening

1. Opening psalm or antiphon (generally based on a text from Psalms).
2. Festive entry of the celebrant and other participants who have a specific role in the celebration. The order of their entry depends on a variety of factors; generally, the higher the person's hierarchical ranking, the later his entry in the procession.
3. The celebrant bows and kisses the altar, makes the sign of the cross, and blesses the congregation. The congregation replies with a fixed response.
4. Words of greeting spoken by one of those accompanying the main celebrant (or by himself).
5. A Penitential rite, which is often a sort of "Public Confession" (sometimes, this part is replaced by sprinkling the congregation with holy water). This act is linked to the idea that before receiving communion a person must confess and be purified of his or her grave sins.
6. Saying of the acclamation "*Kyrie Eleison*" (Lord, have mercy) and, on certain Sundays, holy days, and special occasions, the ancient hymn of praise "*Gloria.*" These hymns are sometimes sung in the original Greek and Latin and sometimes in the vernacular (mainly the "Gloria").
7. Recitation of a short prayer (the content varies but always concludes with the uniform ending "For Ever and Ever" and the response "Amen"). Often, a moment for silent meditation follows this prayer.

Section II: Reading from Scripture ("Liturgy of the Word")

1. First reading. On Sundays and holy days, the reading is usually from the Old Testament. On the other days of the week, the reading is usually from the Old Testament or from books in the New Testament other than the four gospels. The reading appears in a "Lectionary," a book containing all the readings according to their liturgical order. The text is related to the reading from the gospels (the second or third reading). In accordance with local customs, the reader may be either an ordained member of the Church or a layperson, including women. The congregation is seated during the reading. In exceptional instances, for example at a children's Mass, this reading may be omitted.

2. A hymn is sung, regularly based on a passage from Psalms.
3. On Sundays or holy days, there is a second reading from books in the New Testament other than the gospels. Its rules are similar to those of the first reading.
4. Hallelujah and a proclamation of the gospel. The congregation stands. Sometimes the book containing all four gospels is ceremoniously transferred from the altar to the stand on which it will be placed ("ambo" or "lectern").
5. Third reading (second on weekdays). The reading is always from one of the gospels and is almost always done by an ordained man (bishop, priest, deacon). If a number of priests are celebrating the Mass together, it is customary in many places that the main celebrant will not carry out this reading. The reading is according to a predefined order and depends on the liturgical year.[48]
6. A homily is delivered by an ordained man (bishop, priest, or deacon). The homily, which is obligatory on Sundays and holy days and recommended on the other days, must be related to the readings and aims to either supplement or elucidate them. The length of the homily varies according to the person delivering it, the occasion, the type of parish, and the local tradition. In some places, homilies can be rather lengthy, but in many places Catholic homilies are often relatively short in comparison to homilies in neighboring Protestant Churches and take no more than 5–10 minutes.
7. On Sundays and holy days, profession of faith (either the Nicene or Apostles' Creed).
8. The "Universal Prayer" (also called "General Intercessions" or "Prayers of the Faithful"): a prayer for the Church, its leaders, the authorities, the needy, etc.

Section III: Ceremony of Thanksgiving ("Liturgy of the Eucharist")

1. The leader of the ceremony or one of his assistants ("Eucharistic ministers") arranges the altar, placing on it the necessary items: one or more cups ("chalices") for wine, one or more plates for the bread, special napkins underneath and on top of the ceremonial objects, napkins for cleaning the plates and hands, a vessel filled with wine, a vessel filled with water, and the missal (the liturgical book containing all the instructions and texts for celebrating the Mass throughout the year).
2. In special celebratory Masses, the bread and wine will be brought to the altar in a ceremonial procession.

3. On Sundays and holy days, donations are collected for the needs of the parish[49] or any other specified need. The collection is generally carried out by congregants who pass among the rows with baskets or sealed coffers. Apart from the practical reason for the collection of money for one or another need, the collection at that moment in time symbolizes the participation of the community in the bread and the wine, "the work of human hands," which are being brought as a sacrifice to God.

4. Placing of the bread and wine (referred to as "gifts") on the altar. The wafers will be placed on the altar after the celebrant silently recites a number of short prayers upon receiving them. The wine will be poured into the chalice while additional prayers are recited; some water is then added to the chalice. This act is often accompanied by singing, either by the congregation or a choir.

5. Celebratory Masses may add here the spreading of incense: various participants in the Mass (Eucharistic ministers, deacons, priest, or a bishop) will spread incense in a ritualized manner toward the altar, the celebrants, and the congregation. The spreading of incense, which is made from the burning of tree resin over coals inside a special container known as a thurible, is an ancient ritual known in many religions. In the current Catholic understanding, the incense, waved in the direction of particular objects and people is considered to symbolically sanctify them.

6. The celebrant washes and dries his hands.

7. Recitation of a number of introductory prayers: a short prayer that usually emphasizes the sacrificial nature of the Mass, an opening prayer for the ritual of the Eucharist that includes a call for the congregation to appeal to and thank God, and a prayer in praise of God, the substance of which may change, to be followed by the "Sanctus" hymn.[50]

8. The congregation kneels or expresses its devotion in another way. Great differences exist among believers and communities in this regard, and what is the norm in one community might be considered by visitors from another community to be excessively pious or extremely disrespectful.

9. Eucharistic prayer, which describes Jesus' actions and words at the Last Supper. This prayer has four universal and a number of local versions. Besides describing the actions of Jesus, the various versions also include prayers for mercy for the Church, its leaders, and members, Christological and theological statements, confession to God, a plea that God willingly accepts this offering, and more. This prayer, recited by either a priest or a bishop, is one of the most powerful and important in the Church. For this reason, one of its versions (Eucharistic Prayer II), the

most commonly used version today, is presented below in its entirety. It is important to keep in mind that this prayer is accompanied by gestures. The celebrant of the Mass imitates in his gestures some of the supposed gestures of Jesus, while explaining them aloud:[51]

> It is truly right and just, our duty and salvation, always and everywhere to give you thanks, Father most holy, through your beloved Son, Jesus Christ, your Word through whom you made all things, whom you sent as our Savior and Redeemer, incarnate by the Holy Spirit and born of the Virgin.
>
> Fulfilling your will and gaining for you a holy people, he stretched out his hands as he endured his Passion, so as to break the bonds of death and manifest the resurrection. And so, with the Angels and all the Saints we declare your glory, as with one voice we acclaim:
>
> Holy, Holy, Holy Lord God of hosts.
> Heaven and earth are full of your glory.
> Hosanna in the highest.
> Blessed is he who comes in the name of the Lord.
> Hosanna in the highest.[52]
>
> You are indeed Holy, O Lord, the fount of all holiness.
>
> Make holy, therefore, these gifts, we pray, by sending down your Spirit upon them like the dewfall, so that they may become for us the Body and Blood of our Lord, Jesus Christ.
>
> At the time he was betrayed and entered willingly into his Passion, he took bread and, giving thanks, broke it, and gave it to his disciples, saying: "Take this, all of you, and eat of it: for this is my body which will be given up for you."
>
> In a similar way, when supper was ended, he took the chalice and, once more giving thanks, he gave it to his disciples, saying: "Take this, all of you, and drink from it: for this is the chalice of my blood, the blood of the new and eternal covenant, which will be poured out for you and for many for the forgiveness of sins. Do this in memory of me."[53]
>
> Therefore, as we celebrate the memorial of his Death and Resurrection, we offer you, Lord, the Bread of life and the Chalice of salvation, giving thanks that you have held us worthy to be in your presence and minister to you. Humbly we pray that, partaking of the Body and Blood of Christ, we may be gathered into one by the Holy Spirit.

Remember, Lord, your Church, spread throughout the world, and bring her to the fullness of charity, together with N. our pope and N. our Bishop and all the clergy. Remember also our brothers and sisters who have fallen asleep in the hope of the resurrection and all who have died in your mercy: welcome them into the light of your face. Have mercy on us all, we pray, that with the blessed Virgin Mary, Mother of God, with the blessed Apostles, and all the Saints who have pleased you throughout the ages, we may merit to be co-heirs to eternal life, and may praise and glorify you through your Son, Jesus Christ.

During the recitation of this prayer by the priest, and according to Catholic belief, the "transubstantiation" takes place, changing the essence of the bread and wine into the body and blood of Christ.[54] The Church bell or another bell may sound for a few seconds before or at the moment of the transubstantiation, though this is not obligatory. Some are eager for this in order to formally mark the moment of the transubstantiation. Others would rather refrain from sounding a bell in order to emphasize that there is no noticeable moment of transubstantiation, but rather that the entire Mass is one complete unit.

Section IV: The Rite of Communion

1. Prayer: "Our Father."[55]
2. A prayer for peace, after which all members of the congregation greet each other. The custom depends on local culture and may consist of a nod hello, a handshake, or even a kiss or an embrace. The greeter says "Peace," "Peace of Christ," or "Peace be with you," and is answered "Amen."[56]
3. The celebrant (or sometimes a deacon) breaks one of the hosts (often, a special, large one). The breaking of the bread has great symbolic and theological value, as it recreates the actions of Jesus with his disciples at the Last Supper and when he again met two of them after his resurrection: this act helped them recognize him.[57] It also symbolizes the moment when Jesus' body "broke": the moment of his death on the cross. The congregation sings the ancient hymn *Agnus Dei* ("Lamb of God") and ends on the words "give us peace."
4. The celebrant, and some of those assisting him, eat of the bread and drink of the wine. An appropriate hymn accompanies these actions.
5. The Communion procession: The congregation gathers to partake of the bread, often while an appropriate hymn is being sung or an appropriate music is being played. In large churches, long lines may form

in different parts of the church. Most worshippers will approach the priest or Eucharistic minister standing, but in some places, some may go down on their knees. The consecrated bread may be dispensed by priests, deacons or anybody else appointed to the task ("extraordinary ministers"), including women. The minister says to the receiver, "the body of Christ," and the receiver answers, "Amen." The minister may put the host directly into the receiver's mouth, or place it in his or her hand (in which case, the receiver must place it immediately on his or her tongue). The form of dispensation depends on the receiver. Generally speaking, though generalizations should be avoided, direct reception of the bread in the mouth may indicate a more traditionalist or conservative attitude. In some cases, the public is also invited to drink of the wine. If this is the case, they will be served directly from the chalice (and the minister will say "the blood of Christ"), or will dip the bread in the wine (and then the minister will say "the body and blood of Christ"). After receiving the bread and the wine, or the bread only, the receivers return to their seats and sit down or kneel. It is customary to refrain from talking at this stage in particular.

The reception of bread and wine is the only part of the Mass in which participation is limited to members of the Catholic Church (and, some would add, only to those members who are not guilty of a "grievous and ongoing sin.") Their reception by a non-Catholic is considered a great sacrilege. Non-Catholics (or Catholics who are not interested in receiving the Eucharist for whatever reason) should remain in their seats.[58] In various parts of the world, and especially in those where non-Catholics are likely to be present at Mass, a tradition has emerged in recent decades whereby non-Catholics who wish to receive a blessing are welcome to stand in the lines of those waiting for communion, with their hands crossed over their chests (left hand on the right shoulder and vice versa). This sign will indicate to the priest (or the Eucharist minister) that the person is not interested in receiving the bread, but in being blessed.[59]

6. After receiving the bread and wine, or the bread only, and a few moments spent in quiet meditation, the bread and wine that were not consumed will be returned to the altar. The priest or one of the ministers will eat all the crumbs and drink the remaining wine. The dishes in which they were served will be covered in special napkins or cleaned immediately by the priest using napkins made for the purpose. If a significant amount of consecrated bread remains, it will be stored in a small cabinet called the "Tabernacle" in the front of the church, in which the Eucharist is stored and can be venerated outside of Mass.

7. The celebrants of the Mass wash their hands, if needed.
8. The main celebrant says a closing prayer.

Section V: The End of the Ceremony

1. Announcements to the congregation.
2. A celebrant bids farewell to the congregation, makes the sign of the cross, and wishes the members God's blessings.
3. Exit procession of the celebrants.
4. The congregation disperses, often accompanied by a hymn.

Other Ceremonies Incorporated in the Mass

The Mass is the heart of the ecclesiastical liturgy: many of the rites celebrated in Church are incorporated in it. Some may be sacraments in themselves (baptism, confirmation, marriage, ordination, public absolution,[60] anointing of the sick). Others may be ecclesiastical ceremonies of a different kind, such as those carried out during Holy Week (washing of feet, blessing of oil), or sacramentals (such as funerals), which will be discussed forthwith. Ordinarily, these rituals are incorporated between the Mass' two main divisions, the "Liturgy of the Word" and the "Liturgy of the Eucharist."

Major Changes in the Mass in Recent Decades

Very quickly after the Second Council of the Vatican published in 1963 its "Constitution on the Sacred Liturgy," radical changes have been made in the liturgy in general and in the Mass in particular in many places. Some of these changes were related to ideas supported by the "Liturgical Movement" since the beginning of the twentieth century. This "movement" aspired, among other things, to resuscitate some customs of the early Church discovered through modern historical scholarship and to enhance congregational participation in the service. Some changes were instituted preceding the Council, some were an outcome of the its deliberations or the official documents promulgated in its wake, and some (including some very important ones) were the result of changes from "below," coming from grassroots demands of well-organized individuals and associations, not necessarily from decisions made by the upper hierarchy in general or the council in particular.

Among the central changes in the Mass (some of which have been mentioned in passing above) the following can be enumerated: use of the vernacular (instead of Latin);[61] celebration of the Mass with the priest facing the congregation; a major enhancement of the role of laypeople in the Mass;

the creation of a set, defined three-year cycle during which a significant part of the four gospels are read; encouragement of the faithful to receive the Eucharist as often as possible and not just once a year as required; making the altar upon which the Eucharist is celebrated to something resembling a table through the removal of additions placed upon altars over the years (candles, places for storing consecrated bread, crosses, shelves, statues); reinstatement of Masses that had disappeared over the years (Easter Vigil Mass, Holy Week Masses); permission to the congregation, at least on special occasions, to partake of the wine (and not only of the bread); permission for the laity to receive the host in their hand and place it in their mouths themselves (as opposed to the priest placing it upon their tongue); definition of the entire congregation (and not just the priest) as "celebrating the Mass"; enabling several priests to celebrate Mass together ("concelebration"), although only one may direct the ceremony (as opposed to silent watching of the Mass if celebrated by another priest or bishop); placing limitations on the celebration of Masses without a congregation; inclusion of non-priests in various parts of the Mass, including the dispensation of the bread, chanting, and reading from the Scriptures.

First Communion: A Child's First Full Participation in Mass

In the ancient Church, as in Eastern Churches today, children received the Eucharist as part of their baptism, generally through a drop of consecrated wine, which also included what later came to be defined as the sacrament of confirmation. In the Western Church, this practice changed in the Middle Ages when initiation into the Church was split into three different parts. The first part of this initiation, baptism, is now usually carried out in infancy. The second part, confirmation, happens at different ages in different parts of the world, usually between the ages of five and seventeen (depending on local customs). The first time a child partakes of the Eucharist ("First Communion"), the remaining part of the initiation, often takes place around the age of seven.

As is apparent from the discussion of ages above, there are places where confirmation predates First Communion, as well as more numerous places where confirmation occurs several years after it. Those who favor the first option claim that it is more theologically correct, since it maintains the normal order of the three sacraments. Those in favor of the second variant (which is in large part a result of pope Pius X's decree[62] lowering the age of First Communion), would say that a later reception of confirmation makes for a more psychologically meaningful ceremony, one in which the adolescent or young adult may be more serious about his or her religious commitment while still enabling children to feel part of the community and gain spiritual benefit from partaking the Eucharist. Both Confirmation and First Communion are festive occasions, though their character may change quite a bit depending on the age at which they are celebrated.

Contemporary Issues Relating to Mass

Many issues continue to preoccupy the Church in relation to the Mass, the changes made in it, and changes which may still take place. Where does the line pass between conservation of tradition and innovation? Can any kind of music and any musical instrument be incorporated in the Mass? What role is there for local custom? Can dance be included in the rite? Should different cultures be allowed to celebrate the Mass in different ways? When the community is without a priest, temporarily or permanently, how can liturgical life go on without Mass? In such cases, what ceremonies may be celebrated by deacons (if there are any), or even by laypeople? Many cultures do not know wheat and its products, and even when they are familiar with it, wheat and wheat bread are not a major element in their diets. Other cultures are not familiar with the vine and the wine distilled from its fruit. In such cultures, would it not be more appropriate to use basic local foodstuffs, such as rice and traditional liquors, which symbolize joy, success, and plenitude for the local public? Or should one continue celebrating with the foodstuffs known to Jesus, even if they are unknown to his followers? These questions and others once again demonstrate the power and meaning of the Mass for the Catholic public and its role as a catalyst in Catholic culture.

Effect of the Lack of Priests on the Mass

In recent decades the Church has been forced to find ways to deal with the severe shortage of priests in many parts of the world.[63] Due to this fact, several congregations may have to share the services of one priest, and thus it is possible that each parish may have the benefit of a Mass only once every few weeks.[64] Members of communities where the Eucharist is not celebrated regularly and who cannot, for whatever reason, participate in rites celebrated in other congregations in their area have several options. The simplest is of course to wait for a priest to reach the community, even if this means they will not participate in Mass for several weeks at a time. This is a problematic solution. In the past, going without this rite for long periods, sometimes many months,[65] was not considered unusual, but this is no longer the ideal of the Church today. Since the Second Vatican Council, the centrality of the Mass in the life of the Church in general and in the life of the individual faithful in particular, its superiority over all other forms of worship, and the need for frequent participation in it have all been emphasized. For the same reason, participation in prayers in which a priest is not present (as well as, some from the liberal side may say, participation in non-Catholic Christian services)—which be a better solution than no worship at all on Sunday—is seen by many as unsatisfactory.

One solution developed in recent decades is the "Sunday Celebrations in the Absence of a Priest" (SCAP). Central to this ceremony is the dispensation of bread previously consecrated by a priest, accompanied by readings from Scriptures and the saying of various prayers, including "Our Father." This ritual makes it possible for the community to receive the Eucharist but does not include the "reenactment" of the supper of Jesus and his disciples. Despite its many limitations, this ceremony is nowadays a central component in the religious life of many Catholic communities and enables them to maintain a community life despite the absence of a priest. The tough questions it places at the Church's doorstep continue to echo in various contexts: when members of the community are satisfied with the SCAP, questions regarding the necessity of priests are raised; when members are dissatisfied, questions regarding the Church's difficulties to fill its ranks of priests come to the surface.

Reconciliation (Confession)

The status of the sacrament of reconciliation, with confession at its core, varies today quite a bit from region to region and among individual believers. Some perform it regularly every few weeks, some do so once or twice a year, and some almost never confess, at least not individually. The following pages include a short review of the history of the sacrament and its current manifestations in the Catholic Church.

Reconciliation from the New Testament to the Second Vatican Council

The development of the sacrament of reconciliation is particularly complex. In the New Testament the idea of repentance and forgiveness appears several times. The New Testament also includes a few sources for the importance of confession: according to one of these, confession should be made to another member of the community.[66] The idea of the forgiveness of sins by Jesus appears explicitly a few times in the New Testament,[67] but many Christian authors also read the stories in the New Testament in which Jesus does not avoid the company of sinners as symbolizing and indicating the same notion. In addition to these, the central source for the notion that Jesus' disciples are authorized to forgive sins, and the text traditionally considered by the Catholic Church as the basis for this sacrament, is the one in which Jesus says to his disciples, after having arisen from the dead:

> As the Father has sent me, so I send you. . . . Whose sins you forgive are forgiven them, and whose sins you retain are retained.[68]

Baptism is considered to absolve the baptized of all their sins. Thus, for a long time Christian believers delayed their baptism (which, as we have noted, is a one-time affair) as close as possible to their death in order to avoid sinning after it. Among other reasons, it was in order to find a solution for sins committed after baptism that the sacrament of absolution came into existence in the early Middle Ages. Two major issues contributed to its spread: on the one hand, practices coming out of monasteries, and on the other hand, missionaries from Ireland who spread the Christian faith in continental Europe. Not only did the water of baptism brings about forgiveness, said Christian thinkers then and now, but also the tears of contrition have the same power. Penitence can restore the lost grace received during baptism.

During the nineteenth century and the first half of the twentieth century, the sacrament of confession became a central tenet of Catholic life. The public was expected to confess habitually. Sins previously considered quite minor, such as sexual thoughts or absence from Mass, were redefined as very severe and requiring confession. Confession, which was often rapid and quite technical, became an integral part of the Catholic life cycle. With it the consciousness of sin, mortal or venial, became dominant.

The Sacrament of Reconciliation Today

The Second Vatican Council and papal decisions following it brought about a major reform in the sacrament. Among other changes, it was reemphasized that only grievous sins require it. Its name was also changed, and today it is known by an ancient name, "Reconciliation" (*Reconciliatio* in Latin). This name change is quite significant; it implies, among other things, that the sacrament brings about not only forgiveness by God but also peace and renewed harmony between the believer and the Church. Some theologians who worry that the name may bring about a misunderstanding, as if sin were two-sided, might still emphasize that humans are the ones who sin and must repent and "reconcile," not God.

Celebration of the Sacrament

The Church demands that its members celebrate the sacrament of reconcil-iation at least once a year.[69] The customary time is during Lent, the period leading to Easter. In addition, the faithful member is admonished to seek the sacrament every time he or she is guilty of a serious, "mortal" sin.[70] In practice, there are Catholics who perform the sacrament quite often, while others may not seek it for years at a time.

The process of reconciliation may be divided into several parts. The first part is done by the confessant: soul-searching and repentance. Catholics will generally refer to this part as the "Contrition." While this stage ordinar-ily takes place before the sacrament formally begins, it is a part of it, exactly as reading from Scriptures is part of the sacrament of the Eucharist. After one examines one's conscience and discovers grave sins, one must repent. Without true repentance and a real desire not to sin again—both in regard to a particular sin and to all the confessant's other sins—the forgiveness accorded in the sacrament may be considered invalid. Whoever feels that his or her desire for repentance is real may go to a place where a priest awaits those wishing to confess.

Ordinarily, the confession must take place in a church. In many places, a priest will be available for the purpose on Friday, the traditional day of forgiveness and repentance, but also on Saturday, which is a convenient day for many, or on Sunday before Mass. Visitors to many churches may notice the "confessionals": wooden furnishings which include seats for a priest on one end and for a confessant on the other. The priest and the confessant are usually separated by a thick mesh, which prevents the par-ties from seeing each other. These confessionals are relatively new: they appeared in the sixteenth century in Italy. Current Canon Law does not require their use and permits the confessant to choose between having the sacrament done in a room in which confessant and confessor face each other and performing it in a confessional (or a room in which a screen separates the parties). In practice, the custom varies greatly from place to place. There are places where the use of the confessional is quite limited. For example, in many places in France, confession is carried out in a small room with transparent walls at a corner of the church. The con-fessor and the confessant are seated face to face. They can be seen from the outside, but of course their talk cannot be heard. In such churches where the traditional confessionals are retained, it is normally for their historical or artistic value. In other places, confessionals may remain in use today. This is customary, for example, in Italy and in many parts of the Middle East. A shining light bulb may serve to mark a confessional where a priest awaits confessants. In the US, one can find both types of confessional format, open room and confessionals, but not necessarily in the same parish.

After the confessant reaches the priest, the latter greets the former. The confessant will cross him or herself and say, "in the name of the Father, and of the Son, and of the Holy Spirit, Amen." Some might add the opening phrase "Father, forgive me, for I have sinned." This sentence is traditionally associated with the "Parable of the Prodigal Son," one of the most beautiful and famous parables of the New Testament,[71] in which the lost and sinning son returns to his father and says: "Father, I have sinned against heaven and against you; I no longer deserve to be called your son." In the context of the sacrament of reconciliation, this sentence also has a double meaning: it expresses the repentance of the confessant both in front of the priest and before God the Father. After this opening, the priest will invite the confessant and tell him or her, using one formula or another, to trust in God, who awaits those repenting. Sometimes the priest will quote relevant verses from Scriptures.

After this stage, the confessant will begin to describe his or her sins. If he or she did not do it yet, the priest may ask when he or she last confessed, in order to better understand the nature of the confession. Often, this information would be provided earlier by the penitent by adding immediately after the first sentence, "It has been [span of time] since my last confession." In many cases, a conversation will ensue between confessor and confessant. Its nature may vary greatly depending on the place, the character of the two parties, and the relationship between them. The longer their acquaintance and the more time they have, the more likely the conversation will develop and deepen, becoming less mechanical. Some confessants may group their sins into the categories of the "seven deadly sins": pride, greed, envy, wrath, lust, gluttony, and sloth.[72] Generally, priests will not want to hear very specific details of each sin. The priest will ideally help the confessant not only to define the sins but also to reflect on the reasons for committing them and the ways to avoid their recurrence in the future. He should clarify to the confessant that his or her repentance must be complete, and suggest acts that he or she can carry out to reach such completion. In the past, many of these acts were quite technical (such as saying one or another prayer a number of times); today, although not all priests will insist on that, they are supposed to be concretely linked, whether practically or symbolically, to the sin. After this central stage, the confessant will declare that he or she repents and asks God's forgiveness. This declaration may be made using set formulas or in another way. The priest will raise his right arm or both arms over the head of the confessant, and say the formula that gives the penitent the desired absolution:

> God the Father of mercies, through the death and resurrection of his Son, has reconciled the world to Himself and sent the Holy Spirit among us for the forgiveness of sins; through the ministry of the Church may God give you pardon and peace, and I absolve you from your sins[73] in the name of the Father, and of the Son, and of the Holy Spirit.

After the confessant replies "Amen," the priest says a few words of thanksgiving to God, and sends the confessant on his or her way. It is customary for the confessant to remain in the church for a few more minutes and pray. Afterwards he or she carries out the acts stipulated by the priest as soon as possible: Catholics call this part "Satisfaction."

Additional Aspects of the Sacrament of Reconciliation

The content of the confession is protected by absolute confidentiality, unless the confessant explicitly permits the priest to speak of the matter with others—for example, to consult the bishop or a psychologist about one aspect or another of the confession (a very rare occurrence in any case). Without such permission, a priest who divulges details of a confession is automatically excommunicated from the Church and may resume normal relations with it only through a decision of one of the Vatican courts. Although the motif of a priest undergoing moral conflict because of his inability to pass on information about crimes to the police is rather common in literature and films,[74] it is probable that the number of cases in which priests receive significant information of severe crimes is not great. When this does occur, a priest may indeed find himself severely conflicted. As far as the Church is concerned, there is no way to permit the sharing of information obtained during confession, regardless of its content or significance: the information is absolutely protected by the seal of sacramental secrecy.[75]

The steady fall in the frequency of the sacrament of reconciliation in recent decades is of concern to many in the hierarchy. There are different explanations for it: some associate it with social changes and specifically with changes in the conceptualization of "sin" in contemporary society. Others relate it to the certain positive and optimistic "Spirit" they associate, justly or not, with the decisions of the Second Vatican Council; yet others claim that the reason is many Catholics' conviction that the act of contrition at the beginning of Mass is a sufficient substitute for reconciliation.

In various places an effort is made to encourage the public to request this sacrament regularly. Various Catholic writers who have dealt with the matter emphasize the liberating nature of the rite and the feeling that it enables the confessant to open a new page in his or her relationship with God. Only in the future will it be possible to evaluate their success in encouraging this sacrament among Catholic congregants.

Matrimony (Marriage)

Marriage, meaning both a ceremony creating and declaring the existence of a special relationship between two human beings (usually with a significant sexual component and traditionally involving a man and a woman)[76] and the relationship itself which comes after the ceremony, seems to be a universal phenomenon. It is not surprising that many religions, including Catholic Christianity, have created bodies of law and customs institutionalizing and regulating both the ceremony and married life.

Married Life in Catholic Thought

Since the early days of Christianity, many Christian writers and preachers have forged solid visions of married life: they have formulated opinions regarding the very nature of marriage, the sexual life of couples, the status of unmarried people, and so on. In the Gospel of John, Jesus is depicted attending a wedding party in the village of Cana in the Galilee. Of all places, this is where he begins his public activity, by transforming water into wine, thus contributing to the festivities.[77] Some hold that if the author of the Gospel according to John had wanted to attribute a negative perception of marriage to Jesus, he would not have placed his first miracle at a wedding feast. On the other hand, there are texts in which Jesus is described as hinting that marriage may not be the only true road in life, and even that others may be better.[78] Nevertheless, one should keep in mind that in most of the relevant texts Jesus seems to treat marriage as an existing and unquestionable fact: it is on divorce that he gives his opinion, which seems to be negative.[79]

Regardless of Jesus' exact opinions on the matter—to which our access is limited, due to the very nature of the gospels in the New Testament—Paul, in one of his more important epistles, discussed married life, its importance, and necessity in detail. Among other things, he declares:

> Now to the unmarried and to widows, I say: it is a good thing for them to remain as they are, as I do, but if they cannot exercise self-control they should marry, for it is better to marry than to be on fire.[80]

Following texts such as this and incorporating other principles, including some currents in religious and philosophical views accepted by certain groups in antiquity, the dominant view in the Church had for many years been that there are three reasons for marriage, of differing importance. The first and most central reason for marriage was procreation and the raising of children. Mutual aid between the partners was considered the second reason. Its function as an effective means to control sexual desire was the third reason cited. At the same time, those who could manage without it were leading a life of a higher status.

The Second Vatican Council dealt differently with marriage.[81] Without defining a hierarchy between the different reasons for marriage, it was declared as important and beneficial for the couple, for society, and for children, and not inferior to celibate life. For children, marriage creates an optimal environment to grow up in, said the Council. For society, the family nucleus serves as a building block. For the couple, the intimate bond of love enables development and self-realization. Marriage was defined as an "intimate community of conjugal life and love."[82] Although for long periods in the Church's history sexual relations had been seen as a necessary evil, this was no longer so in the Council's declarations. Sexual relations among married partners that were carried out with love and fidelity were good and proper, even if their purpose was not exclusively procreation. Marriage thus earned an honored position in the Church, one it had not always held.

History of the Sacrament

Many thinkers in the first few centuries of the Church discussed married life and sexuality, but they were often less interested in the ceremony establishing the married state. Thus for hundreds of years most Christians were accustomed to marry according to local custom and law, without the Church playing a significant role in the process. The Church, for its part, recognized these marriages *a posteriori* almost without hesitation. This historical fact is of significance even today: the Church treats any marriage of a single man and a single woman made willingly, at least *a priori* and especially when both spouses are not Christians, as valid. The laws of the Church ritual have to be upheld only when at least one of the participants is Catholic.

Only beginning in the twelfth and thirteenth centuries, during which official lists of the seven sacraments appeared, did the act of marriage of two validly baptized individuals become considered a sacrament. This made it into a Church rite, which therefore must be celebrated in accordance with Church law.[83] The ceremony's sacramental status has great theological significance: not only did marriage became a fully respectable state of life, but also, when the two partners are baptized, the fact that the marriage act is a sacrament grants them a special divine grace according to the Church's doctrine, whose purpose is to assist them in conjugal life. Moreover, if their union is sanctified as a sacrament and if it is later consummated, their union is equated with the relations between Jesus and his Church. As the latter link cannot be broken, the same is true of the former.[84] Declaring marriage a sacrament did not make all concerns the Church had with sexuality disappear though: there was still something sinful about it. Yet, the sacrament of penitence, in which people could confess their sins and get absolution, created a tenable balance enabling people not only to be married but also to engage in marital relations.

The Sacrament of Matrimony Today

The Council of Trent set in the sixteenth century the basis for the ritual, upon which Catholic marriages to a large extent are still based. The most up-to-date law on this matter is the Code of Canon Law of 1983, which is influenced by the decisions of the Second Vatican Council.

Unlike the situation in some other religions, such as traditional Judaism, Catholic marriage is strictly equal. Neither the husband nor the wife is considered primary. Thus, any reference to Catholics in the following pages refers to men and women in equal measure.

Order of the Ceremony

When two Catholics marry one another, the marriage is normally part of a Mass. After the readings from Scriptures, which, depending on the date, may join texts related to the occasion with those linked to the liturgical season, the ceremony itself begins. More than any other sacrament, the marriage ceremony is quite flexible and may include local customs, including those of non-Christian provenance, so long as these have been permitted by local bishops. Usually it will include questions from the celebrant to the couple, in which he (or she[85]) may ask if they have come of their own will and if they intend to respect their partner for the rest of their lives. In accordance with the partners' ages and status, the celebrant may also ask if they are open to the possibility that this marriage will bring children into the world. The two answer the questions in the positive and declare their desire to marry. After this part, the core of the sacrament begins—the moment in which both sides declare their commitment to the other:

> I promise to be true to you in good times and in bad, in sickness and in health. I will love you and honor you all the days of my life.

The formula may differ slightly from place to place, but it must minimally include an absolute and eternal commitment of the partners to each other.[86] This exchange of vows is what constitutes the marriage. After this crucial moment of the ceremony, the celebrant will bless the newlyweds using the following formula or one like it:

> You have declared your consent before the Church. May the Lord in his goodness strengthen your consent and fill you both with his blessings. What God has joined, man must not divide.

After the rings each partner presents to the other have been exchanged,[87] the celebrant once more blesses the couple with a special nuptial blessing. Although in the Western Church the legal meaning of this blessing is marginal, many consider it to be one of the highlights of the ceremony. Historically speaking, they are certainly not wrong: a nuptial blessing, delivered by a priest following a wedding previously celebrated according to local secular customs, existed centuries before a full-fledged Christian marriage ritual was established. In accordance with local custom, family members or the entire assembly may symbolically participate in the blessing, for example by raising their hands. After this blessing, if the ceremony is part of a Mass, the liturgy of the Eucharist will begin, followed of course by communion: the dispensation and reception of consecrated bread and wine.

Marriage between a Catholic and a Non-Catholic

A Catholic may be wed in church with a non-Catholic Christian, with a person of another faith, or with a person who does not belong to any religion. It might happen that family members, priests, or bishops may try to dissuade Catholics from marrying non-Catholics, but Church law is not on their side: so long as certain minimal demands are met, a single Catholic has the right to marry any single person of the opposite sex in church, regardless of their religion or lack thereof. The couple has to commit to raising their children as Catholics, though in many places the clergy will now be content with a statement by the Catholic partner, that he or she will do his or her best to bring this about.

Often such a wedding is carried out without a Mass, since it is probable that many of those present will not be Catholic: they and one of the partners will not be able to take communion. The celebration of a Mass may bring about a situation in which the marriage and the Mass, two sacraments symbolizing unity, perversely become rites demonstrating more than anything a rift between all those present.[88]

Ordination (Holy Orders)

Reception of the sacrament of ordination brings a man (and until ecclesiastical law changes, a man only) into the ranks of the clergy[89] and grants him a particular authority to lead in the celebration of various sacraments. Like baptism and confirmation, ordination to a particular rank is a one-time sacrament, which according to Catholic faith leaves an indelible spiritual mark on its receiver. Thus, a person may not be ordained twice as deacon, priest, or bishop, but he may be ordained a number of times, each time to the next rank among these, until he reaches the most "complete" ordination: that of a bishop.

This sacrament has various names. One of these, "Holy Orders," is particularly important, since it emphasizes the true aim of the sacrament, and the fact that, as with marriage, the ceremony itself is only the beginning of a new form of life.

Preparation for Ordination into the Diaconate and Priesthood

In the vast majority of cases, the entire ordination process will be geared towards ordination into the priesthood. The following describes the most common procedure, although in practice things may be slightly different depending on the candidate's particular case and personal biography.

Ordinarily, a baptized and confirmed young man will present himself to the local bishop and say to him that he believes the priesthood is his vocation. Many candidates do indeed feel that they have been called by God for this vocation. The bishop will speak with him and ask for opinions of people who know this young man: his parish priest, acquaintances, and former teachers and mentors. If the candidate is a member of an Institute of Consecrated Life, the opinion of his superior will be of utmost importance.

If the bishop decides that the candidate is worthy, he will be sent to begin his theological studies. These studies may take place in a seminary—a Catholic institution created for this very purpose—or in a department of theology in a university. The study period is normally about four or five years long and is approximately equivalent to bachelor's and master's degrees. The candidate will take basic and advanced courses in theology, Bible, classical languages (Hebrew, Greek, and Latin), the sacraments, ethics, philosophy, history, sociology, psychology, and more. He will usually live with other candidates (unless he is a member of an Institute of Consecrated Life). Normally he will be attached to a local congregation: by aiding in the activities of the parish, he will gain valuable practical work experience. Throughout this preparatory period, his suitability for the role will be examined through his academic achievements and the opinions given by those with whom he lives and works. The assessment of the director of the seminary, if he is enrolled in one, will be crucial. The process is not easy, and the dropout (or dismissal) rate is quite high: in many places, more than 30 percent of those who begin the process will not finish it, either because they decide to leave or are asked to. When the candidate has finished his studies or is close to finishing them, if opinions of him continue to be positive and if he has passed the age of twenty-five, he will be ordained as a deacon, a temporary role he will generally fill for about a year, after which he will be ordained as a priest.

For a man interested in becoming a permanent deacon,[90] the process will usually be different. The age of the candidates is usually higher, and many of them are married. Their training process will be much more flexible. Although there are also clear rules for this training, it is, among other things, dependent on the academic opportunities available in the region where the candidate lives: unlike candidates for the priesthood who are usually young, and, in the Western Catholic Church, single (and can thus be easily sent to study elsewhere), those on the track to become permanent deacons are often more rooted in a specific place.

Overview of the Ordination Ceremony

The ordination of a person as deacon, priest, or bishop may be done only by a bishop. Sometimes, mainly when a bishop is being ordained, it is celebrated by a number of bishops; nevertheless, even in this case one of them will be considered the main consecrator in the Western Church. The ordination ceremony is carried out during a festive Mass, usually on a Sunday or holy day. It is not unusual to see a number of men ordained at the same time.

The ceremony, whether it is celebrated for a single man or a number of candidates, is an impressive, complicated, and symbol-laden event. Nevertheless, the heart of the sacrament is simple and made up of two elements: the silent laying of the consecrator's (or consecrators') hands on the head of the ordained and a special prayer of consecration.

The laying on of hands, an ancient ritual gesture in the Church, is considered to be the continuation of a Biblical custom that appears both in the Old and New Testaments. Thus Jacob laid his hands on the heads of his grandsons, the sons of Joseph, when he blessed them, as did Moses with Joshua upon appointing him as his successor. In the New Testament it is mentioned, among other places, when the apostles appointed seven assistants. In Christian context, the gesture has become related to the descent of the Spirit.[91]

The act of laying on of hands is the same in terms of its performance whether a deacon, priest, or bishop is being ordained. The prayer of ordination is that which distinguishes between the levels of ordination. Symbols and ritual acts also differentiate, certainly visually, between these three categories.

Ordination of a Deacon

The ceremony in which a deacon is ordained opens with the presentation of the candidate to the bishop by a priest. The priest will say to the bishop that the Church requests the candidate's ordination. The bishop will ask the priest if he considers the candidate worthy. The priest will answer that after inquiries, and following the recommendations of those involved in the training of the candidate, this is the case. The bishop will then declare his election of the candidate, and the public will assert its support for the decision through applause or a set formula. This seemingly marginal part of the ceremony is of great importance. Its purpose is to emphasize that the bishop chooses the candidate, but that he does so with the assent of the entire community. Immediately following this, the bishop will give a homily on the role of the deacon. It will hopefully be related to the candidate's biography and the type of diaconate (transitional, permanent, permanent married) he is ordained for.

In the Western Catholic Church, men who take Holy Orders are obliged to remain celibate, unless they are ordained as permanent deacons when already married[92] (in the Eastern Catholic Churches a married man can also be ordained as a priest).[93] If this is not one of the cases of a married candidate, the commitment to celibacy is made during ordination into the diaconate. After the sermon, the bishop will ask the candidate if he is willing to commit to a life of sexual celibacy as a symbol of his devotion to Christ and for the sake of his service to humankind and God. The candidate will answer in the affirmative. This moment of commitment is significant: even if the deacon later becomes a priest, he will not be asked to repeat his promise.[94]

After this stage, the bishop will publicly present the candidate with a number of questions. Among other things, he will ask if the candidate desires to be ordained, if he intends to fulfill his role with humility and love, to teach the Gospel according to Church tradition, and to diligently pray the "Liturgy of the Hours," a duty imposed on him from the moment of ordination. The candidate will answer these questions in the affirmative; he will also declare, sometimes while symbolically laying his palms between those of the bishop, his intention to follow the orders of his superiors now and in the future.

Now, after the nature of the candidate has been ascertained, begins the most dramatic part of the ceremony, with the "Litany of the Saints," a powerful prayer used on festive occasions, when the aid of the saints is explicitly wished for. Throughout this prayer, which is not short, and is usually chanted as a dialogue between the congregation and a cantor, the candidate for ordination (no matter what role he is being ordained for), if physically capable, lies flat on the ground between the congregation and the altar, facing the ground. This act symbolizes his fidelity to the Church on one hand, and his acknowledgment that he will need aid from above in his new role. The voices of the faithful will ring in his ears:

St. Andrew,	pray for us
St. John,	pray for us
St. Mary Magdalene,	pray for us
. . . St. Augustine . . .,	pray for us
Lord have mercy,	Lord have mercy
Christ have mercy,	Christ have mercy
Lord have mercy,	Lord have mercy
Holy Mary, Mother of God,	pray for us
St. Michael,	pray for us
Holy angels of God,	pray for us
St. John the Baptist,	pray for us
St. Joseph,	pray for us
Sts. Peter and Paul,	pray for us

[. . . additional saints, including those selected by the candidate . . .]

Jesus, Son of the living God	Lord, hear our prayer
Christ, hear us,	Christ, hear us
Lord Jesus,	hear our prayer
Lord Jesus,	hear our prayer

The prayer ends with the bishop beseeching God to help the candidate in his role. With this, the candidate gets up, goes to the bishop, and bows before him. The moment of ordination has arrived: the bishop lays his hands on the candidate's head in silence. After the laying on of hands, the bishop will read a prayer aloud, all the while raising his hands over the candidate. This prayer, the prayer of ordination, is what marks this ordination as that of a deacon. It includes a theologico-historical summary of how the class of deacons came into existence. In it, the bishop asks God to invest the candidate with the Holy Spirit and to fortify him so he may perform well the role to which he has been appointed.

When the prayer ends, the new deacon will be dressed in appropriate liturgical vestments. As a symbol of his new role, he will receive a book containing the Gospels. The bishop will bless him and say: "Believe what you read; Teach what you believe; Practice what you teach." The bishop and the new deacon will give each other a kiss of peace as a symbol of their fraternity and the special bond created between them.

In the liturgy of the Eucharist immediately following the ordination, the new deacon will assist the bishop in celebrating the Mass and dispense the consecrated bread (or the consecrated wine, if wine is offered), to the congregants.

Ordination of a Priest

In many ways the ordination of a priest is similar to that of a deacon. Certain parts are not included in it, for example the commitment to celibacy, which, if necessary, has already been made. Other parts are adjusted to the occasion: the homily will deal with the status and actions of the priest, as will the prayer of consecration. When a deacon is being ordained, only the bishop lays his hands upon him. When a priest is being ordained, all the priests present will come to the candidate and lay their hands upon him after the bishop does so. This act, which of course does not replace that of the bishop nor equals it in importance, nevertheless symbolizes the reception of the new priest into the community of priests.

After the prayer of consecration, and after the new priest is dressed in his liturgical vestments, the bishop will anoint the new priest's hands with holy oil. This ritual is associated with the centrality of the administration of the Eucharist, the sacrifice to God, in the new priest's life. In his hands, anointed with consecrated oil, he will from now on perform this blood-less sacrifice it in the name of the entire Church.[95]

After the new priest and the bishop have given each other the kiss of peace, the liturgy of the Eucharist begins. The new priest will celebrate the Mass together with the bishop.[96]

Ordination of a Bishop

The ordination of a bishop (also referred to as "Episcopal Consecration") is, naturally, a particularly festive occasion. The main consecrator, a bishop of course, will be joined by two other bishops and sometimes more.[97] The presence and involvement of various bishops in the ceremony is meant to emphasize the fact that the new bishop is joining the *collegium* of bishops, and that these accept him joyously.

After the reading of the Gospel, the sacrament itself begins with an ancient and festive hymn, *Veni Creator Spiritus,* used at various moments of the liturgy when the descent of the Holy Spirit is desired.

In the Western-Latin Church, the decision to ordain a new bishop is made by the pope.[98] Therefore, as opposed to the above-mentioned cases, the ordaining bishop will not ask the priest presenting the candidate for his opinion of the candidate and the information he has received regarding him and will not declare that he has found the candidate worthy. Instead, he will ask the presenting priest if he has a letter of appointment from Rome for the candidate, and after answering in the affirmative, that priest will be asked to read the letter out loud.

In accordance with an ancient custom, and because of the crucial importance for the Church that only appropriate persons will be consecrated as bishops, the candidate for Episcopal ordination will be asked to clarify through affirmative answers to a battery of questions the quality of his faith and his intention of serving the Church properly. Among other things, the bishop-elect will be asked whether he intends to defend the Church's traditional doctrine; to maintain unity with the other bishops under the pope, "the successor of Peter"; to obey him and stay loyal to him; to lead the congregation together with the priests and deacons; to be generous and compassionate to the poor, foreigners, and all those in distress; to attempt as a good shepherd would to bring the stray sheep of his flock back into the fold; to pray for the People of God; and more.

During the ordination of a bishop, a symbolic ritual is added between the laying on of hands and the prayer of consecration: a book containing the Gospels is set on his head. With the support of two deacons, it is held there during the entire prayer of consecration.

After the prayer, the main consecrator anoints the head of the new bishop with scented holy oil, symbolizing that from now on he shares in the priesthood of Christ (a term which literally means, as mentioned before, "the anointed one") and alluding to the descent of the Spirit upon him. After he is given a book containing the Gospels, he will also receive the objects symbolizing his new status: a bishop's ring symbolizing his fidelity to the Church, the consort of God, and his resolve to protect Her; a mitre, or bishop's cap; and a shepherd's staff ("crosier"), symbolizing his function as shepherd and guardian of God's flock. Before the bishops kiss their new colleague as a symbol of peace, the main consecrator will lead the bishop to his chair or *cathedra*. This moment, in which the bishop is granted a specific charge, is also very significant, especially if the ordination is carried out in the cathedral where he will serve.

Anointing of the Sick

The sacrament of anointing of the sick consists, as its name indicates, of a sacramental anointing of an ailing person with oil. This sacrament rests upon various verses in the New Testament, including the following:

> Is anyone among you sick? He should summon the presbyters of the church, and they should pray over him and anoint (him) with oil in the name of the Lord, and the prayer of faith will save the sick person, and the Lord will raise him up. If he has committed any sins, he will be forgiven.[99]

In opposition to the custom preceding the Second Vatican Council, today the sacrament is carried out even when there is no imminent danger of death: any person whose health is seriously impaired by sickness or old age, is able and entitled to receive it. This is also the reason for its current name, different from the pre-Council "Extreme Unction." Many theologians today agree that the sacrament's role is to fortify the spirit of the ill and to aid them in their struggle against despair, worry, and even sinful thoughts that the illness may bring about. The ceremony is also designed to counteract the distance that the disease may create between the ill person and the Church. Many will say that this distance is not necessarily brought about by sin: the illness might be partially its cause. For exactly this reason, the sacrament demonstrates that the sick person is an integral part of the Church. Although the sick person is the only one anointed, the message of hope sent by the sacrament is also intended for those surrounding him or her, and indeed for the whole Church. To exemplify this, the sacrament is carried out, when possible, in the presence of those close to the sick person and other members of the Church. Again, as with almost all the other sacraments, their public aspect is nowadays emphasized.

The unshakeable Catholic beliefs in the existence of a world beyond this one and in the immortality of the soul are essential to understanding this sacrament. It is not a healing ritual, and there is no promise that it will contribute to the physical well-being of the sick person. Even if Catholics believe that God answers their prayers, they have no certitude that the answer will always be positive. Miracles happen extremely rarely, the average Catholic will say: in most cases, nature follows its preestablished rules. Nevertheless, whatever the patient's fate, the Church believes that the sacrament will help him or her in the next stage of life, in body, spirit or both, including by absolving his or her sins.

The Church recommends separation of this rite from the sacrament of reconciliation: if the sick person wishes to confess, the confession should, if possible, take place at a preceding visit with the priest. If this is impossible, the sacrament of reconciliation may take place during the first part of the ceremony.

The sacrament of "Anointing of the Sick" may take place in the home of the sick person, in a hospital, or in a church. It may be the only sacrament celebrated, or it may be integrated with a Mass. The celebration of this sacrament in public, and its granting to many sick or older people at the same time is today more and more frequent.

Administration of the Sacrament

Only a priest can celebrate this sacrament. After the priest blesses the sick person, he may sprinkle him or her with holy water, recalling the sick person's baptism. Then, depending on the person's state, the priest, another participant, or the sick person reads relevant passages from Scriptures. If appropriate, the priest may give a short sermon. Afterwards, the priest blesses the sick person and assures that person that the Church is praying for him or her. He may ask the sick person to pray for others as well. It is commonly suggested that this request may assist the sick person in retaining dignity and realizing that he or she also has something to offer the Church. Then, in silence, the priest will lay his hands on the sick person's head. After the laying on of hands, using sanctified olive oil (or, if necessary, another kind of vegetable oil), the priest will make the sign of the cross on the sick person's eyes, ears, nose, and mouth, and say:

Through this holy anointing, may the Lord in his love and mercy help you with the grace of the Holy Spirit.

The anointed and those present say "Amen." The priest once again makes the sign of the cross in oil, this time on the palms of the sick person, and says:

May the Lord who frees you from sin save you and raise you up.

After the anointing, the priest will pray and ask God to help the anointed. The prayer is adjusted to the person's state: a prayer used for a patient entering surgery which may bring about recovery is likely to differ from one for a person who is expected to pass away in the coming days. After this request for mercy, all those present will together say an "Our Father,"[100] which ends the ceremony.

Unlike baptism, confirmation, or ordination, anointing is not a one-time-only affair: if the patient revives, the Church recommends that he or she participate in a prayer of thanksgiving. If his or her state deteriorates, he or she may receive the sacrament again.

Viaticum

When there is a high probability that the sick person is nearing his or her end, another ritual, that of the *Viaticum,* may take place in addition to the anointing (or without it). During this ritual, the dying person will receive, if possible, a piece of consecrated bread to serve as "provisions for the road" (the Latin name of the ceremony) when he or she goes to meet God, according to Catholic belief. In unusual cases, a person might receive the Viaticum more than once: pope John Paul II was given it for the first time after being seriously injured in an assassination attempt in 1981, and then again for the second and last time in 2005, a few hours before his death.

Prayers and Sacramentals

In addition to the seven sacraments, which form the heart of public worship in the Church, Catholics also perform many other ritual acts that have a religious meaning. The general name for these and the objects associated with them is "sacramentals." Some say that if the sacraments are Catholic food for the soul, sacramentals are additives or "vitamins" that should accompany this food. Many prayers unconnected to the sacraments also exist in Catholic tradition. This chapter cannot encompass all of the prayers of the Catholic Church nor all of the sacramentals, both of which are very numerous. We shall make do with mentioning a small number of prayers that are considered basic and elementary and then quickly reviewing some sacramentals.

Christian Prayer

It is often said that one of the most important elements of Christian faith is the idea of having a direct connection between humanity and God. Although many religions affirm the same idea, Christianity, by virtue of the existence of Jesus, a human who is also divine, has something that the mainstream branches of the two other Bible-related religions, Islam and Judaism, do not have (but some Eastern religions do). The believer is not obliged to turn to God the Father, whose essence is sublime and ineffable.

He or she may turn to Christ, a human like him or herself, knowing that Jesus is, at the same time, God Himself.

The person addressing God in His manifestation as Father, Son, or Holy Spirit, may choose to do so in a few words of prayer or in silence. The instructions given by Jesus in the Gospel According to Matthew serve for many as an invitation to do so:

> But when you pray, go to your inner room, close the door, and pray to your Father in secret. And your Father who sees in secret, will repay you. In praying, do not babble like the pagans, who think that they will be heard because of their many words. Do not be like them. Your Father knows what you need before you ask him.[101]

And indeed, many Catholics may kneel in front of Jesus' effigy on the cross, facing the consecrated bread set in a corner chapel, or in front of another icon in silence and for a long while. They may try to focus their thoughts on God and sometimes ask his blessing and aid. They might do this by addressing a saint, especially Mary, but others as well. For many Catholics, this form of worship well expresses the central idea of prayer: a link to Christ. Such an internal connection with the divine needs no words.

Those who wish to use words in their prayers may also find formulas and biblical references supporting such a practice. The rest of this chapter will concern itself not with silent prayer but with those prayers built around fixed words. Nevertheless, the importance of silent prayer for many Catholics, and of more spontaneous types of prayer should be kept in mind, even when the discussion turns to the practical and "external" aspects of the modalities of the prayer under discussion and not to its mystical meanings.[102]

The Lord's Prayer

The main and most important prayer for many branches of Christianity is the one known as the "Lord's Prayer," or by its Latin name, *Pater Noster,* which is based on its first words, "Our Father." Its importance lies mainly in its attribution, by two of the gospels, to Jesus himself. Immediately after he asserts the unimportance of verbiage, Jesus suggests a formula for prayer.[103] The following is the version of the prayer given in the Gospel according to Matthew:

> Our Father in heaven,
> hallowed be your name,
> your kingdom come,
> your will be done,

on earth as in heaven.
Give us today our daily bread;
and forgive us our debts,
as we forgive our debtors;
and do not subject us to the final test,[104]
but deliver us from the evil one.

In its liturgical version, the prayer usually ends in a hymn of praise ("doxology"):

For the kingdom, the power, and the glory are yours,
Now and for ever,
Amen.

This coda appears in some manuscripts of the New Testament, but not in the most important ancient ones. Thus, although it is generally not included in modern editions (Catholic or others) of the Christian Bible, nevertheless, in accordance with a longstanding tradition it is usually included in contemporary Catholic prayer. In order to distinguish it from the ancient body of the prayer, it is customary to separate the main text from the later addition through the use of a buffer sentence.

This prayer, as its name indicates, addresses the Father. The fact that it originates with Jesus himself, the Son, gives it its special character. Without a doubt, this prayer could also have been included in a Jewish liturgy, as it does not contain any particularly "Christian" element. Its resemblance to the Jewish *Kaddish* prayer, though it has been exaggerated at times, is undeniable. It is remarkable that, nevertheless, in a Catholic context and for other Christian denominations who also practice a rite of communion of some kind using bread, the sentence "Give us today our daily bread" takes on a particular meaning, especially when it is said during such a ceremony. The frequent use of this prayer means that even Catholics who rarely attend church are likely to know it by heart.[105] It is one of the basic building blocks incorporated in many hymnals, sacraments, and sacramentals.

Hail Mary (Ave Maria)

One of the most renowned prayers in the Catholic world is the "Hail Mary" or *Ave Maria:*

Hail Mary, full of grace, the Lord is with thee; blessed art thou amongst women, and blessed is the fruit of thy womb, Jesus.

Holy Mary, Mother of God, pray for us sinners, now and at the hour of our death. Amen.

This prayer is known both for its content, which is considered by many—including non-Christians—to be beautiful, moving, and very "human," as well as for its innumerable musical renderings. The two most famous settings are by Schubert[106] and Gounod.[107] Even today, many performers consider singing it a particular feat. In recent years, the *Ave Maria* has been rendered by Luciano Pavarotti, Celine Dion, Aaron Neville, Dolores O'Riordan, and many others.[108] The prayer itself is composed of a number of elements stitched together over many generations. Its basis is two greetings to Mary, which appear in the first chapter of the Gospel According to Luke: the greeting of the Archangel Gabriel, and that of Elizabeth, the mother of John.[109] Their concatenation into one unit for the liturgy apparently occurred in the twelfth century. The names Mary and Jesus were added to the text some time later. The coda ("Holy Mary, Mother of God, pray for us sinners, now and at the hour of our death"), which transforms this greeting into a true prayer, was added in the sixteenth century. The *Ave Maria* plays a central role in the prayer of the rosary, to be described below, and in the *Angelus,* among other prayers.

Angelus

The *Angelus* ("angel") is a short Catholic prayer whose origin, if not its current form, is probably to be found in the fourteenth century. Its name is taken from its opening word. It is said three times a day, in the morning, at midday, and in the evening. Its purpose is to recall and remind the faithful of the Incarnation of the Son of God and of the moment it was announced to Mary. Its centerpiece is the "Hail Mary," said three times. Traditionally, the *Angelus* is accompanied by three sets of three rings of a bell. Since many generations, it has been considered not only a prayer of the "common people"[110] but also one that has had an important role in the life of popes. One of the pope's weekly public appearances above St. Peter's Square revolves around it. If possible, the *Angelus* is said as a dialogue (between A and B):

A. The Angel of the Lord declared unto Mary.
B. And she conceived by the Holy Ghost.
A. Hail Mary, full of grace, the Lord is with thee; blessed art thou amongst women, and blessed is the fruit of thy womb, Jesus.
B. Holy Mary, Mother of God, pray for us sinners, now and at the hour of our death.

A. Behold the handmaid of the Lord.

B. Be it done unto me according to Thy word.

A. Hail Mary . . .

B. Holy Mary . . .

A. And the Word was made Flesh.

B. And dwelt amongst us.

A. Hail Mary . . .

B. Holy Mary . . .

A. Pray for us, O holy Mother of God.

B. That we may be made worthy of the promises of Christ.

A. Let us pray. Pour forth, we beseech Thee, O Lord, Thy grace into our hearts, that we, to whom the Incarnation of Christ Thy Son was made known by the message of an Angel, may by His Passion and Cross be brought to the glory of His Resurrection. Through the same Christ Our Lord.

B. Amen.

Kyrie Eleison

The prayer of *Kyrie eleison* ("Lord, have mercy") is the only Greek prayer included in its original language in the prayer book of the Latin Catholic Church. This short, ancient prayer appears at the beginning of the Mass. Today it is sometimes said in the original language and sometimes in translation, using Gregorian melodies:

> *Kyrie eleison* / Lord have mercy
> *Christe, eleison* / Christ have mercy
> *Kyrie eleison* / Lord have mercy

The Liturgy of the Hours

Many religious traditions have made a point of instituting a link between certain prayers and specific times. By the fourth and fifth centuries a Christian system of prayers existed, correlating with the hours of the day. In the sixth century, this system was integrated in the *regula,* or system of rules for monks instituted by Benedict of Nursia,[111] but it has gone through several changes since then. This system of prayers has received multiple names, but the most common of these today is "The Liturgy of the Hours."

Prayer according to the "Liturgy of the Hours" is obligatory for all clergy from the moment of their ordination as deacons. In accordance with the rules of their group, parts or all of it may also be obligatory for lay and ordained members of Institutes of Consecrated Life: monks and nuns, friars and sisters. In fact, the prayer of these is, as mentioned above, the very origin of the "Liturgy of the Hours." The hierarchy also encourages laypeople to observe this liturgy, but for them it is optional. While the Liturgy of the Hours may be said by a group or an individual, in any case it is considered a communal prayer, the prayer of the Church. Thus, unlike the case of a spontaneous personal prayer, the person praying may not change it at will: He or she should use the "Breviary," the book containing these prayers. The importance of this liturgy in the life of the Church is great, practically and theologically speaking: through it the Church prays together ceaselessly to the Father, the Son, and the Holy Spirit.

In the system based on Benedict's *regula,* seven prayers are said during the day and three at night. In monasteries, this liturgical system forms the main axis around which community life revolves. The Second Vatican Council decided to reform this system of prayer, simplifying it and making it more convenient.[112] It must be noted, though, that the main object of the Council was the order of prayers intended for bishops and priests, whose central activity is not prayer, and not the prayer of monks and nuns. Following the decisions of the Council, a new "Liturgy of the Hours" was promulgated in 1971 under pope Paul VI, mainly intended for those who are not members of Institutes of Consecrated Life. The latter were allowed to keep their old customs if they so desired.

Since its revision, the system instructs ordained men to observe at least the morning and evening prayers. These two prayers are considered to be the basis for the entire system, and they should be particularly emphasized, even if the person recites other prayers as well. In addition, when possible, they should be said in public. The morning prayer symbolizes both the opening of the day, its dedication to God's service, and the resurrection of Christ. The evening prayer is one of gratitude for the day and is related to Jesus' last supper, his sacrifice, and the expectation of his return. The clergy should also include in their daily prayer the "Office of Readings," a prayer that had no exact parallel in the pre-reform system, in which writings that are not a part of Scriptures but that are written by highly regarded Church Fathers, authors, and saints of the past have a special place. In addition to these three prayers, two more were created: a day and a night prayer. The new system thus includes five daily prayers made up of hymns, Psalms, readings from Scriptures, and other traditional Church writings and petitions.

The Rosary

The rosary is a complex meditative prayer cycle observed by many Catholics, especially those who see themselves as somewhat "traditional." The Virgin Mary, mother of Jesus, is at its center. Many consider it "a glorious expression" of the Catholic faith. Pope Pius XII said it is a "summary of the entire Gospel,"[113] an expression reiterated by several of the more recent popes.

Often the rosary is said using a special string of prayer beads, also called a rosary. The prayer itself is fixed, but the ideas and themes upon which the worshipper reflects depend on the day of the week. Today, there are four themes for reflection.[114] Each one is divided into five "mysteries" related to the lives of Jesus and Mary:

> *Monday, Saturday*—the five "Joyous Mysteries": the announcement of Jesus' upcoming birth ("The Annunciation");[115] Mary's visit to her relative, Elizabeth, the mother of John;[116] the birth of Jesus;[117] the presentation of the infant Jesus in the Temple;[118] the finding of Jesus in the Temple after his parents lost him.[119]
>
> *Tuesday, Friday*—the five "Sorrowful Mysteries": Jesus' agony in the garden upon understanding that his death is near;[120] the lashes he receives;[121] the crown of thorns placed upon his head;[122] the carrying of the cross;[123] his crucifixion and death.
>
> *Wednesday, Sunday*—the five "Glorious Mysteries": the resurrection;[124] Jesus' ascent to Heaven ("The Ascension");[125] the descent of the Holy Spirit on his disciples;[126] the ascent of Mary to Heaven ("The Assumption");[127] and her coronation there as "Mother of God."[128]
>
> *Thursday*—the five "Luminous Mysteries": the baptism of Jesus by John in the Jordan River;[129] the wedding at Cana and the miracle performed there;[130] Jesus' declaration of the "Coming of the Kingdom";[131] his transfiguration and shining, glorious appearance to the disciples ("The Transfiguration");[132] the initiation of the Eucharist at Jesus' supper with his disciples.[133]

After the daily theme has been ascertained, the worshipper begins to say the rosary. He or she crosses him or herself and then says the Apostles' Creed, the Lord's Prayer, and three times "Hail Mary." After this, he or she would say the short prayer "Glory Be to the Father"[134] and announces the first mystery. After the announcement and a moment of silence, the Lord's Prayer is said, followed by ten "Hail Marys" while contemplating the mystery. The contemplation may be aided by the use of a painting, icon, written text, or nothing. Every cycle is ended with a "Glory Be to the Father" (and in some traditions, a short final prayer) after which the worshipper announces the second (third, fourth, or fifth) mystery of the day.

The rosary, an act of devotion to Mary, which was created in its current form by Dominican friars in the fifteenth century, was apparently intended to replace the reading of the 150 Psalms, a tradition attested among both Christians and Jews. Many miracles have been associated with it. According to Catholic belief, the Mother of God has aided and continues to aid those who turn to her using this prayer. One must remember, though, that not all Catholics assign the same significance to the rosary. Some are accustomed to saying it every day. Two of the most important popes of the twentieth century, Paul VI and John Paul II, had great affection for it. Conversely, many Catholics have never performed it and may even treat with scorn those who say it.

Other Prayers

In addition to the prayers and prayer cycles described above, a Catholic person may say other prayers related to particular acts or times of day, or to feelings and needs. Thus, some say a short prayer before they go to sleep, some say grace before or after meals, and some may light a candle in front of an icon and pray for themselves or those close to them. Some prayers are said one time only, and some are part of extended cycles, such as a *novena*, a cycle of nine units (nine consecutive days, nine Mondays in a row, etc.). A novena may be said as part of a process of mourning, of repentance, or in another context. For these prayers and others, a Catholic may improvise a text, recite one by heart, or read from a printed page. Some texts may pertain to a local or family tradition, and some have been composed by various famous figures throughout the recent and ancient history of the Church. Today, many of the personal prayers have no obligatory formulation, although certain versions may be customary in certain places.[135]

Sacramentals

The distinction between a sacrament and a sacramental is solely based on the ecclesiastical classification of the act: accepted religious acts that are not defined as sacraments are considered sacramentals. Obviously, this makes for a very large number of sacramentals. Some might say that the sacramentals are closer to what scholars of religion call "popular religion" if compared to the sacraments, as they are less regulated by the hierarchy and can be performed without the involvement of clergy. Although such categorization of the sacramentals has problems of its own, there is surely some truth in it.

Some of the sacramentals are personal and simple: making the sign of the cross, wearing particular medals, using holy water and holy oil, contemplating paintings and icons, lighting candles, and so on. Some are more complicated: pilgrimage, usage of prayer beads, and more. Some are carried out in public: wakes and funerals, the taking of monastic vows, consecration of objects and buildings, reenactment of Jesus' last hours, and many others. This chapter will discuss only a tiny fraction of the innumerable sacramentals of Catholic culture: rituals related to death, making the sign of the cross (or wearing one), and the lighting of candles. After these, mention will be made of a subject related to many sacramentals: saints in Catholic culture. Another chapter deals with the significance of the saints' role as part of the Church;[136] here we will discuss the acts performed by members of the terrestrial Church in order to show their regard for the members of its celestial counterpart and to beseech their aid.

Death-Related Rituals

Sacraments can be celebrated for living humans only. Even if the Church believes that the dead can benefit from a Mass celebrated in her or his memory, a funerary mass is intended for the living who take part in it. All other rituals that are related to death are thus in the category of sacramentals.

The historic evolution of the Catholic rituals of death is very complicated. Today, the Church generally marks the death of a person with three consecutive rituals, called together "The Rite of Christian Burial."

The first part of the Rite is the Vigil (or Wake, or Viewing). After the deceased's body is prepared according to local customs, the coffin will be presented, open or closed, in a church, home, or a funeral home. During that time, people pass near the coffin to pay respect, prayers are recited by a priest or another person who celebrates the ceremony, and appropriate readings from the Bible are be read. A short homily is also commonly given. For many, the Vigil is a time not only to say goodbye to the deceased but also to celebrate his or her life. This is why in some cultures the Wake can seem at times as a rather joyous event.

Following the Vigil the Funeral Liturgy, with a Mass at its core, will take place. It can be celebrated immediately after the Vigil or several days later. Other than in exceptional cases, it will be celebrated, like any Mass, in a church. Generally the coffin will be placed in the front of the church and it will be sprinkled with holy water, a reminder of the baptism the deceased had in the past. Christian symbols, such as a cross and a Bible, might be placed on the coffin. The readings from the scriptures during the mass will be adapted to the event. They will often deal with death, but generally with an optimistic view, discussing things such as resurrection, the just judgment of God, the grace of Christ, or the goodness reserved for the dead. With these readings, the Church emphasizes its belief in eternal life and the world to come. Despite the sadness, focus is on hope for the future and gratitude for the life of the deceased. It is common that in such a Mass the Catholic faithful take communion from both the bread and the wine. By the end of the celebration a hymn of farewell will be said or sang and a special prayer, the Prayer of Commendation, will be recited.

Generally immediately after the Mass, the procession (by foot or car) to the cemetery will begin. There, the last and third part of the ritual, "The Rite of Committal," will take place. Not all who took part in the previous two rituals will come to the cemetery. In fact, often only those close to the deceased will be present. This part is often short. After reciting some biblical verses and short prayers, and following some words of condolence to the relatives, the corpse will be buried and the ceremony will end.

In some countries today a cremation of the deceased is common, and the rituals described will be adapted accordingly, considering that there might be no coffin in the Mass and that the burial itself will be of an urn with ashes. If the cremation is not a sign of a rejection of the world to come, the local Church can allow it. Dispersal of the ashes without burial, however, is not considered legitimate.

A child that was not baptized and a person who wished to be baptized but did not have his or her wish fulfilled are also entitled to a Catholic funeral. In fact, even a non-Catholic person, if there is a good reason to believe he or she would not object to it and if this is the wish of the family, can have such a funeral with some changes.

Making and Wearing the Sign of the Cross

Making the sign of the cross while evoking the Father, the Son, and the Holy Spirit (the "Trinity"), an act reminding the worshipper both the Trinity and the crucifixion, is a well-defined element of the Catholic liturgy but may also be done outside of it. Often its performance is dependent on local culture and the particular person. There are Catholics who cross themselves when passing a church, before eating, when they succeed at some act, or when they feel in danger. Others will refrain from doing so almost entirely outside of a liturgical context.

The act of making the sign of the cross, an ancient Christian custom, can take various forms. First, one should differentiate between making the sign over others (in the air in the direction of a person or object, or touching him, her, or it directly), an act performed mostly by clergy in a liturgical context, and between making the cross over oneself ("crossing oneself"). This latter act will be analyzed here.

In the Western Churches one crosses oneself by touching the forehead with the right hand and saying "In the name of the Father," drawing the hand downwards vertically towards the chest, touching the area of the sternum, saying "and of the Son," then drawing the hand to the left shoulder, touching it and saying "and of the Holy . . . " and finally drawing the hand horizontally to the right shoulder, touching it and saying " . . . Spirit, Amen."

In many Eastern Churches, the horizontal movement is made from right to left and not from left to right. There is also another way to cross oneself, which is usually used during Masses. In order to symbolize the aspiration that God's word in the Gospel reaches the thought, speech, and heart of the believer, the faithful at Mass will make with the thumb the sign of the cross in "minuscule" fashion on their forehead, lips, and heart.

Many Christians, male and female, wear a pendant displaying the sign of the cross. Among Catholics, this cross often has the figure of Jesus on it: this is a "crucifix." Wearing such a pendant is also, in a certain sense, a sacramental. The meaning of the pendant may be very different for different people. For some, it may be a gift from a beloved person. Some may consider it a fashion accessory. Some see it as a cultural symbol. Others desire to declare their religious identity through it, and yet others may regard it as a protective talisman.

Lighting Candles

Although the personal lighting of candles has no definite and agreed religious meaning in Catholicism, it may be one of the ritual acts most visible to an observer who explores a Catholic church. It is a common and customary sacramental, which many Catholics may see as a significant element in a visit to church, especially when it does not include participation in Mass or another public prayer. Many Catholics also see it as a continuation of personal prayers for themselves, for others who are sick, or for some other purpose. When the worshipper has left the church, the candle's flame will carry on the memory of his or her prayer. The fee, which the visitor is usually asked to place in a special box near the candle, often includes a contribution to the local church.[137]

Veneration of Saints

The regard given to saints causes many, especially those outside the Catholic Church but occasionally also Catholics, some discomfort. Others see it as completely legitimate and even desirable. The following will very briefly detail various sacramentals related to the saints. I shall not use the phrase "worship of saints," heard occasionally from mostly non-Catholic speakers. Although not all Church members always observe the distinction, since antiquity theologians have distinguished between the Greek words *latria* or "worship," which is exclusively directed at God, and *doulia,* "service" or "veneration," which may be legitimately used to describe the regard, the respect, and the honor given to saints. Catholics are supposed to venerate, or honor, the saints: not to worship them.

In order to understand the matter, one must also keep in mind that for the Catholic Church the saints are not "dead" in the secular sense of the word. The saints, together with many others who have passed away, are "living" in "Heaven" close to God. Thus, expressions of appreciation for them, as for any deserving person, are not without significance. Even addressing them in a petition for help is understandable, much as a request for aid from a person close to high authorities is not an illogical act. Some would say that they pray "with" the saint: a way of thinking that would appease probably even the most judgmental theologian.

Many types of liturgical and non-liturgical activity include the mention of saints. For some of them—Mary, Joseph, Matthew, John, and others—this happens on a daily basis. Others, such as Augustine or Thomas Aquinas, are evoked on special occasions. Not rare, though, are those saints who may be addresses and remembered only on the day assigned to them, in the church carrying their name, by those named after them, or almost never at all.

Some Catholics petition occasionally to a particular saint, asking for his or her help. They may place his or her image in their home, car, or workplace. Such saints are "patron saints." At times, the link between a person and their patron saint will be a common first name: Thomas will turn to St. Thomas, Claire to St. Claire. Parents often name their children after the saint on whose day they were born.[138] A patron may also be chosen by reason of a particular event in his or her life or an element of his or her character that is connected to a particular place, subject, profession, illness, or the like. Thus, for example, Thomas Aquinas, a major medieval theologian, is considered the patron of academic institutions. Joseph, who hesitated for a moment but eventually chose the right path defending the honor of Mary, his betrothed, the mother of Jesus, is the patron of hesitating people. A carpenter himself, he is also the patron of those who take up this ancient profession. St. Francis, of the city of Assisi in Italy, is one of the patrons not only of Italy but also, due to various stories about him, of birds. St. Gertrude—for reasons not entirely clear—is the patron of those among us who happen to be cats. An angel may also function as a saint: St. Michael is the patron of the terminally ill. Some people may also believe that a particular angel, their "Guardian Angel," is protecting them.[139]

Sites of Pilgrimage

Pilgrimage to a place where a saint was active or to his or her burial place is a major aspect of the Catholic veneration of saints.[140] There are many sites of pilgrimage all over the world, but in different epochs certain places have drawn more pilgrims than others for various reasons. Among the most popular sites today are the basilica of Our Lady of Guadalupe in Mexico City, built to commemorate the appearance of Mary to a native of the area in the sixteenth century, whose Christian name (if he ever existed) was Juan Diego; a cave in the city of Lourdes in France, which is visited every year by millions, mostly people seeking a cure for themselves or those dear to them, and which is said to be where the Virgin has appeared in the nineteenth century to Bernadette, a young girl;[141] Santiago de Compóstela in north-western Spain, which is, according to medieval belief, the burial place of James, one of the apostles; and the basilica of St. Anthony, born in the thir-teenth century in Padua, Italy, a saint credited with many miracles, among them help in the finding of lost objects.

Relics

The relics of saints, real or forged, have accompanied the Church from its earliest days. In a certain sense they are regarded in the same way as people regard the objects left behind by a beloved or admired person, such as pictures of loved ones carried in a wallet or hung up in an office, auto-graphs of celebrities, or objects belonging to relatives who have died. All these have the function of recalling the beloved or admired person and helping to feel their spiritual presence despite their physical absence. The regard given to relics by Catholics is no different, with one possible excep-tion. Some Catholics may see these relics as objects that, with the proper faith and prayer, can bring about miracles. Many theologians object to such beliefs, though the New Testament contains sources that attest that such beliefs already existed in the Church's earliest days.[142] These same theologians will emphasize that when miracles, which seem related to the relics, do occur—and various events may indeed be defined by the Church as miracles, if rarely—it is God, and only God, who has performed them after being asked to do so by the saint, to whom the believer addressed himself or herself. They may add that the relic demonstrates and expresses the connection between the terrestrial Church, with its living members, and the celestial Church, whose members have died—and that therein lies the relic's importance. Some Catholics will see relics in such a way. Others might have different opinions.

Needless to say, like any object of desire, the distribution and commerce of relics involved not only sincere spiritual beliefs but also often pure financial greed. In a fictional description of the treasury of an imagined fourteenth-century Benedictine monastery in Northern Italy, Umberto Eco includes the following objects:

> There was, in a case of aquamarine, a nail of the cross. In an ampoule, lying on a cushion of little withered roses, there was a portion of the crown of thorns; and in another box, again on a blanket of dried flowers, a yellowed shred of the tablecloth from the last supper. And then there was the purse of saint Matthew, of silver links; and in a cylinder, bound by a violet ribbon eaten by time and sealed with gold, a bone from Saint Anne's arm. I saw, wonder of wonders, under a glass bell, on a red cushion embroidered with pearls, a piece of the manger of Bethlehem, and a hand's length of the purple tunic of Saint John the Evangelist, two links of the chains that bound the ankles of the apostle Peter in Rome, the skull of Saint Adalbert, the sword of Saint Stephen, a tibia of Saint Margaret, a finger of Saint Vitalis, a rib of Saint Sophia, the chin of Saint Eobanus, the upper part of Saint Chrysostom's shoulder blade, the engagement ring of Saint Joseph, a tooth of the Baptist, Moses's rod, a tattered scrap of very fine lace from the Virgin Mary's wedding dress.[143]

This list superbly presents the varied types of relic that a wealthy church or monastery actually could have had. In fact, the relics of saints recognized by the Catholic Church are traditionally divided into three types. A relic of the first degree is a remnant of the body of a saint or of objects related to the life and death of Jesus. These relics are the most sought after, a fact well known to those individuals, pious or otherwise, who have busied themselves throughout history in supplying this demand. Among these, those linked to Jesus himself and his mother Mary are undoubtedly the most important.[144] A second-degree relic is a remnant of an object belonging to a saint or one relating to his or her death. The importance of these depends on their nature and the saint with which they were in contact. Eco's list includes relics of both types. A relic of the third degree is one which has come into contact with a first- or second-degree relic, for example a piece of cloth which has been laid on a saint's tomb. These are mainly used by individuals who desire a memento of the relic itself. In the Middle Ages, as today, some Catholics would treat such objects with awe and respect and others would sneer at them, or at least at some of them, either openly or privately.

Sacraments and Sacramentals in Everyday Life

The very use of a sacramental, and moreover the frequency of such use, are very dependent on local culture as well as personal preferences. A village church in South America will typically contain more statues of saints than an urban church in North America, and more parishioners will typically spend time praying in front of these. On the other hand, both these churches may very well count among their parishioners one who is continuously engaged with sacramentals (wearing devotional objects such as scapulars, crossing him or herself several times a day, hanging up pictures of saints at home, lighting candles), and another who refrains from all these practices and even disdains them.

The sacramentals, acts of worship that often carry a personal note, are for many the heart of Catholic culture. Many theologians who may accept and even support the existence of sacramentals insist repeatedly that they are legitimate only if connected practically and spiritually to the seven sacraments.

Notes

1. See for example in his *Quaestiones in Pentateuch*, Book 3, question 84. For a fascinating and thought provoking modern discussion of what sacraments are, see Leonardo Boff, *Sacraments of Life, Life of the Sacraments*, trans. John Drury (Portland: Pastoral Press, 1987).
2. Such "rituals" exist in all cultures. Some might have a religious connotation, some not. The classic study of such rituals remains the 1909 book bearing this name by the ethnographer Arnold Van Gennep: Arnold van Gennep, *The Rites of Passage*, trans. Gabrielle L. Caffee and Monika B. Vizedom (London: Routledge, 2010).
3. Only a tiny fraction of groups that consider themselves to be Christian do not perform the ritual of baptism. The most well-known are the Society of Friends (Quakers) and the Salvation Army.
4. See for example, Matthew 3, and parallels.
5. See for example, Mark 1:9, and parallels.
6. Matthew 28:19.
7. Exodus 14.
8. Joshua 3.
9. Genesis 3.
10. See Acts 2:38; Acts 8:16.
11. Commonly, texts such as Matthew 10:32 & 39 are used as a proof for the idea of "Baptism of Blood," while Luke 23:42–43 and John 14:21 are used as proofs for the existence of "Baptism of Desire." "Baptism of Desire" can be understood in a limited, conservative, way or in a very open and liberal one, making many "People of good will" who are looking for God as theoretically falling in this category.
12. *The Apostolic Tradition*, chapter 21. Until recent decades, this book was attributed to Hippolytus, an important Christian theologian who lived in Rome in the third century. Today, this attribution is questioned by some.
13. The Church today does not condone this belief. For hundreds of years, up until the Second Vatican Council and the subsequent changes, it was widely believed in the Church

that infants who died before being baptized were not destined for salvation. They do not enter Paradise, but instead are destined to remain in "Limbo," an interim state or in-between place. While Church law encourages emergency baptism of babies whose lives are in danger, the Church today states its belief that God redeems children who have died before they have been able to be baptized (see for example the *Catechism of the Catholic Church*, par. 1261). The doing away of the idea of limbo from Church teaching certainly helps Catholic parents to cope with what might be a double tragedy: the loss of an unbaptized child.

14. On the early history of baptism, see the massive work of Everett Ferguson, *Baptism in the Early Church: History, Theology, and Liturgy in the First Five Centuries* (Grand Rapids: William B. Eerdmans, 2009).

15. The revival is connected to the activities of the "Liturgical Movement," a mix of experts in liturgy, historians, members of the hierarchy and orders, and laypersons who demanded changes in the liturgy beginning in the late nineteenth century. One of their first major successes was the renewed introduction of the Easter Vigil ceremony in various countries. On this, see p. 120.

16. Mark 7:31–37, especially verse 34.

17. On this prayer see pp. 141–142.

18. See Augustine, Treatise on the Gospel of John VI, 1, 7. See also in the *Catechism of the Catholic Church*, par. 1127.

19. Council of Trent, Seventh Session, Canons on Baptism, par. 4.

20. On Ecumenism, see also pp. 221–224.

21. In the East, this sacrament is known as "Holy Anointment" or "Chrismation." It should not be confused with the sacrament known as "Anointing of the Sick."

22. See for example John 14:16–17; Acts 1:7–8.

23. Acts 8:14–17. See also Acts 19:1–6; 2 Corinthians 1:21–22; Hebrews 6:1–2.

24. It is important to keep in mind that this event took place, according to the story, after the Holy Spirit descended upon the apostles themselves while they were gathered in Jerusalem during the festival of *Shavuot* ("Feast of Weeks," Pentecost), seven weeks after Jesus' death and presumed resurrection; see Acts 2:1–4.

25. The same happens also today in Eastern Churches, Catholic as well as Orthodox.

26. For a thorough exploration of the evolution of the ritual (as well as of the Eucharist and Baptism, the two other Christian "Rites of Initiation"), see Maxwell E. Johnson, *The Rites of Christian Initiation: Their Evolution and Interpretation* (Collegeville: Liturgical Press, 2007).

27. See more on this term later in our discussion of the Eucharist, pp. 114–115.

28. Note that unlike the case in a celebration of ordination, they do not place their hands directly on the heads of those receiving the sacrament.

29. A well-publicized example of this sort of conversion in recent years is that of the former British Prime Minister Tony Blair, who in 2007 converted from the Anglican Church to the Catholic Church, to which his wife and children belong. Blair continually pointed out that this was a natural move both personally and in terms of his family, and not one that stemmed from complex doctrinal or ideological reasons. On the possibility that entire communities belonging to the Anglican Church and its offshoots move to the Catholic Church for ideological and theological reasons over the next few years, see pp. 227–228, n. 56.

30. I will later discuss briefly the origin of this name for the ritual. The term "Mass," when used to describe a particular type of musical composition, may be misleading. These musical works, performed generally in concert halls, were in some instances written for use in the celebration of Mass, and in others were inspired by but never intended to be performed as part of an actual ritual. The musical composition is not the Mass itself.

Today such complex musical compositions are rarely performed in the context of a liturgical celebration of the Eucharist.

31. Matthew 26:26–29; Mark 14:22–25; Luke 22:14–20; 1 Corinthians 11:23–26.

32. This is the expression in Luke (in the Greek, *to haimati mou*) and in the Epistle to the Corinthians. It is important to clarify that when we say here that "all versions" mention Jesus' words, we refer to the accepted printed text of Luke. Important early manuscripts point to a wide range of longer and shorter versions of this account. In some versions, the crucial verses 19b and 20 do not appear. Most of the members of Bruce Metzger's committee, a committee of scholars who oversaw the preparation of a scientific critical edition of the New Testament, were of the opinion that the longer version, similar to the printed one, is the more ancient one. See the detailed discussion in Bruce M. Metzger, *A Textual Commentary on the Greek New Testament, Second Edition* (Stuttgart: United Bible Societies, 1994): 148–150.

33. John 6:22–59.

34. *Didache*, chapter 9.

35. Today, this evening is known in the Jewish calendar as the "Seder." Due to the fact that the Jewish Temple of Jerusalem, the place where the sacrifices were offered, was destroyed almost two thousand years ago in the year 70 CE, this meal does not include a sacrificial meat.

36. See for example Matthew 26:26–28.

37. Quite a number of Protestant Churches, particularly in the United States, prefer grape juice in their celebrations or even use it exclusively. Many of them explain this simply by referring to the possibly negative side effects of wine without making additional historical claims. A few of them go further by claiming that Jesus himself used only grape juice (a claim which is questionable for exegetical, historical, and technological reasons). The Catholic Church acknowledges the possibility that some of its members may not be able to or should not consume even small quantities of wine for various reasons. In such cases, *Mustum* (or Must) grape juice, in which fermentation has begun, may be used. Catholics who cannot consume gluten are allowed to partake of low-gluten hosts or to receive communion through wine only. Because the host must be made of wheat, gluten-free hosts are not liturgically valid.

38. The terms "Eucharist," "host," "consecrated bread," and sometimes even "bread" (over which the Eucharist prayer has already been said) are usually equivalent and interchangeable in the following pages.

39. See John 6:34–35 and 1 Corinthians 10:4.

40. On this, see for example Eugene LaVerdiere, *The Eucharist in the New Testament and the Early Church* (Collegeville: Liturgical Press, 1996).

41. Like our discussion with regard to the resurrection (p. 44) and its meaning as defined in an ancient Jewish and Hellenistic context, so is the definition of this belief connected to the philosophical context of the time in which it was articulated in the Middle Ages, and to the fact that the opinion of one side in the debate won, even though there were other opinions as well. And again, as with the resurrection, even if theologians and members of the Catholic hierarchy are careful not to trample this traditionally accepted definition and try to improve the public's understanding of it, its central meaning is identical to that of the resurrection: Christ is present in the life of his Church and leads it.

42. Malachi 1:10–11.

43. The extremely influential book *The Imitation of Christ* by the fourteenth-to-fifteenth-century author Thomas à Kempis provides, in the author's discussion of the Eucharist (chapter 4), a striking example of this approach. See Thomas à Kempis, *The Imitation of Christ* (New York: Dover Publications, 2003): 115–139.

44. For a thorough exploration of the history of the Eucharist and the ways it has been understood, see Edward Foley, *From Age to Age: How Christians Have Celebrated the Eucharist,* revised and expanded edition (Collegeville: Liturgical Press, 2009). Another major work, more than a thousand pages in length, was initially published in 1909, and while certainly dated, it was recently reprinted and can still be of great use: Darwell Stone, *A History of the Doctrine of the Holy Eucharist* (1909; reprint, Eugene: Wipf and Stock Publishers, 2007).

45. This "un-relatedness" is not entirely true. In a deep way, the "New Order of the Mass" described below is more suitable to the understanding of the Mass as a communal event, while the "Tridentine Mass," especially when celebrated in Latin to a non-Latin-speaking congregation, reflects better the Mass as a sacrificial act, with less concerns about the congregation's active participation in it.

46. Even though his actual input was limited, because pope Pius X (1835–1914) was the last pope to be involved in the adaptation of this version of the Mass, particularly in the comments and instructions that accompanied it before it was rejected, this version is sometimes referred to, mainly by its supporters, as the "Mass of Pius X."

47. Moto proprio Summorum Pontificum.

48. A discussion of the two types of liturgical cycles can be found in the chapter devoted to the Catholic calendar: see p. 171 and p. 180, n. 10.

49. In countries such as the US, in which the Church does not get public funds, the money collected during the Mass is likely to be one of the main financial sources of the local church.

50. The "Sanctus" is an ancient Christian hymn based on a verse from the book of Isaiah: "Holy, holy, holy is the Lord of hosts . . . all the earth is filled with his glory" (Isaiah 6:3). The Christian exegetical tradition interprets the thrice-repeated word "holy" to be a hidden reference to the Trinity.

51. As is the case in other places in this book, the text used here is the one promulgated by the United States Conference of Catholic Bishops, used in the US since November 2011.

52. This part, the "Sanctus," is said together by the priest and congregation.

53. The version used for this prayer is based on descriptions of the last supper as they appear in Matthew 26:26–29; Mark 14:22–25; Luke 22:14–20; 1 Corinthians 11:23–26.

54. See more on this concept on p. 111 and p. 156, n. 41.

55. See on this prayer on pp. 141–142.

56. A first-time visitor to a Catholic Mass may be surprised at this moment, when those present come into contact—if only for a moment. There is no need to abstain from shaking a hand proffered to the guest. Even if one is not Christian, the word "peace" in the local language is considered an appropriate and polite response.

57. See Luke 24:13–35, and especially 30–31.

58. For practical reasons, it may be appropriate to reiterate this matter for non-Catholics who wish to visit churches after reading the above: the vast majority of members of the Catholic Church are happy to have non-Catholic guests in their churches, so long, of course, as they show respect for the Church and its members. Throughout the Mass, the visitor should sit down when the congregation sits and stand up when it stands. There is no obligation to say prayers or sing hymns; neither is it forbidden. The visitor is barred only from participation in Holy Communion, and should remain quietly seated while the Eucharist is dispensed. Catholics may also abstain from taking the Eucharist for various reasons, as will non-Catholic Christians present at a Catholic rite. Therefore, remaining seated will not necessarily expose the visitor's identity, as the visitor is very likely to not be the only one abstaining from receiving communion.

59. Of course, there are places where priests or Eucharist ministers might not understand this sign, especially places where the presence of non-Catholics is relatively rare.

60. This is a public form of the sacrament of reconciliation, to be discussed later on.

61. This is a clear example of change from below, pushed by liturgists and not by the bishops. The Council reluctantly allowed the limited use of local languages: "The use of the Latin language is to be preserved in the Latin rites. But since the use of the mother tongue . . . frequently may be of great advantage to the people, the limits of its employment may be extended. This will apply in the first place to the readings and directives, and to some of the prayers and chants" (*Sacrosanctum Concilium,* par. 36). And yet in some places, for example in the United States, a complete abandonment of Latin happened almost overnight, even before the Council completed its deliberations. The limitations placed on a celebration in the vernacular were ignored, and wishes for change that existed in some quarters well before the council were swiftly implemented. Today, celebrations in Latin are extremely rare. They might be found occasionally in places where the congregation is of varied origins and lacks a common modern language, when done for aesthetic reasons, or in very conservative (and numerically marginal) groups who use the Tridentine version. The next change mentioned above, regarding the direction in which the priest faces during the Mass, is not a result of explicit directions by the Council either.

62. *Quam Singulari,* August 8, 1910.

63. For more on this see pp. 189–193.

64. At times this happens even if the priest in charge celebrates three Masses every Sunday, the maximum allowed by Canon Law (on other days, two is the maximum).

65. There were also cases in which Catholics did not have the opportunity to be in a Mass for years, but this was considered an undesired and unfortunate situation. See, for example, regarding early Americans in James M. O'Toole, *The Faithful: A History of Catholics in America* (Cambridge: Harvard University Press, 2008), 11–49.

66. James 5:16.

67. See for example Matthew 9:1–7, and parallels.

68. John 20:21–23.

69. Code of Canon Law, c. 989.

70. On the definition of sin in general, and mortal sins in particular, see pp. 27–28.

71. Luke 15:11–32.

72. See pp. 27–28.

73. Or "I forgive you your sins."

74. Two wonderful examples are found in Alfred Hitchcock's *I Confess* (1953), and Antonia Bird's *Priest* (1994).

75. The situation might not be much different from that faced by a doctor or psychologist, who knows that a patient harmed others, but that revealing this might have negative impact on the treatment, even though in such cases the law is generally very clear. In many countries, legal clauses traditionally protect priests' right to keep secret such information, although in recent years, particularly following cases of sexual abuses, such clauses were challenged in various places, for example in Ireland. Those defending the confession secrecy say, among other things, that priests encourage those who committed crimes to turn to the police, and if offenders become afraid that the content of their confession might be revealed, they will simply not come to speak with priests anymore, thus possibly closing the only chance they might speak with anyone. Obviously, others disagree with these arguments.

76. On the issue of gay rights and same-sex marriages, see pp. 204–208.

77. John 2:1–12.

78. Matthew 19:10–12.

79. In 2012, a possible discovery of an ancient manuscript in which a "wife of Jesus" was mentioned made news headlines all over the world. Since then, serious arguments

claiming it is a forgery were raised. Regardless, one should remember two important facts. On the one hand, even if this text is ancient, it reveals only that some authors in the first centuries claimed Jesus was married: it does not provide information about the historical Jesus. On the other hand, many scholars would say that regardless of texts, it is almost certain that among Jesus and his male disciples most were married. Any other situation would be unusual for first century CE Jewish men.

80. 1 Corinthians 7:1–16 and 25–40. The verses cited are 8–9.

81. See *Pastoral Constitution on the Church in the Modern World* (*Gaudium et spes*), par. 47–52.

82. "Intima communitas vitae et amoris coniugalis" (Gaudium et spes, par. 48).

83. Of course, many other Christian Churches also hold marriage ceremonies, but they are not necessarily considered rites instituted by Christ ("Dominical Institutions"). Whether this theological distinction is of significance to their members is another question.

84. On this, see also pp. 208–213.

85. Catholic marriage is a sacrament that the spouses give to one another. The "celebrant" has thus only a limited role from a legal and theological perspective. For this reason, the "celebrant" does not have to be a priest. A deacon, or even a layperson (male or female), if appointed to the role, can perform the act. Although such occurrences are still rare in many places, they are not unheard of and are likely to become more and more common, for reasons of both choice and necessity.

86. Another famous version ends in the words "till death do us part." This form is valid and in use, but many prefer the variant quoted above, as it refrains from mentioning death at the very moment of marriage.

87. One must remember that the exchange of rings, although perhaps deep in symbolism, is not what "makes" the marriage: the two crucial parts of the sacrament are the marriage vows and the later consummation. Therefore, if an exchange of rings or even the existence of wedding rings altogether is not part of the local culture, this section of the ceremony can be dropped.

88. Probably not everyone will be convinced by this common legal and practical explanation. Some may argue that this distinction hints at reservations the Church has after all about such a match. In some places, priests may allow the non-Catholic spouse to exceptionally take communion.

89. For more information on the ordained members of the Church, see pp. 60–86.

90. For the essentials of this office, see pp. 84–86.

91. References for events or narratives mentioned above: Genesis 48; Numbers 27:15–23; Acts 6:1–6; Hebrews 6:2.

92. Another exceptional case, which is interesting and important for reasons of principle, is that of a married man who was a priest or a pastor in another Christian Church and later joined the Catholic Church. In many cases in recent years, the hierarchy has authorized the ordination of such people as priests in the Catholic Church despite their married status. Since many of them live in Western Europe and North America, where the Catholic public is unused to having married priests, this is not insignificant. In the coming years, more married priests of this type are likely to join the Catholic Church. See more on this on pp. 227–228, n. 56.

93. Such a candidate will be limited in one respect: he cannot be ordained as a bishop. If his wife dies, he cannot in principle marry again, since marriage can only take place before ordination, not after. In practice, especially if he has small children, such a priest may nevertheless be allowed to marry again.

94. The celibacy of the clergy began to develop in the fourth century under the influence of the monastic movement, but only became obligatory beginning in the twelfth century. See a good summary in Charles A. Frazee, "The Origins of Clerical Celibacy in the Western Church," *Church History* 57 (Supplement: Centennial Issue, 1988): 108–26 (Article

originally published in *Church History* 41, no. 2 (1972)). Nevertheless, this is a commitment and not a vow like that of members of religious Institutes of Consecrated Life. It is a disciplinary matter, not a doctrinal one. Even if the difference has little practical meaning, it demonstrates that in the West as well, the obligation to celibacy is not an immutable principle of priestly life, and that its annulment, if it occurs, will not be revolutionary in doctrinal terms. If fact, it can happen with a few short pen strokes of a daring pope.

95. Although after this ritual the priest and bishop wipe the oil off their hands in order to continue the ceremony, at the end of the ordination people may approach the priest, wishing to touch or kiss the hands of the man who was just blessed with this anointment and with the descent of the Spirit which is associated with it.

96. Preceding the Second Vatican Council and for hundreds of years, ordination was one of the only events in the Western Church in which a number of ordained men, in this case a priest (or priests) and a bishop, celebrated Mass together. Today this practice of "con-celebration" is common and done regularly.

97. Although Canon Law requires one bishop only, a single bishop will ordain another bishop only in exceptional circumstances. In the Eastern Churches, none of the bishops is designated as the "main consecrator."

98. See our earlier discussion of this matter, p. 65.

99. James 5:14–15. See also Mark 6:13.

100. On this prayer, see pp. 141–142.

101. Matthew 6:6–8.

102. On major changes with regard to American Catholics' attitudes towards prayers in recent decades, see James P. McCartin, *Prayers of the Faithful: The Shifting Spiritual Life of American Catholics* (Cambridge: Harvard University Press, 2010).

103. Matthew 6:9–13; Luke 11:1–4.

104. Another common translation: "and lead us not into temptation."

105. One of the things that tend to surprise many non-Catholic Christians who visit a Catholic service for the first time is the relatively large number of texts Catholics know by heart.

106. 1797–1828.

107. 1818–1893.

108. Some of these and other renderings do not include the original text but rather adaptations thereof.

109. Luke 1:28, 42.

110. A famous painting by the nineteenth-century French painter Jean-François Millet shows a man and a woman standing in a field praying. In the background, a church belfry is visible. Despite having previously chosen another title for the painting, upon its presentation to the public Millet decided to name it *Angelus,* thus charging it with unmistakable meaning for anyone acquainted with Catholic culture. The painting hangs today in the Musée d'Orsay in Paris.

111. Circa 480–543. We mentioned previously Benedict and his "Rule." See p. 56.

112. *Sacrosanctum Concilium*, par. 83–101.

113. *Acta Apostolicae Sedis* 38 (1946), p. 419.

114. The last, one "The Luminous Mysteries," was instituted by pope John Paul II in 2002.

115. Matthew 1:18–21; Luke 1:26–38. These citations and the following may aid the reader in understanding the theme, though a person saying the rosary may also use descriptions of the events which are not taken directly from the New Testament, such as mystical writings, paintings, and the like. These references intentionally contain long passages. In practice, the practitioner will usually focus on one or two verses from each passage.

116. Luke 1:39–56.

117. Matthew 2:1–12; Luke 2:1–21.

118. Luke 2:22–40.
119. Luke 2:41–52.
120. Matthew 26:36–39; Mark 14:26–32; Luke 22:39–42.
121. Matthew 27:26; Mark 15:15; John 19:1.
122. Matthew 27:27–31; Mark 15:16–20; John 19:2–16.
123. Matthew 27:31–34; Mark 15:20–23; Luke 23:26–32; John 19:16–17.
124. Matthew 27:32–61; Mark 15:21–47; Luke 23:33–53; John 19:16–42.
125. Matthew 28:1–20; Mark 16:1–20; Luke 24:1–53; John 20:1–18.
126. Mark 15:19; Luke 24:50–52; Acts 1:1–11.
127. John 20:21–22; Acts 2:1–4.
128. The last two events are not mentioned in the New Testament. To mark the first of them, some may contemplate Song of Songs 2:4 or Psalms 45:14–18. For the second, some may use Genesis 3:15, Judith (a book not included in the Jewish and Protestant Bibles) 15:10–13, or Revelations 12:1.
129. Matthew 3:13–17; Mark 1:9–11; Luke 3:21–22; John 1:19–35 (in a certain sense).
130. John 2:1–11.
131. Matthew 4:17; Mark 1:14–15; Luke 4:16–21.
132. Matthew 17:1–5; Mark 9:2–7; Luke 9:28–32.
133. Matthew 26:26–29; Mark 14:22–25; Luke 22:14–20; 1 Corinthians 11:23–26.
134. "Glory be to the Father, and to the Son, and to the Holy Spirit: as it was in the beginning, is now, and ever shall be. World without end. Amen."
135. For a good collection of Catholic prayers, see Michael Buckley and Tony Castle, eds., *The Catholic Prayer Book* (Ann Arbor: Servant Books, 1986).
136. See pp. 87–90.
137. Since these are not sacramentals in the precise sense of the word, I have not discussed the candles that are sometimes incorporated in public rituals, such as processions, baptism, and certain Masses. A candle (or even a small light bulb) shining over the "Tabernacle" (a kind of chest, usually ornamented) in the front of the church signifies that a consecrated host lies within. Many Catholics will kneel when passing the altar only if this light is on, signifying by this that their gesture honors Christ, not the church's furnishings.
138. Regarding the place of saints in the liturgical calendar, see pp. 179–180.
139. The other side of the belief in angels is the belief in demons: angles who "fell" by disobeying God. The belief in the existence of demons is part and parcel of the Catholic faith, although not all Catholics relate to it in the same way. Those who do might also believe that, at times, a sacramental of exorcism might be appropriate.
140. It should be noted that many sites of pilgrimage are associated mainly with events that occurred in them, especially apparitions of the Virgin, and not with the activity of a particular person (though, of course, the Virgin has often appeared to people who were subsequently recognized as saints).
141. On this topic in contemporary Catholic culture, see Robert A. Scott, *Miracle Cures: Saints, Pilgrimage, and the Healing Power of Belief* (Berkeley: University of California Press, 2010).
142. See for example Acts 19:12.
143. Umberto Eco, *The Name of the Rose,* trans. William Weaver (Orlando: Harcourt, 1994): 423.
144. It is important to remember that, leaving aside various oddities which appeared in different periods of the Middle Ages (such as "Jesus' foreskin" or one of his milk teeth), relics of Jesus' body cannot exist, since, according to the faith, he was resurrected and rose to Heaven. The same applies to Mary, who according to Catholic belief was also elevated in her body.

CHAPTER **5**

The Catholic Calendar

It is hard to overstate the importance of the calendar for the understanding of any culture. Through their calendars, groups commemorate historic or mythic events of significance and safeguard their memory. Through the calendar, members of the group, wherever they may be, may mark these days as a community. The calendar provides the group with memory and unity, two elements without which its very existence might be cast in doubt.

The Catholic Calendar

All this is also true of the Catholic calendar. It provides Catholics with yearly opportunities to mark crucial events in the history of their faith and to do so in synchrony. In compliance with the immense cultural variation within the Catholic Church, the calendar enables different sub-groups to add to the calendar days and events of particular significance for them while maintaining the "universal" dates. This chapter will deal mostly with the latter.

The current universal calendar of the Catholic Church was promulgated by pope Paul VI in 1969 and came into effect the following year. It is influenced by the decisions of the Second Vatican Council, which adjourned a few years earlier. This calendar, like its predecessor, consists of events and holy days which take place on fixed dates, as well as of moveable feasts and events whose date may change from year to year based on astronomical considerations or on the requirement that they take place on Sunday. Most components of this calendar are also present in the calendars of many other Christian groups: the description given here may also be useful, at least in part, in understanding the practices of these other denominations.

The Ancient Roman Calendar

The Catholic calendar is based on a modified version of the ancient Roman calendar, created by Julius Caesar in the year today known as 45 BCE, and which is called the "Julian calendar" in honor of its originator. The first month of the Julian calendar was January.

In the more than two thousand years since the creation of the calendar, it has undergone several reforms. The last of these was carried out more than four centuries ago on the order of pope Gregory XIII. The calendar used throughout most of the world ever since is thus known as the "Gregorian calendar."

Up to about ten or eleven hundred years ago, years were sometimes reckoned in Europe in relation to the traditional year of the foundation of Rome, sometimes in relation to the reign of the third-century Roman Emperor Diocletian, and more often in relation to the coronation of the reigning king or emperor. Then during the eighth and ninth centuries, partially through the reforms of Charlemagne, Europe began to take up a calculation made several centuries earlier by Dionysius Exiguus, or "Dennis the Small," a monk who was living in Rome. Dionysius calculated the date of birth of Jesus, and came to the conclusion that it happened 525 years before his day. He gave that year the number 1.

Even if Dionysius' calculation was imprecise, since according to scholars (including Catholic scholars) Jesus was most probably born a few years earlier, this is of no great practical or religious consequence: the calculation was accepted and institutionalized and has been current in the use of European and European-influenced societies ever since.

Catholics (both Eastern and Western), as well as members of the other Western Churches and some Eastern Churches, use the Gregorian calendar. Most of the non-Catholic Eastern Churches use the Julian calendar, since, naturally, they do not recognize the authority of a sixteenth-century Roman pope to change the calendar.

Sunday

In spite of the aforesaid, the most basic holy day for most groups calling themselves Christian is related to neither calendar nor astronomy, but to a tradition regarding the human-made (or, according to the Bible, divinely made) weekly cycle: this is the day of the week during which, according to the faith, Jesus rose from the dead.

The special regard Christians hold for the day that follows the Jewish Sabbath is attested to since the beginning of the second century CE. The first Christians would congregate on Sundays for a fraternal feast (*agape,* a Greek term describing love or affection), in which they prayed and sang hymns to their Lord. Various modern languages of Latin origin retain this meaning in the name of the day itself. The terms *dimanche* (French) and *domingo* (Spanish) are cognate to the Latin *Dies Dominicus,* "day of the Lord." In other languages of Germanic or Nordic provenance, the day's name retains the Roman pre-Christian meanings of the day of the sun (*dies solis*), which became in English "Sunday" and in German "Sonntag."

Sunday is the day on which the main Mass of the week is celebrated, and Catholics are supposed to attend it. Before the changes related to the Second Vatican Council, the idea that missing a Sunday mass is a mortal sin that can condemn one, if not absolved, to damnation, was a given in Catholic culture. Today, the situation is not as clear. The *Code of Canon Law* (*CCL*) speaks in strong terms about the obligation of Catholics to attend this Mass, and the *Catechism of the Catholic Church* (*CCC*) says missing it if not for serious reasons is "a grave sin."[1] And yet, many Catholics today do not consider it to be a cardinal sin requiring confession.

In many churches, the main Sunday Mass is celebrated in the late morning. Additional Masses may be celebrated earlier or later the same day. Since the liturgical day begins in the evening (in accordance with Jewish and Roman tradition, as well as that of medieval Europe), a Mass said on Saturday evening is also considered to be a Sunday Mass. Unlike the Sabbath for practicing Jews, there is no religious prohibition of work on Sunday for Catholics (so long as part of it is given over to worship). Nevertheless, today Sunday is considered a day of rest in countries of Christian culture.

Annual Observances

Around the middle of the second century, Christians began to celebrate Jesus' resurrection on an annual basis. Generally, the date for this celebration was based on the date of the Jewish Passover. Various Romance languages have retained a term cognate with the Hebrew name of this festival, *Pessach: Pâques* in French and *Pascua* in Spanish are examples. Other languages, like English and German, use a different word, which preserves the name of a pre-Christian spring festival (*Easter* in English and *Ostern* in German).

The two special days discussed above—weekly and yearly commemorations of the Resurrection—take their content from the most basic statement of Christian faith: "the Lord has risen."[2] Only later, after many saints' days had already been integrated into their calendars, did Christians in various places begin to celebrate holy days related to the first appearance of Jesus during the winter. Some marked the "Incarnation" of the Son of God, while others celebrated his birth.

The following discussion of the Catholic holy days will follow the order of the liturgical calendar, not the order of their historic appearance or importance. This calendar opens with the Christmas season.

The Christmas Season

There is no reason to believe that Jesus was born on December 25th of all days. Neither is this an article of Christian faith, though various Christian authors of different periods have tried to prove that the date is historically precise. It was chosen for various reasons and became standard in the fourth century. The conventional view that the Church adopted a Roman festival, "the Birthday of the Invincible Sun," or *Dies Natalis Solis Invicti,* or at least tried to replace it with a Christian celebration, is probably only partially correct. This festival's existence may have contributed to the dating of Christmas, but Jesus' birth was also celebrated around midwinter in places where the date apparently had no special pre-Christian meaning. When the reckoning of years was gradually tied to Jesus' birth year, it apparently added impetus to the date of his reputed birth, December 25th. The Orthodox Churches also celebrate Christmas on December 25th but according to their own Julian calendar, which translates to January 7th in the Gregorian calendar.

The name of this holy day in various languages, such as the French *Nöel* or the Spanish *Navidad,* hints at its nature through an etymology connoting birth. Its English name has to do with the manner of celebration and not the reason for it: "Christmas" derives from the Old English "Christ's Mass" (*Christes Maesse*).

Celebration of the period before Christmas began in the early Middles Ages but made its way into the calendar of the Church of Rome only in the tenth century. Thus, the one-day holy day became the centerpiece of a complex liturgical season. Today, this season is composed of two parts:

1. *Advent,* a period that opens the liturgical year. It begins on the fourth Sunday before Christmas (in other words, the Sunday closest to November 30th is the "Liturgical New Year's Day"), and ends on December 24th;

2. *Christmas Time,* which begins on Christmas Day and ends in principle on January 5th, the eve of Epiphany which is celebrated on January 6th, but in practice on the following Sunday. This second period, between Christmas Day and Epiphany, is sometimes known as "the twelve days of Christmas."

The original reason for beginning the liturgical year with the Christmas season and not with the Paschal cycle (due to which decision liturgical books traditionally begin with the Christmas season) is related to the fact that the Roman calendar begins in January. Regardless of this initial reason, the commemoration of Jesus' birth before his death makes, after all, some sense.

Liturgical Colors

In the Catholic Church (and in many others Christian Churches), certain colors are associated with particular events and dates. Like all other parts of the liturgical year, the Christmas season has its own dominating colors used in ceremonies and decorations. Traditionally, the color of Advent has been violet, a "royal" color considered appropriate for expectation of a king. Today, this color is sometimes replaced by dark blue in order to distinguish it from the period before Easter, which is also associated with violet. The use of green, red, gold, and silver during the Christmas season is unrelated to the liturgical schema. On the third Sunday of Advent, the liturgical color is pink.

Character and Customs of the Season

Advent is a period of expectation, primarily of the coming of Jesus to the world in his Incarnation, but also of his future "[Second] Coming," his *parousia,* at the end of days. Many of the readings from Scriptures during this season are also related to this aspect. The character of the season is complex: like the period preceding Easter, to be discussed later, it includes elements of contrition and repentance as well as elements of joy and expectation of a savior. This mixture is due more than anything to the complex evolution of this liturgical season.

The origin of many of the customs of Advent is hard to identify. Some have been customary in the Church since the early Middle Ages, some were instituted during the period of the Reformation and Counter-Reformation, and others are much more recent. Many of these are common to various Christian groups and are not unique to Catholicism. Thus, for example, many churches are decorated with green leaves and wreaths, and round Christmas wreaths are hung up in many homes. In many places, it is customary to have a four-armed candelabra in the home (or to place the candles on the wreath), lighting an additional candle every week. Many people send greeting cards to friends and family during this period. "Advent Calendars" with a "window" for every passing day are also common in many houses. Every window includes some appropriate message, and, when intended for children, a sweet. The construction of a "nativity scene" ("manger," "crèche") in which the scene of Jesus' birth is displayed, with representations of the infant Jesus, Joseph, Mary, an ox, and a donkey,[3] as well as the three Magi,[4] is very common in many countries. Francis of Assisi, who assembled a "living manger" with various animals in the thirteenth century, may have contributed to the perpetuation of this custom.

Christmas

Christmas Day, December 25th, has liturgical colors of its own—white and gold—as well as many customs unique to it. Theologically speaking, many hold that Easter is much more important than Christmas: it is the resurrection of Jesus after his crucifixion, and not his birth—almost a "private" event—that, according to the Christian faith, announced the salvation of humankind. The fact that Jesus' birth and childhood are only recounted in two of the four Gospels, Matthew and Luke, as opposed to the crucifixion, which is described in all four, probably indicates the relative unimportance accorded to the story of Jesus' childhood in some ancient Churches. The absence of the infancy story from the Gospel According to Mark, considered the most ancient of the four Gospels, might hint that it took significant time for this story to appear and become accepted. Nevertheless, beginning in the Middle Ages and certainly today, Christmas garners plenty of public attention, much more so than Easter. There are various probable reasons for this. The cold weather with which it is associated in the Northern Hemisphere contributes indirectly to the "cozy" and "warm" feeling that gives it a domestic character. The commercial aspects of Christmas, created in order to encourage people to go shopping at a time when they might prefer to stay at home, may also be a factor. Its proximity to New Year's Day and the joy associated with the beginning of a new year certainly also add to the day's aura. Beyond all these, there may be another more internal reason for Christmas' success: many find it easier to relate to the happy story of a young mother and the birth of an infant that accompanies this day, rather than to the complicated narrative of suffering, death, and resurrection that accompanies Easter. Some of the most beautiful songs and hymns of the liturgical year celebrate these aspects, and preachers will often emphasize the peaceful, pure, humble, and serene idea that the redemption began with a baby who was revealed to simple shepherds.

Christmas has become so central to the culture of many countries that its religious significance may be completely lost: people who are not observant Christians or even Christian at all celebrate the domestic aspects of this festival in many countries. Some, especially in Europe, argue that historically there is nothing wrong with such a secular Christmas, pointing out that midwinter celebrations existed in Europe before and regardless of Christmas. The very fact that in many languages the name of the day has nothing to do with Christianity supports their claims. Nevertheless, for Christians the theological importance of this day should not be forgotten, as it has probably also played an essential part in its historic development: Christmas, the day celebrating Jesus' birth, emphasizes the mainline Christian belief that Jesus of Nazareth was not only God but also fully human.

"Secular" Customs and Traditions

The popular centerpiece of Christmas is a family meal, often on the evening preceding Christmas day or in the afternoon of the day itself, in which traditional dishes, depending on the region or country, are served. In addition to the food, one of the most famous elements of Christmas today is the Christmas tree. Its origins lie in the late sixteenth century in Alsace (along today's French-German border), and it is probably related to an ancient custom of decorating the home with green branches during the winter and perhaps also to a domestic adaptation of a popular medieval play on the story of the Garden of Eden, which included the use of a fruit-laden tree. Only in the nineteenth century did the custom of bringing a decorated tree into the house become popular in many countries. The tradition of Santa Claus, who brings gifts to children on Christmas, is well known in the United States but it is not a universal one. In many other countries, other figures, and not necessarily friendly ones, are associated with the period. Santa Claus is an admixture of the fourth-century figure of St. Nicholas with medieval Dutch customs and pre-Christian German traditions, forged together by North American settlers, defined in a song in the nineteenth century, and popularized by Coca-Cola ads during the first half of the twentieth century. No wonder, then, that many Christians are scandalized and disturbed by the fact that for many children this character symbolizes the essence of this Christian holy day.

The Liturgy

The nocturnal Mass (which, despite its occasional designation as "Midnight Mass," is often celebrated earlier in the evening) represents the culmination of Christmas and even the culmination of the religious year for many. Many Catholics who do not regularly attend services throughout the year make an effort to be present at this Mass. Many famous carols, such as "Silent Night," originating in Austria during the first half of the nineteenth century, give the service an especially festive flavor. The readings from the Old Testament included in the various Christmas Masses[5] (the one celebrated on Christmas Eve and those celebrated during the day) are taken from chapters considered by the Christian tradition as "Christological," or related to Christ, in the book of Isaiah: chapters 9, 52, and 62. The second reading is taken from the Epistle to Titus or the Epistle to the Hebrews, and is also related to the subject. The third reading, from the Gospels, is taken from the chapters detailing the birth and genealogy of Jesus, from the beginning of the Gospels according to Matthew, Luke, or John.

The Holy Family, New Year's Eve, and New Year's Day

The first Sunday after Christmas is the "Feast of the Holy Family," comprised of Joseph, Mary, and Jesus. The last day of December and the first day of January are of no particular religious importance. Nevertheless, since the eighth day or "octave" after various holy days is considered worth marking in many cultures, January 1st, eight days after Christmas, has been given various designations in the history of the Church. Up to 1969 and until today in several non-Catholic Churches it has been celebrated as the day of the circumcision of Jesus: the Jewish practice of ritualized male circumcision is regularly done on the eighth days of the child's life. In 1969, this designation was removed in the Catholic Church, and today it is mostly celebrated as the "Solemnity of Mary, Mother of God." In 1967, the Church also declared it the "World Day of Peace." December 31st has no religious significance.[6]

Epiphany

Epiphany ("manifestation, revelation"), a feast of Eastern Christian origin, which was adopted by the Western Churches at an early stage, is celebrated immediately at the end of the Christmas cycle. Its liturgical colors are identical to those of Christmas: white and gold. Traditionally, Epiphany falls on January 6th, but today, in order to accommodate the public and enable people to participate in it, it is celebrated in many countries on the Sunday between the 2nd and the 8th of January. Epiphany's meaning has changed quite a bit over time. Today it marks, among other things, the revelation of Christ's nature to the peoples of the world, which is understood to be symbolized in the New Testament story in which three wise men of the East (or shepherds) come to adore the infant Jesus in Bethlehem.[7] In many countries, this day is known as the "Three Kings' Day": quite early on, these mysterious visitors were described as magi and kings. In many countries there are local customs celebrating the day: special types of cakes and cookies, parades, or visit of homes by three children dressed as the magi. The children ask for a donation for some good cause, and in return sign on the door with a prior-blessed chalk "C+M+B" and the year, to tell all that the three magi, traditionally named Caspar, Melchior, and Balthasar, visited the place and as a reference to a Latin sentence *Christus Mansionem Benedicat*, "May Christ bless this house."

In churches, the revelation of Jesus' divine nature at his baptism in the Jordan River and at the wedding at Cana[8] are also celebrated on this Sunday or the next one as the "Feast of the Baptism of the Lord."

Ordinary Time

The period after the feast of Epiphany is, like most of the year, part of the "Ordinary Time."[9] Its liturgical color is green. Insofar as days of observance do not occur during this period, the parts of the Bible read at Sunday Mass are arranged according to set schedules, which depend on the year's place— A, B or C—in a three-year liturgical cycle.[10] The readings on other days of the week are arranged according to a different cycle of two years: odd years are designated as "I" and even years as "II."

The Paschal Cycle

The second cycle of the year is the Paschal cycle. Since Easter, unlike Christmas, does not always happen on the same date, the entire cycle is moveable. Like the cycle around Christmas, this cycle includes different periods:

1. Lent, which starts between the beginning of February or the middle of March, forty-six days before Easter, and ends two days before it on the eve of Holy Thursday;
2. The *Triduum* ("three days") of Easter;
3. Paschal Time (or "Eastertide"), the period beginning on Easter Sunday itself and ending fifty days after Easter on Pentecost.

The Date of Easter

The history of Easter is as complicated as that of Christmas. Christians began to celebrate the resurrection of Jesus in the spring during the middle of the second century at the latest. Some observed it on the 14th of the Jewish month of *Nissan,* following the Jewish calendar, and some on the following Sunday. In the interests of the unity and autonomy of Christianity, the Council of Nicaea, which met in 325 CE, decided to decouple Easter from the Jewish Passover, and to base it on an independent astronomical calculation: Easter would fall on the first Sunday after the first full moon after the spring equinox. This did not succeed in bringing about full uniformity, since Alexandria and Rome—the two centers which would proclaim the date of Easter each year—sometimes calculated different dates. The calculation was only synchronized in the sixth century, but to this day, there is usually a discrepancy between the date used by Western Christian Churches and the Eastern ones. This gap is caused by differences in calculation (the "equinox" referred to in the calculation is not necessarily the astronomical one), as well as by the use of different calendars, and by the fact that for the Eastern Churches Easter can never happen before the Jewish Passover. In the Western world, Easter may fall between March 22nd and April 25th, but unlike Christmas, it will always be on a Sunday.[11] Today, Orthodox Easter sometimes falls on the same day as the Catholic/Protestant Easter, sometimes a week later, sometimes four weeks later, and sometimes five.[12]

The possibility of anchoring the moveable feasts, first and foremost Easter, to a particular date has been discussed a few times in recent decades at ecumenical meetings attended by representatives of many Christian denominations. One of the Catholic Church's official offers was to celebrate Easter every year on the Sunday after the second Saturday of April. The idea was not accepted, and it appears that, for the moment, no other idea has a better chance to be accepted by all Christian Churches.[13]

Lent

Like Christmas, Easter is also preceded by a period of preparation. Its liturgical color is violet. This period connotes repentance, since it leads up to the death of Jesus, who died for the sins of the world. In the past, the public was required to eat moderately and even, in many periods, to abstain completely from certain foods, such as meat, wine, and often dairy during this forty-day period. Beginning in 1966, these limitations were minimized considerably and relegated to the Fridays of Lent and to "Ash Wednesday," which opens the period.[14] As in the ancient Church, today this period is considered the culmination of the process of preparation of adults for their baptism, which is carried out on Easter Night. Some sacramentals are emphasized in it, for example the recreation of the "Stations of the Cross," which will be discussed later. For many Catholics, Lent forms the religious peak of the year. It is then, many say, that they feel Catholic, even if, practically speaking, their participation in worship is limited. Many choose to limit their diet in some way, for example by giving up on sweets (often in addition to avoidance of meat), as a reminder of the period and as a personal sacrifice.

Since Sundays are considered days of joy, when bodily castigation is forbidden, and since in the Western world there was a desire to create a period including forty days, in which penitential acts are possible, the period actually begins forty-six days before Easter, on Ash Wednesday.

Ash Wednesday

On this day, a special ceremony takes place in churches. During the celebration of Mass or independently of it a priest (or another person appointed to do so) makes the sign of the cross on the foreheads of all those present using ashes (at times, mixed with oil), or, in some places, sprinkles ash over their head. The ash, which is sometimes made of the palm fronds (or other plants) saved from the previous year's "Palm Sunday" (to be discussed soon), is a biblical symbol of mourning, repentance, and contrition,[15] as well as a reminder of human mortality. Accordingly, the act of marking the cross is accompanied by the words "For you are dirt, and to dirt you shall return."[16] The readings from Scriptures on this day have to do with contrition and repentance.

This supposedly marginal ceremony is considered today in many parts of the world to be one of the most popular yearly Catholic events. The reasons for this are probably multiple. In addition to the fact that it opens an important liturgical season and makes use of ashes, a "primeval," "raw" element and therefore perhaps a particularly attractive one to us "post-moderns," the rite enables many Catholics to physically demonstrate their faith. In accordance with local customs, and especially if the rite involves an actual marking of the cross on the forehead, participants may leave the church at its end and enter the public sphere, with the fact of their Catholicity quite literally marked upon them.

The day before Ash Wednesday, "Fat Tuesday" ("Shrove Tuesday," "Mardi Gras"), was traditionally the last day upon which the eating of meat was allowed. In many places (in the United States, the most famous is New Orleans), it is celebrated as Carnival (a word originating, apparently, from the Latin for "removing of meat"). It has no deep religious meaning.

Holy Week

The "Holy Week" begins thirty-eight days after Ash Wednesday. Of particular importance during this week are Sunday, Thursday, Friday, and Saturday, though the other days of the week also have customs of their own. The habit of marking some of the days of Holy Week, especially the three days before Easter proper, is quite ancient. The customs pertaining to the other days were adopted in the Roman calendar only starting in the eleventh century.

Palm Sunday

Palm Sunday (also known as "Passion Sunday") commemorates on the one hand the entrance of Jesus and his disciples into Jerusalem, and on the other hand the beginning of Jesus' suffering ("Passion"), death, and resurrection. According to various sources in the New Testament, the Jerusalemite public received Jesus with branches spread along the road, and calls of "Hosanna to the son of David!"[17] In many places, it is customary to bless branches or flowers outside the church and then to bring them into the church in a festive procession. The readings from Scriptures are related to the entry of Jesus into Jerusalem but also to the later, less joyous days of that fateful week. These texts are often read theatrically by several readers. Thus, the joy of entry into Jerusalem is mixed with the sorrow to come. The blessed branches used in the procession are kept in many homes until the next year.

Holy Monday, Tuesday, and Wednesday

Monday, Tuesday, and Wednesday of the "Holy Week" are considered relatively minor, but various customs are kept in homes and churches on these days as well. They are seen as particularly opportune for reception of the sacrament of reconciliation as preparation for participation in Easter Mass.

On Holy Tuesday or Wednesday[18] a special ceremony is held in every cathedral, the church of the local bishop. In this ceremony, the "Chrism Mass," the bishop blesses the oils of anointment used throughout the year by himself and by the other priests of the diocese: scented oil for baptism, confirmation, and ordination; oil for anointment of the sick; and oil for the anointment of catechumens, those preparing for baptism. It is a particularly impressive ceremony, not only for the ritual itself, but also for the fact that, for the most part, it is the only annual occasion upon which all the priests of the diocese are present under the leadership of the bishop.

Holy Thursday

Holy Thursday leads into the *triduum,* or the three days (Friday, Saturday, and Sunday) that form the heart of the Holy Week. The events of the "Last Supper" of Jesus with his disciples have a special place in this day, and a ritual reenactment of Jesus' washing of his disciples' feet is performed in churches.[19] The Mass of the day is particularly festive, and special efforts are made so that as many parishioners as possible may receive a Eucharist consecrated therein. During the washing ceremony (a very theatrical act), the celebrant, priest, or bishop, passes with a bowl of water and a towel among twelve parishioners seated in a row alongside the altar and washes their feet.[20]

After Mass, the consecrated Host, the body of Christ, is ceremonially transferred to a side chapel in the church. The consecrated Host will remain in the chapel, and some congregants will spend time sitting or kneeling before it for a while after the ceremony as an act of respectful worship.[21] It will be distributed and consumed the next day, the only day of the year in which no Mass is celebrated. The coverings of the altar are removed, and the preparation for Good Friday begins: the atmosphere at the end of the Mass is tense.

Good Friday

Good Friday is a day of mourning, the day of Jesus' crucifixion and death. Its English name—which apparently derives from an original meaning of "sacred," not "good" in the sense of an opposition to "bad"—may be misleading. In the past, it was a day of complete fast, or at least a day upon which eating was severely limited. Today, the extent of the fast is very dependent on local custom and even more so on the feelings and piety of the particular believer.

The mourning is expressed visually in churches, where coverings are removed from the altars, and tabernacles are displayed open and empty. It is also apparent in the liturgy itself. Readings describing the passion and crucifixion of Jesus, often featuring several readers, are included in a prayer said in the afternoon. Many consider this a particularly impressive prayer precisely for its subdued nature. A ceremony in which the congregants kiss a cross may also be included in this prayer. Mass is not said on Good Friday, but bread consecrated the day before is dispensed.

Another well-known custom of the day is the recreation of the "Stations of the Cross," the path Jesus walked to his death. The *Via Dolorosa* ("Way of Suffering"), a path in Jerusalem, is its focal point in a certain sense, but it may be enacted in any church, religious institution, or even, temporarily or permanently, outdoors or in public space. Thus, for example, today it is carried out in Paris on Montmartre, in Rome at the Coliseum, and in New York on the Brooklyn Bridge. The faithful walk through fourteen stations, each commemorating a historical or legendary event of the earthly Jesus' last day.

In some churches, the removal of the figure of Jesus from a cross and its "burial," are also reenacted. This ceremony is very theatrical and impressive. The attitude of members of the Church towards it differs greatly, regionally and individually.

Holy Saturday

Holy Saturday, the day on which Jesus died and, according to medieval tradition, descended into Hell to save the souls of the righteous who died before him, does not itself manifest liturgical motifs of any particular importance. In the Middle Ages the liturgy originally intended for the night between Saturday and Sunday was celebrated on Saturday. When this ceremony was returned to its original place in the middle of the twentieth century, Holy Saturday reverted to a time of preparation both material and spiritual, and of waiting for the significant night ahead.

Easter Night and Day

According to the Gospels, Jesus died on Friday. He remained dead on Saturday. On Sunday morning, when women came to his burial cave, he was not there. "Why do you seek the living one among the dead?" two mysterious figures asked the women. "He is not here, but he has been raised," continues the author of the Gospel according to Luke.[22] Thus, it was during these hours—the early morning of Easter Sunday—that Christians celebrated the Resurrection for hundreds of years. Later, this ceremony gradually disappeared in the Catholic Church, and the night Mass between Saturday and Sunday was pushed up to the morning of Holy Saturday. The primary Mass of Easter was that of Sunday morning. Many other events of Holy Week also lost their importance. In 1951 the Easter Night ceremony was resuscitated, and since then, at least in parts of the world, and for those Catholics practically and spiritually involved in the life of the Church, it has been considered the central event of the entire year. Mass is also celebrated on Sunday morning, just as it is every Sunday, and there are places where this service is the most frequented. The discussion here will nevertheless focus on the night Mass.

The festive Mass of Easter night is considered a "vigil": this is the greatest night of the year, on which the faithful await salvation. It opens with a ceremony often referred to as "The Liturgy of Fire." If possible, the public congregates in darkness and silence outside the church, each holding an unlit candle. Then, a great fire is lit: Christ, the light of the world, has arrived. After the fire is blessed, it is used to light the "Easter Candle," a large candle stamped with the sign of the cross and the Greek letters Alpha and Omega. These letters, which begin and end the Greek alphabet, symbolize Christ, who is said to be "the Alpha and the Omega, the first and the last, the beginning and the end."[23] To these are added the year, whose numerals are written between the arms of the cross, and five waxed grains of incense in the form of "nails," symbolizing the wounds of Jesus on the cross. After the Easter Candle is lit, the candles held by the entire congregation are lit from it, and the public marches into the dark church. The world, darkened by the death of the Son of God, is cast into light by his resurrection. The Easter Candle is set in a central location, near the altar.

One of the special elements of the night Mass is the large number of readings from Scriptures integrated into it. The "Liturgy of the Word" on this night includes nine texts considered essential in Christian theology: they proclaim Jesus, his resurrection, and its meaning. These include the creation of the world (with emphasis on the creation of man in the image of God),[24] the binding of Isaac (the son who, unlike Jesus, was not sacrificed),[25] the parting of the waters of the Red Sea and the passage from slavery into freedom (a symbol of Christian baptism),[26] chapters on salvation from Isaiah and Ezekiel,[27] and a description of the Wisdom living among humankind, from the Book of Baruch, understood in Christian eyes to refer to Christ.[28] From the New Testament, a famous passage is read regarding baptism,[29] as well as, of course, the description of Jesus' resurrection on the first day of the week.[30] At least three of these texts must be read: in many churches most or all of them are read. It is easy to understand why, while the readings from Scriptures were made in Latin, a language with which the public was not entirely acquainted with, many decided to forgo this lengthy Mass (as do many parents of small children today, even when the texts are read in the vernacular).

One of the climaxes of the Mass of Easter night is the moment of baptism of not-yet-Christian adults (if there are any of these), who have been preparing for a long time for the ceremony. If this baptism is carried out, and even when it is not, each believer is enjoined to reflect on his or her own baptism and to renew the declarations of faith included therein. Sprinkling the entire congregation with holy water makes this element even more concrete.

As mentioned above, the Mass on Easter Sunday morning also attracts many. In one of its readings, which are not lengthier than those of an ordinary Mass, Simon-Peter proclaims the rising of Christ and its meaning.[31]

Additional customs and symbols have been attached to Easter over the years. Among these may be found the painting and hiding of eggs, special cakes, and more. Many of these customs originate in various European spring and fertility festivals and have no essential or primary Christian meaning. Nevertheless, quite naturally, over the years many of them have obtained interpretations related to Easter.

"Easter Monday," while a vacation day in many countries, has no religious meaning.

Paschal Time ("Eastertide")

Following Easter, a period called "Paschal Time" or "Eastertide" begins. It is seven weeks long. The Book of Acts, which describes the life of the first disciples after the death and resurrection of Jesus, is central to it. The fortieth day after Easter is the "Ascension of the Lord": a day celebrating Jesus' ascent to heaven after staying with his disciples and teaching them.[32] Nine days later, forty-nine days after Easter, Pentecost (from the Greek word for fifty) is celebrated. This holy day is parallel to the Jewish *Shavuot,* and in it the Church marks the descent of the Spirit on the disciples of Jesus gathered in Jerusalem, an occasion often considered as the "birthday" of the Church.[33] The liturgical color for this day is red, symbolizing among other things the Holy Spirit and the images of fire in the description of the event. After Pentecost, the liturgy returns to "Ordinary Time."

Other Observances

Most of the holy days described above represent events related to the life of Jesus and are therefore known, together with others, as "The Solemnities of the Lord." Other holy days pertain to the category of "Feasts of Mary." These are also numerous, and central among them are the "Feast of the Immaculate Conception," celebrated on the 8th of December, and the "Feast of the Assumption of Mary," celebrated on the 15th of August.[34] An example of the third category, saints' feasts, will be mentioned briefly at the end of this chapter.

The Catholic calendar also contains, in addition to the cycles and feasts described so far, additional days of observance. Among these there is a clear hierarchy: some are "Holy Days of Obligation," in which all Catholics worldwide are expected to attend a Mass, barring exceptional circumstances.

Other more numerous days are of lesser weight. They are marked with a Mass, but their practical importance varies greatly from place to place. We shall mention five such days from among the observances listed in the universal calendar. Three of them open the period of "Ordinary Time" after the "Paschal Time"; the fourth is dedicated to the saints; the fifth ends the entire liturgical year.

The "Feast of the Holy Trinity" has been celebrated in the Catholic Church since the fourteenth century, on the first Sunday after Pentecost. Its liturgy, not surprisingly, concentrates on the central theological principle whose name it bears.

Thursday of the same week (or the following Sunday) is the "Solemnity of the Most Holy Body and Blood of Christ," known also by its Latin name *Corpus Christi*. This day celebrates the body and blood of Christ incorporated in the sacrament of Mass. Traditionally since the Middle Ages, this feast has centered upon a procession outside of the church, during which the consecrated host—the body of Christ—was displayed with great pomp. At the time, most Catholics refrained from frequent reception of the host, and viewing it was therefore of great religious significance. Today, when most practicing Catholics are used to partaking of the host regularly at Mass, the importance of this passive viewing has declined. The customs of this holy day have therefore also changed, and in many places a Mass celebrated outside of church has replaced the procession. In some other places the processions go on with great splendor, integrating expressions of local culture.

On the Friday following the second Sunday after Pentecost, the "Solemnity of the Sacred Heart of Jesus" is celebrated. This day marks the love of Jesus for all of humankind, a love born of his human heart. A pious image of his heart, sometimes pierced by the spear with which he was stabbed according to the Gospel of John,[35] may also be used in the ritual.

The first of November is "All Saints' Day." On this festival, which dates back to the Middle Ages, honor is paid to all the saints known and unknown. Many visit cemeteries on this day or on the following one (November 2nd). In Ireland, the United States, and in many other places today, the night before it, known as "Halloween," is marked by references to the dead and ghosts. Many of the customs of this night are Celtic in origin, but the connection between Celtic traditions regarding the dead and the Church's decision to venerate its saints on this day is not accidental.

"The Feast of Christ the King" is celebrated on the last Sunday of the liturgical year, during the second half of November. This is a relatively new holy day, instituted in 1925 by pope Pius XI.

In addition to the universal days, other holy days are celebrated in particular areas of the world. Since the universal calendar leaves quite a few days bereft of any particular significance, it is possible to add observations of the days of "local" saints or those particularly venerated locally. Examples are the celebration of the "Feast of Our Lady of Guadalupe" on December 12th, particularly among Spanish-speaking Catholics, of St. Patrick's Day on March 17th in Ireland (and some particular aspects of that celebration in many other countries today), or of St. Rosa of Lima in South America on August 30th.[36]

Notes

1. Code of Canon Law (*CCL*), canons 1246–1248; *Catechism of the Catholic Church* (*CCC*), par. 2181. On the *CCC*, see p. 48.
2. See for example Luke 24:34.
3. An allusion to Isaiah 1:3.
4. See Matthew 2:1–12. In Luke's parallel text the visitors are shepherds; see Luke 2:1–20.
5. For a detailed overview of the Mass, see pp. 107–123.
6. For a well-done and very readable exploration of the Christmas season, see Greg Dues, *Catholic Customs & Traditions, a Popular Guide, Revised and Updated* (Mystic: Twenty-Third Publications / Bayard, 2000): 42–69. The cycle of Lent and Easter, to which we will devote the coming pages, is described in that book on pp. 70–100.
7. Matthew 2:1–12; Luke 2:8–20.
8. John 1:19–2:12.
9. The actual meaning of the term is related to the word "ordinal," due to the fact that the weeks during this time are numbered in the calendar. At the same time, the understanding that refers to this season being more "regular" is also not wrong.
10. The liturgical year begins at the end of November, and thus is not exactly contemporaneous with the calendrical year. In A years (liturgical years divisible by three, such as 2016–2017 and 2019–2020), almost all readings from the New Testament are taken from the Gospel of Matthew. In B years (which leave a remainder of one when divided by three, like 2014–2015 and 2017–2018), most readings are taken from Mark and some from John. In C years (likewise with a remainder of two, such as 2015–2016 and 2018–2019), almost all readings are from Luke.
11. For example, these are the dates of Western Easter for the five years following the publication of this book: April 5, 2015; March 27, 2016; April 16, 2017; April 1, 2018; April 21, 2019.
12. The dates of Eastern Easter for the five years following the publication of this book: April 12, 2015; May 1, 2016; April 16, 2017; April 8, 2018; April 28, 2019.
13. Despite these global difficulties, local solutions have been found in many places. Thus, for example, in many towns and villages in the Middle East where mixed Christian populations live, Christmas is often celebrated according to the Western calendar, and Easter according to the Eastern date.
14. See the apostolic constitution *Paenitemini* by Paul VI, February 17, 1966.
15. See for example 2 Samuel 13:19, Jeremiah 6:26, and Esther 4:1.
16. Genesis 3:19. Another common translation used in the liturgy is "For you are dust, and unto dust you shall return."
17. Matthew 21:1–11 and parallels. The Hebrew-Aramaic expression "hosha na," which means "Please save us!" (see also Psalms 118:25) was received into the Christian liturgy as *Hosanna*, as were at least three other words of Hebrew or Aramaic origin, *Amen* ("I believe," "I agree"), *Hallelujah* ("Praise God!"), and *Maranatha* ("The Lord comes").

18. Until some decades ago, this ritual took place generally on Thursday.
19. John 13:1–20.
20. In recent years, controversy has arisen in some parts of the world over the inclusion of women among the twelve chosen for this honor. Those in favor stress the equal status of women in the congregation, while opponents point to the fact that all twelve disciples were men. This is of course yet another permutation of the larger debate over the place of women in the Church. The pope reigning at the time this book was finalized, pope Francis, celebrated this ritual two weeks after his election in March 2013, in a prison in Rome. Among those whose feet he washed were two women, one of who was not even Catholic, but Muslim.
21. On the meaning of such silent contemplation, see also the discussion on prayers, p. 27 and p. 41.
22. Luke 24:1–12, and parallels.
23. See Revelation (the book also known as The Apocalypse of John, which ends the New Testament) 1:8, 21:6, and 22:13.
24. Genesis 1:1–2:2 (or only 1:26–31).
25. Genesis 22:1–18 (or parts thereof).
26. Exodus 14:15–15:1. This text is obligatory.
27. Isaiah 54:5–14 and 55:1–11, Ezekiel 36:16–28.
28. Baruch (a "deuterocanonical"/"apocryphal" book: of Jewish origin, but not included in Jewish and Protestant Bibles) 3:9–15 and 3:32–4:4.
29. Romans 6:3–11.
30. The reading from the Gospels is chosen in accordance with the liturgical year: Matthew 28:1–10 on A years, Mark 16:1–7 on B years, Luke 24:1–12 on C years. On the determination of the liturgical year, see p. 180, n. 10.
31. Acts 10:34–44.
32. Acts 1:1–11.
33. Acts 2. The idea that the descent of the Spirit marks the birth of the Christian Church is current not only in the Catholic world. Some Evangelical and Pentecostal Churches put great emphasis on another aspect of the event: the descent of the Spirit on all the members of the Church, exciting a kind of religious ecstasy known as "speaking in tongues": a state in which the believer emits sounds which are not words in a language known to him or her (or, as skeptics would have it, talks gibberish).
34. On these two feasts, see also pp. 45–46.
35. John 19:34–35.
36. For more information on the saints, see pp. 87–90 and 150–153.

CHAPTER **6**

Catholic Challenges

This chapter, though the last in the book, does not attempt a summary. Its purpose is rather to outline the main challenges faced by the Catholic Church today, at the middle of the second decade of the twenty-first century. Its main premise is that identifying these challenges may be helpful to those seeking to comprehend potential developments in the Church in the coming years.

The challenges to be discussed can be divided into three categories: structural issues, issues related to gender and sexuality, and topics that involve the complicated relations of the Church with its past (both distant and recent), its future, and those that are not among its members.

In the first category, one can think of shifts in geography and demography in the Catholic Church, the status of the laity, the topic of collegiality, the shortage of priests, and the interpretation of the Second Vatican Council. The second category includes discussions about the challenges related to women and feminism in the Church, sexual abuse of young people, birth control and HIV/AIDS, abortion, homosexuality, and divorce and remarriage. In the final category we mention several other thorny issues, such as how the Church as a whole and Catholics as individuals are coming to terms with the past, secularization, relations with Judaism and with Islam, ecumenism, and competing with other Christian groups.

Though other commentators may emphasize different challenges faced by the Church, all those versed in the subject would no doubt include the vast majority of these topics under one name or another on their list.

Shifts in Geography and Demography

If for many centuries the center of Catholicism was indeed in Europe, this is no longer the case. Only about a quarter of the world's Catholics live in Europe. Sixty percent of Catholics today live in the southern hemisphere, and this number will rise. The average Catholic today is not white, not rich, not European or North American, and not male. At the same time, vast financial resources and the power that accompanies them, are still found in the northern hemisphere. Balancing this gap between north and south will be one of the major challenges for the Church in the coming decades.

The Catholicism found in the southern hemisphere is often quite different from the Catholicism of Europe and North America. In many places the questions and concerns that are most pressing for the population are not the same. In some cases, rules and traditions that came from Europe are ignored or rejected and considered to be a form of colonialism. The Catholicism that is characteristic of the southern hemisphere, which is often the result of a more recent conversion to and adoption of Catholicism, frequently shows local cultural characteristics that are different from the European ones. Non-Christian customs were absorbed into European Catholicism many centuries ago, and thus are seen by European and North Americans as authentic and inherent parts of their Christianity. When Europeans and North Americans look at the current practices among Catholics in the southern hemisphere, they are likely to consider many of these practices to be "non-Catholic." Tensions, objections, and misunderstandings on both sides are rather easy to come by.

The Catholic Church has a long history of spreading itself to new territories and dealing with inculturation. Sometimes the process has been smooth and successful, at other times disastrous. Today, when the majority of Catholics live in the southern hemisphere, the north no longer spreads the gospel to the south. Sometimes, in fact, conversion and proselytization efforts happen in the opposite direction, and this is likely to become even more common in the future.

The southern hemisphere also presents Catholicism with a challenge it has not had to face in Europe for several centuries: serious competition with other Christian groups. Thus in South America for example, Evangelical and Pentecostal groups attract large numbers of people that were previously considered Catholic. The Catholic Church, if it wants to retain its members and attract new adherents, must find ways to answer the spiritual needs of current Catholics and potential converts that are more compelling than the available alternatives.

Pope Francis is the first pope in almost 1,300 years to be born outside of Europe, and the first ever to be born in the New World. His election perhaps marks the moment in which the Old Catholicism of Europe gave way to the New Catholicism of the southern hemisphere. Many Catholics from the north and south will watch with interest for the possible implications of this shift.

The Status of the Laity

Most people living today, Catholics included, probably see democracy as the best form of government in spite of its drawbacks. The Church is not democratic, and many Catholics would like it to continue this way. On the other hand, many Catholics feel that various elements of democracy can and should be integrated into their Church. Although most Catholics believe that ordained members of the Church should have a unique author-ity, most are interested in limiting this authority to specific fields, mostly those related to actual rituals, so that the voice of the laity can be heard and taken into consideration before important decisions are made.

In practice, on the local level the involvement and power of the laity depend on local Catholic and secular culture. In some countries, priests and bishops assume, correctly or not, that they can make many decisions without taking the opinion of the community into particular consideration, while in other countries the voice of the laity is carefully listend to. The issue usually surfaces when a decision made by a bishop or a priest draws oppo-sition from the community: it is then that laypeople make their influence felt. Indeed, various lay organizations and movements have succeeded in bringing about changes in the Church, although the hierarchy is sometimes loath to admit this.

Still, while, numerically speaking, the laity is thousands of times larger than any other group in the Church, it is prevented from fulfilling many roles within it and is almost always powerless with respect to ordained Church members. The conception that only ordained priests may preside over most sacraments is difficult to argue with, so long as one remains a Catholic. The same is true of the idea that bishops are invested with the responsibility of overseeing the sacraments and the orthodoxy of faith in the Church. The remaining question is where, among the other aspects of ecclesiastical life, laypeople can make their contribution. Since, as remarked above, in many parts of the world laywomen are one of the strongest and most involved groups in Church life, this issue also bears upon the status of women in the Church.

It may be argued that the laity has more power in the Church today than it has had in many previous generations. One could also assert that this power is growing, sometimes with the support of parts of the hierarchy and sometimes against its will. Nevertheless, many believe lay power should still significantly increase. The slogan "We Are (the) Church" (or the more nuanced one, "We Are Also the Church") is used today by many progressive lay organizations to remind the hierarchy that without the laity the Church is but a fleshless skeleton. In many minds, one of the biggest challenges faced by local churches in the coming decades is the necessity of cooperation between the various groups making them up, striking the balance between a measure of democratization on the one hand, and the maintaining of the distinct status of the Catholic clergy on the other.

Collegiality

While some use the term "collegiality" to refer to micro-level relationships between laypeople and priests (as well as between priests and bishops), in its most narrow and precise sense the term refers to the macro-level relationships between the bishops (as individuals and as a group) and the pope. In other words, the term refers in the main to the global Church and not the local one. Yet this relationship has repercussions for the local churches as well. Even if it does not apply to local behavior, it may be perceived as a model for it.

In its most extreme sense, the principle of collegiality states that all bishops have equal authority over the entire Church, and that each bishop holds absolute authority and autonomy over his diocese. In the eyes of its proponents, the principle is based upon the relationship between Jesus and his disciples. According to their interpretation, all the disciples enjoyed equal status.

The principle raises many problems. Practically speaking, what happens when the majority of bishops are opposed to the actions of one of their colleagues within his diocese? Does the majority override local authority, or vice versa? What is the precise status of the pope, the bishop of Rome, in this system? When a council votes, does he get only one vote, like any other bishop? Can he veto the decision of the entirety or majority of bishops?[1] What happens when he opposes a local bishop on actions taken in that bishop's diocese?

For the most part, these questions are no more than an intellectual exercise for the Catholic Church, and a slightly dangerous one at that. Within the Church, consensus has held for centuries that the bishop of Rome enjoys greater authority than other bishops. Thus the debate on collegiality may focus on the precise definition of the primacy of the bishop of Rome over all others and its practical consequences, or on the question of the authority of bishops within their dioceses, in other dioceses, and in the universal Church.

Those in support of a high degree of collegiality and relative independence for bishops are not hard put to find grounding in the ancient history of the Church. In the Eastern Churches, a similar principle is expressed in the idea that a patriarch is "the first among equals" (*"Primus inter pares"*). The idea also appeals to contemporary attitudes, which seek to grant collectivities of people the greatest possible autonomy without forcing upon them principles that may be opposed to their desires, culture, and mentality. Those upholding local freedom wish to emphasize and even fortify the multicultural aspect of the Church. Any growth in the authority of the pope, which always comes at the expense of the bishops, would in their minds bring about a system in which the Vatican's way of thinking aspires to impose its opinion on groups of different mentality, whether these are located within walking distance of the Vatican or a many hours' flight away. They also remind the Church of the concept of "Subsidiarity," widely praised in Catholicism, which requires that difficult situations be handled by the lowest and least centralized competent authority.

Their opponents, who are interested in strengthening the pope's power at the expense of the other bishops, can point to historical examples of periods in which bishops were seen as emissaries of the pope and not autonomous leaders. In their opinion, the centralization of power in the hands of the pope and the Vatican Curia contributes to the Church's unity. The curia's involvement in local affairs ensures a certain homogeneity in the global Church, which may be necessary for its maintenance as a coherent unit. What would happen, they ask, if a bishop or an Episcopal conference of some country were to make a decision that drew the ire of others? In the pre-modern Church, regional differences, which were usually discovered accidentally, often brought about fierce debates; what would happen today, when every decision made somewhere in the world is known within minutes on the other side of the globe? What would conservative bishops in one country do if the bishops of another country decided to reinstate priests who had married? On the other hand, how would progressive bishops react if in another country women were excluded from all active participation in the liturgy? Those who support centralization see it as the only force that can protect the Church, the "Noah's Ark" floating upon stormy waters, from breaking into pieces and sinking.

The supporters of greater independence rebut that the many subterranean streams flowing through the Church may someday explode in full force and destroy this semblance of unity if not allowed to express themselves. According to them, a high level of collegiality, enabling local Churches to make their own way, can serve as a pressure valve. This independence would not detract from the pope's *de jure* authority, even if it did constrain his practical ability to intervene in particular local affairs.

Finding the right formula to solve these conundrums is a major challenge for all Church members. One must remember that subjective reasons are also at play: when a pope seems to be liberal, progressive Catholics suddenly hope for his involvement in local affairs against local conservative trends. When a pope seems conservative, it is the conservative side that calls for his intervention while progressives defend liberal decisions made at the grassroots level.

Events in the Anglican Communion which is characterized by a high degree of collegiality and which has been engulfed in recent years by controversy with regard to the ordination of openly gay bishops, are being watched with great interest by many Catholics. If the Anglican Church splits over this issue, it may strengthen the argument of those Catholics who warn against greater collegiality. If the Anglican Communion weathers the crisis, united in practice and not only in name without too much damage to its principle of collegiality, the partisans of collegiality in the Catholic Church may use its example to argue the viability of their road.

The issue of collegiality was discussed in the Second Vatican Council mostly as part of the debates around the document that came to be known as *Lumen Gentium*, or "The Dogmatic Constitution on the Church." Yet the final version of this text did not really clarify the issue. The paragraphs dealing with it are rather obscure, and the almost impossible combination of different approaches is quite visible in the final document. Traces of the debate between different groups are in fact so salient that both of the main camps—the one calling for greater freedom for bishops and the other upholding the absolute authority of the pope—can find grounds for each of their cases in its phrasing.[2]

The reigns of popes John Paul II and Benedict XVI were characterized by a growing centralization of power in the Vatican and heavy interventions by its officials in the affairs of local churches. This might not be only related to the personality of these two popes but also to developments in communications and in the ability of modern institutions to give orders from their center to their peripheries. Many claim that the idea of collegiality, which was developed to some extent at the Council at any rate, was emptied of its content during this period, though formally the innovations instituted by the Council were maintained. Others emphasize that while decisions in the Church are certainly not made democratically, various mechanisms make it possible for members of the Church, both lay and clergy, to make their opinion on various subjects heard at the top hierarchical echelon. There is no doubt that the debate over the interpretation and implementation of the principle of collegiality at both micro and macro levels will continue to constitute a complex and challenging issue for the current and future popes.

The Shortage of Priests

One of the most difficult issues faced by the Catholic Church in recent decades has been the ongoing shortage of priests. In theory, today slightly more than 400,000 living priests serve more than 1.2 billion Catholics worldwide. Practically speaking, many of these priests are inactive due to old age or other reasons. Moreover, about a third of these priests are members of Institutes of Consecrated Life (living in monasteries or other types of communities), and though they sometimes assist parish priests, the vast majority of them do not head lay congregations. It is often assumed that, ideally, one priest should serve not more than two thousand parishioners. In reality, many priests, due to their small number, are obliged to serve much greater groups of laypeople. Conversely, from the perspective of the laity, laypeople must settle for a very small number of clergy to handle their religious needs. The shortage also affects the lives of active priests: many feel worn down by the extent of their charges, and surveys show that this feeling often plays a significant role in the process that leads many priests to eventually leave the priesthood.

This deficit is not a new problem. In the years following the Second Vatican Council, many priests left the priesthood. In some places, such a decision was made by more than 20 to 30 percent of the clergy. The question of whether this exodus was related to the Council, and if so, how, is rather contentious.[3] Even when this drop in the number of priests leveled off, the number continued to go down—or at least, in relation to the number of Catholics, it never grew again. In 1978, the year in which John Paul II was elected pope, the worldwide ratio was one priest for every 1,800 Catholics. At the time of writing, the situation is much worse, and the ratio has grown by more than 50 percent. In some countries, particularly outside of North America and Europe, five and even ten thousand laypeople must make do with the services of one priest. Since the number of priests over the age of fifty is significantly greater than the number of younger priests (including priests to be: those studying in seminaries), the situation is expected to get much worse over time.

Some claim that these calculations distort reality. Distinguishing between active and inactive Catholics, they agree that the number of priests has gone down, but point out that the number of churchgoers has also declined. According to this interpretation, the situation is indeed worse than it was a few decades ago, but is not catastrophic.

In the last few decades, many sociologists have conducted research on Catholic priests. Their work has brought the many reasons for the shortage to light. Among these, it appears, one is the enhanced status of the laity in the ecclesiology of the Second Vatican Council. The sexual revolution of the second half of the twentieth century has also made the idea of celibacy more alien. For many priests and young men considering a career in the priesthood, the approbation of lay life, including repeated Church declarations about the value and sanctity of heterosexual marital life, create doubts regarding the value of a priestly life demanding sexual abstinence. At the same time, the growing acceptance in many parts of the world, including in progressive Catholic circles, of a homosexual lifestyle makes it possible for Catholic men of such an orientation to consider such a life "outside the closet" without leaving the Church they are members of. The advantage of holy orders as a good excuse for not marrying a woman is therefore less and less needed for many of them.[4] Another reason for the falling number of candidates for the priesthood is the general downturn, in the developed world at least, in the prestige accorded to professions such as teachers, clergy, social workers, and the like. The opportunity for a certain upward social mobility once granted by the priesthood is no longer relevant in many countries: other professions in which many men considering the priesthood could doubtless succeed enjoy greater prestige, and may also proffer a more materially comfortable existence.[5]

Many members of the Church are involved in attempts to find a way to make up the deficit. Some of them believe that there is only one solution: prayers beseeching the Father, the Son, and the Holy Spirit to instill young men with the realization that the priesthood is their vocation.[6] These Church members may try to increase the chances that their prayers will be answered through the organization of seminars and lectures and the dissemination of written information on the topic. Through these programs of encouragement, they hope to induce young men who may be contemplating a priestly vocation to seriously consider this option.

More realist Catholics may see these methods as vital while admitting that without a sudden miracle doubling or tripling the number of candidates for the priesthood, the shortage will not be made up. They suggest a number of more practical solutions. One of these is to import priests from certain developing countries, where the number of young priests is still relatively large, to developed countries, where they are needed. Such a solution, like other forms of migrant labor, can help and is already of assistance in particular situations, but its limitations are clear. Not all young priests are likely to succeed on a foreign continent and with a congregation culturally different than the one they grew up in, and not all congregations will easily accept someone who comes from far away. Moreover, even if in many developing countries the number of young priests is high, it is nevertheless low, often even lower than in developed countries, when compared to the size of the Catholic population. Rich western dioceses may cause a certain brain drain (or at least sacrament drain) in poorer places through this practice.

Another supposedly simple solution to the lack of priests is the integration of laypeople and deacons into the work of the Church, as far as doctrine allows. Thus, the supporters of this solution state correctly, there is no reason that baptisms, funerals, or marriages should not be carried out by deacons or even by laypeople who have received the proper instruction and training. In practice, such solutions may also be found lacking: surveys have repeatedly shown that the majority of Catholics want priests, and not deacons or laypersons, to provide for their liturgical needs, even in rituals where this is not required by Church law.

Another solution is the ordination of married men. Married men are ordained in the Eastern Catholic Churches, and the Western Catholic Church has also ordained as priests a number of married men who entered its ranks from other denominations where they already served as pastors or priests.[7] These facts favor those who highlight the point that the celibacy of the priesthood is not a matter of doctrinal principle. Nevertheless, such an act may be conceptually difficult for many Catholics. A related idea is to authorize priests who have left the priesthood and married to return to their posts.[8] Among the other advantages of this use of married ex-priests is the fact that in many cases these experienced men can rather easily be integrated into their home congregation. Some Catholic thinkers have proposed allowing priests to marry (as distinct from ordaining already married men). The assumption is that young heterosexual men who are not certain of their future plans may thus be ordained for the priesthood, knowing that this will not prevent them marrying later if they so wish. Since this option, in principle, does not exist in the Eastern Churches either (although in practice, a priest whose wife has died might be allowed to remarry), it is more doctrinally problematic to put into effect. Another idea that has been proposed is priesthood for a limited term, similar to what is commonly done with soldiers, young teachers, or members of the Peace Corps. The ordained would commit in advance to serve a set number of years, and if he wishes to leave the priesthood after this period, the Church would not put obstacles in his way or relate negatively to his decision.[9]

Finally, the solution that is considered by many to be the most radical one is the ordination of women. Some estimate that such a step would immediately double or even triple the number of candidates for the priesthood, since in many places female theology (and related fields) students already outnumber the males. The advantages of such a solution are clear, even disregarding its significance as a message of equality between men and women in general and in the Catholic world in particular. Surveys have shown time and again that in many parts of the world a large percentage of the Catholic public supports such steps, as do many clergymen.

The upper hierarchy rejects the last four ideas. It treats two of them, in particular, with strong disdain: granting priests permission to marry (thus enabling men who do not want to give up the possibility of marriage to consider ordination, and making it possible for priests who want to marry to keep their position), and the ordination of women. In order to make this crystal clear, in 2011 the Vatican removed an Australian bishop from his position because some years earlier he had suggested ordaining women and married men to solve the crisis. In the same year, a Portuguese cardinal, the Patriarch of Lisbon, was seemingly forced to make a declaration denying a previous hint that he was not opposed to women's ordination.

It is hard to believe such an attitude will be sustainable in the long run. Many believe that sooner or later the shortage of priests will become so severe that proactive steps beyond prayer, encouraging young men to consider the priesthood, and doctrinal declarations will become inevitable. Sometime in the coming years or decades, many say, the ordination of married men and the readmittance of ex-priests who have married will be allowed simply because the Church will have no choice if it wants to continue providing its members with the spiritual support they are entitled to. It is not impossible to imagine that this might happen during pope Francis' reign. The ordination of women may take longer, but the chance that the Church can avoid it forever appears slim. It is hard to imagine that in some decades, when in all likelihood the very idea that there are jobs only men can do will become simply inconceivable, the Catholic hierarchy will still succeed in convincing members of the Church that an exception with regard to its priests is justified. Allowing priests to marry also seems unavoidable: here again, in the long run, the Church is unlikely to be able to offer a strong argument as to why married men can fulfill the most demanding positions on this planet but not serve as priests.

Not just the issue of attracting candidates to the priesthood is at stake; no less important is finding the right method of retaining those who have chosen it already. Surveys and studies carried out in various places in recent years have shown clearly that celibacy, a thing that many may guess would be a crucially difficult issue for priests, is not so. When asked about potential reasons for leaving the clergy, most priests mentioned overwork and tension with their superiors, leaving the issues of celibacy and the inability to raise a family and have open intimate life far behind. Clearly, while these priests had advanced knowledge of the vocation's sexual constraints (and at times, also the various ways priests may deal with them, including not living in complete chastity, regardless of their sexual orientation), they were less likely to have a prior understanding of the job's other difficulties.

Still, many believe that these findings need addressing by the hierarchy, especially if it does not want to lose those who have already chosen the way of holy orders.

Interpretation of the Second Vatican Council

The topic of the Second Vatican Council, which convened between 1962 and 1965 and published its decisions in sixteen documents, is still rather sensitive today.[10] Many in the Church puzzle over the myriad questions associated with that major meeting. One kind of question deals with the texts promulgated by the Council: what is the correct way to interpret them? Should they be read literally, or is it permitted (or desirable) to try to comprehend the "spirit of the Council" behind them? When texts appear to contradict each other, is there a hermeneutic method for resolving the contradictions? If so, what is it? Who has the authority to interpret and explain the texts? Another kind of question deals with the Council itself and its aftermath: was the convocation of the Council a good idea? How did it make its decisions? Was it beneficial for the Church, or did it do more harm than good? Was it an "event," a "watershed," with clear demarcations of "before" and "after," or was the Council merely one link in the never-ending and continuous chain of continuity and change in the Church?

Although from the beginning of its deliberations the Council was clearly divided into two camps, a larger one (known also as the "progressive" or "liberal" camp) and a smaller one (the "conservative" faction), all of its decisions were made by absolute majorities. This is mainly the doing of pope Paul VI, who pushed the Council Fathers to strive as much as possible for consensus. This process had its price: not only did the documents become much more moderate than both sides desired them to be, they were also sometimes formulated vaguely and in a way that left much room for interpretation. Some even contain internal contradictions, including statements in accordance with both progressive and conservative approaches.[11] Both sides could find grounds for their position in the final documents and feel that victory was on their side. It is no wonder that at its adjournment most members of the hierarchy, as well as the rest of the Church, felt that the Council was a success and its decisions salutary: great hopes were entertained for a period of growth in the Church.

Great expectations often lead to great disappointments. In a rather strange statement, usually cited by the extremist opponents of the Council, but whose veracity is not in doubt, pope Paul VI said in 1972 that contrary to the great hopes that the Council would inaugurate a period of radiance for the Church, darkness had taken over. He added that although he did not know the reason, it may be that at the Council "from some crack, the smoke of Satan . . . entered the temple of God."[12] Leaving aside the exact meaning of the term "Satan" in Paul VI's words, this statement clearly and dramatically expresses the feeling in various parts of the Church that something had gone awry—that the Council had not just brought light to the Church but also shadows.

Even today, half a century after its conclusion, many point to the Second Vatican Council and its legacy in order to explain the Church's current woes. Liberals often claim that the Council was too hesitant in its proposals for reform: if it had avoided this, many problems would not have arisen afterwards. Centrists claim that the Council's decisions were correct but not always applied successfully. Conservatively minded Catholics argue that many of the Council's decisions were too liberal, and that this is the source of current difficulties.

Even before the closure of the Council, and certainly after, it was clear that a new period had dawned on the Church: the Council's decisions became binding, and the question now was how to interpret them. The "natural" interpreter of the Council's decisions was the pope who presided over its three final sessions, Paul VI. It was he who headed various workgroups in charge of preparing new prayer books and missals, rewriting Canon Law, instructions on application of Council rulings on the media, relations with other Christian groups, and more. Some of these tasks were carried out swiftly (including various injunctions on the Mass, promulgated between 1964 and 1966), some took several years (for example the new calendar, published in 1969), and some only came about many years later (such as the new Code of Canon Law, ratified only in 1983 by pope John Paul II). Some of Paul VI's decisions, like the new missal, ratified in 1969 and published in 1970, angered conservative Catholics. Neither did the progressive wing rest easy: many were furious, and expressly so, when Paul VI published in 1968 his encyclical *Humanae Vitae* on the use of birth control.[13] While this subject was not itself discussed at the Council, the explicit conservative line of the document seemed to many to contradict what they believed to be the "Spirit" of the Council, closed only a few years earlier, and the tendency of the majority of its participants.

Pope John Paul II, who led the Church from the end of 1978 to mid-2005, participated in all of the Council's sessions, though he was not a central player, perhaps due to his young age (he was then in his forties). Karol Wojtyła, as he was known then, attended the first two sessions in his capacity as auxiliary bishop of Krakow and the final two as archbishop of the same city. Later, in spite of his papal authority, he did not enjoy the same renown as Paul VI as exegete of the Council. Though both conservatives and progressives in the Church suspected him of supporting the opposite wing, it seems fair to characterize him, cautiously, as a conservative pope. Many progressives felt that during his reign he managed to block many trends they had expected to triumph in the wake of the Council. As far as they were concerned, John Paul II had attempted, successfully to a certain extent, to turn back several processes that the Council had inaugurated. He, naturally, saw things differently. In his view, his path was absolutely faithful to the path suggested by the Council.

Pope Benedict XVI, born Joseph Ratzinger and elected in 2005, was also privy to the debates of the Second Vatican Council, though in the capacity of a consulting theologian without a vote: he was ordained bishop in 1977, more than a decade after the end of the Council. During the Council, Ratzinger was considered a rather liberal theologian;[14] a few years later, many began to see his opinions as more and more conservative, and probably rightly so. Ratzinger himself has argued that it was the views of others that have changed, not his own. In his opinion, the Council was a major milestone but one that should be seen as part of a continuous and permanent process of development within the Church, and certainly not as a break with the old in favor of the new. On the day after his election as pope he announced, unsurprisingly, that he would continue to apply the decisions of the Council. Whether he did it or not is a question open for debate.

The story of the Council and the interpretation of its declarations will continue to affect the Church for a long time. The eventual passing of all those involved will transform it, in a few years' time, into a fully historical event. The current pope, pope Francis, was not part of the council itself,[15] and this will also be the case of all future popes. He and they will have to make practical decisions on its interpretation and implementation. Among them, a particularly bold pope may arise and decide to convene an additional council, almost inevitably to be called the Third Vatican Council. If and when this future council does convene, will it ground itself in the decisions of the Second Vatican Council? Or will it try the almost impossible, to turn back the clock in one field or another?

Women and Feminism

The status of women in the Church is, without a doubt, one of the more perplexing challenges faced by Catholics today. Throughout the Church's history, women have played significant roles in it: like men, they were to be found among the saints and the sinners, they were theologians, founders of Institutes of Consecrated Life, teachers, mystics, martyrs, parents of Catholic children, or simple loyal members of the Church. Women play these same roles today. In many places, laywomen form a distinct majority among active Church members, whether in terms of attendance and participation in the liturgy or in terms of educational, medical, academic, volunteer, and other work carried out under Church auspices. The absolute majority of members of Institutes of Consecrated Life are nuns. At the same time, women currently cannot be ordained in the Catholic Church as deacons, priests, or bishops. Moreover, since Canon Law states that the non-ordained may not make any decisions binding on the clergy, women are excluded not only from the liturgical practices monopolized by ordained men (including the not insignificant act of preaching during Mass) but also from almost every other decision-making body in the Church. Women may assist and consult, but the final decision will almost always be made by priests or bishops—that is, by men.

Clearly, then, the possibility of the ordination of women is a central goal of many Catholic women's organizations in their struggle for recognition and equality in the Church. Surveys carried out in many parts of the world in the last two decades have shown that a rather high percentage of Catholics support the idea (in some places, more than 50 percent), or are at least willing to consider it. This attitude is no doubt the result of the fact that women are to be found today in all professions, and forbidding them to fulfill specifically this role seems to many Catholics strange and inappropriate. In addition, the practice of women's ordination in many non-Catholic Churches, which has been common for many years now and is generally regarded as successful, has also had some impact on the opinions of Catholics, especially those who live in places where there is a significant presence of such Christian groups. Catholics observe their neighbors' Churches, see their female clergy, and wonder why in their own Church this is not done.

When authorities in the Vatican realized the idea was no longer limited to some intellectual, liberal, margins of the Church, they ensured that the hierarchy made its position on the matter clear. In 1994, pope John Paul II declared "that the Church has no authority whatsoever to confer priestly ordination on women, and that this judgment is to be definitively held by all the Church's faithful."[16]

The document promulgated by the pope did not explicitly invoke the dogma of infallibility for its content,[17] but many in the Church, and especially in its conservative wing, chose to see the statement as final and absolute, obviating any further discussion of the matter. Their position was strengthened by an explication subsequently published by then-Cardinal Joseph Ratzinger (who later became pope Benedict XVI). The liberal branch of the Church continues to emphasize that, formally speaking, the statement is not absolute dogma, but it is quite clear to all concerned that the chance that the Vatican will allow ordination of women to the priesthood anytime soon is small. Pope Francis, who many see as a champion of some liberal ideas, expressed his loyalty to the statement of pope John Paul II (even though, many might argue, not in a particularly enthusiastic way). He will not allow the ordination of women.

The debate flares up sporadically, with a major peak in 2002 when an Argentinian bishop celebrated what he and those involved considered as an ordination of seven women in Germany, as well as more recent cases in which priests and occasionally some bishops openly supported the idea. Leaving aside such moments, the recognition of the status quo has muted the issue to some extent, or at least the public attention devoted to it.

Despite the centrality of the subject, women's concerns vis-à-vis their status and position in the Church do not end with the issue of ordination. As various theologians have argued, most women cannot and do not wish to become priests anyway, much like most men. Indeed, some make the more radical claim that the Church's hierarchical structure is designed in accordance with masculine conceptions, and that therefore women should refuse to join this male hierarchy even if they are invited to do so. At times, female theologians who profess this attitude demand the ability for women to carry out liturgical acts on their own and to design them as they see fit. The more radical among them would like to see a total overhaul of the Church's worldview, based, in their opinion, on masculine and patriarchal conceptions. The less radical would like to see, for example, a systematic use of gender-neutral language in the liturgy[18] as a starting point.[19]

All recent popes have been adamantly opposed to the ordination of women. Unsurprisingly, some of them, for example Benedict XVI, called on Church tradition and Scriptures to support their position. Their main arguments were the fact that all of Jesus' apostles were men (and therefore, all priests should also be), and the fact that the Church never ordained women (and therefore, the Church should not suddenly start to do so).[20]

Despite this, several recent popes had said that women must be maximally integrated within the Church, including in key roles. The previous pope, Benedict XVI, has made positive references to a variety of feminist approaches and claims, including full equality of rights and opportunity, demand for state recognition of the economic value of domestic work, recognition that various social distortions and problems are rooted in discrimination against women, and so on. Pope Francis expressed also a strong support for integrating women in decision-making roles in the Church. How this will be done is still to be seen, but it might require a relaxation of the Catholic rule that only ordained men can make decisions regarding other ordained men.

One should remember that even without ordination or formal authority, the impact of women on the Church is very important. In many families women are the main transmitters of the faith to children, and there are certain traditional practices and sacramentals that are, in some places, primarily associated with women.

The feminist revolution, which has in several decades brought about the integration of women in almost all spheres of society in developed countries and in many developing ones, represents a complex challenge for the hierarchy and the entire Church. In the coming decades, it will certainly become apparent to what extent this revolution affects the order of things in the Catholic Church itself.

Sexual Abuse of Young People

Since the late 1980s, the Catholic Church in various parts of the world has had to deal with the surfacing of many cases of sexual abuse of minors by priests. The vast majority of these cases happened decades earlier, with a peak in the 1970s. Without a doubt, the novelty was not the phenomenon but the attention devoted to it by the media and criminal justice authorities in the 1990s and 2000s: acts carried out covertly for many years, while authorities turned a blind eye and victims were intimidated into silence by the perpetrators or society, suddenly appeared in the public sphere thanks to the thorough investigations of journalists and judicial authorities. Bishops around the world did not always know how to respond, and did so in widely varying manners. One of the main allegations against the hierarchy has been the proven claim that many bishops worldwide (including possibly the Bishop of Munich, who later became pope Benedict XVI) ignored crimes they knew about and sometimes transferred offending priests from one parish to another. They did so without warning parishioners about the identity of their new priest and the danger posed to their children. In other words, although it is clear to many that child abuse is not a particular characteristic of Catholic clergymen but can unfortunately be found anywhere—including in secular education systems, other religious frameworks, and even, perhaps most commonly, in family settings—the willful blindness of senior members of the hierarchy and the often systematic way by which information was not transmitted to or actively hidden from secular legal authorities, was what angered many Catholics most of all.[21] Many dioceses, especially in the United States, were obliged to pay out astronomic sums in compensation to victims and fees to lawyers representing the Church. Church members who suddenly realized their donations were being used to compensate for the sins of priests and bishops felt cheated. Following these disclosures,

voices were heard arguing that the existence of a class of clergymen officially barred from intimate relations with other adults is "abnormal," and
thus a potential reason for child abuse. These claims have been rejected by
many experts, who often rely on psychological findings showing that the
connection between various sexual activities is quite complex, and that one
type of act does not necessarily serve to replace another. After all, the general assumption among experts regarding the sexual abuse of minors is that
most offenders are married, heterosexual men who attack children in their
own family. Moreover, the statistics about those incidents showed certain
patterns of rise and decline which bore no correspondence to changes in the
obligation of priests to remain chaste. At the same time, the fact that about
80 percent of minors abused by priests were young boys and not girls, as the
case is in the general population, left some still questioning issues such as
the sexual orientation of many priests. The most thorough study done on
the matter in the United States concluded that 4 percent of the clergy were
involved in such cases. Whether this is a high or low percentage compared to
other groups of men is not clear, due to the lack of comprehensive parallel
studies on other populations.[22]

The crisis of confidence caused in local churches by these events has yet
to dissipate. Bishops' Conferences around the world create guidelines that
are supposed to help the Church fight such cases, but it will surely take time
for the hierarchy to convince the faithful that the system was fixed and that
things like this cannot happen again. Some characteristics of past Catholic
mentality, for example, the feeling that priests are "Fathers" and "Holy Men"
with whom one can safely and calmly leave one's children, are most probably gone forever.

Birth Control and HIV/AIDS

The use of various means of contraception has been a contentious issue
since the earliest days of the Church. It is not discussed in the New Testament, although Paul declares that couples are permitted to abstain from
sexual relations by mutual agreement for spiritual reasons.[23] Other methods
have most often been seen by Church authorities as prohibited,[24] although
this of course does not mean they were not used by the faithful. In 1951, two
decades after scientists began to understand the female menstrual cycle and
formulated the "rhythm" method, which relies on abstinence from sexual
relations during the days when conception is most probable, pope Pius XII
allowed the use of this method. Theoretically, this gave many Catholics the
opportunity to control their own fertility. In practice, the method has many
drawbacks and its effectiveness is limited. In the modern developed world,

in which infant mortality has become rare, Catholic families have begun to stand out for their size: the refusal of effective modern means of birth control has almost become a hallmark of Catholicity.

And yet, as time went by, this seemed to many to be an unsustainable situation. When the Second Vatican Council was declared, they thought the bishops would discuss the topic and perhaps allow modern contraceptive methods. In reality, despite their expectations the Council did not debate the subject. The two popes who presided over its sessions, John XXIII and Paul VI, reserved the discussion for a special committee they appointed. It appears this was possible in part because, for various reasons, the vast majority of attending bishops did not place the topic on the top of their agendas.[25]

The committee appointed by John XXIII and Paul VI adjourned in 1966, and its findings, which were supposed to be divulged to Paul VI only, were leaked to the press. The world Catholic community found out that most committee members recommended a change permitting the use of any birth control method considered medically safe within the context of a marriage committed to bringing children into the world.[26] Many in the Church, including important bishops, openly supported these conclusions and expected pope Paul VI to do the same. In the summer of 1968, Paul VI publicized his decision in an encyclical called *Humanae Vitae* ("Human Life"). He considered the various arguments in favor of the use of birth control seriously and respectfully, but finally ruled unequivocally against them. According to the encyclical, almost any act that is likely to prevent sexual relations from being potentially procreative is forbidden. Excepting abstinence, the only method open to Catholics interested in regulating their fertility remained the already permitted "rhythm method."

Catholic centrists and progressives, many of whom had expected change and even considered the decision inevitable, were dumbstruck. Birth control was in the headlines at the time, perhaps even more so than today. The feminist revolution and the gradual integration of women into all spheres of life, especially in the developed world, enlivened the debate on women's rights to control their fertility and limit the number of children they had. The great demographic leap of the second half of the twentieth century, especially in the developing world, was also of concern, as the conventional wisdom was that it would be impossible to meet even the minimal needs of such a large population. The issue was also central to medical discourse: the birth control pill, which for the first time in history enabled women to control their fertility easily, safely, and very effectively, appeared on the scene a few years prior and had already become part of the daily life of many women.

The complex arguments of Paul VI, who supported the "natural" rhythm method but opposed methods involving the active prevention of conception, were unconvincing for many. Among other things, many were disturbed by the text's absolute emphasis on the physical aspect of the sexual union and disregard to questions such as the couple's intention. The opinion that the arguments for birth control included at the beginning of Paul VI's encyclical were more convincing than the arguments against it at its end was widespread among theologians. A growing feeling among Catholic laity that a supposedly celibate clergy had no right to "get into their bedrooms," dictating rules on matters of which they had no direct experience, also played a role in the controversy.

The absolute majority of the Catholic public, especially in developed countries where contraceptive pills were easily available, did not accept the pope's position. All sociological studies show that the use of birth control is now prevalent among the Catholic public, and that in many countries Catholics use birth control at the same rates as their non-Catholic neighbors.[27]

Paul VI's successor to the papacy, John Paul II,[28] had been interested in questions of sexual ethics ever since his days as an academic. His opinions were clear and solid, and in many ways his opposition to the use of birth control, based on the complex "Theology of the Body" he developed, was even stauncher than that of Paul VI. No wonder, then, that during his papacy John Paul II often expressed his support of Paul VI's encyclical both directly and indirectly.

The Catholic public at large will surely not cease using contraceptives. The challenge for the Church, then, is to deal with the fact that many Catholics reject an explicit teaching of a pope, yet still see themselves as faithful members of the Church. Simultaneously, the Church must find a way to minimize as far as possible the gap between the instruction of the top echelon of the Church on the matter and the way the majority of the Catholic public sees the issue.

The gap between the reality of contraceptive use among Catholics and the instructions of Paul VI had been evident even before the appearance and rapid spread of the HIV/AIDS epidemic in the 1980s. But when it appeared, a specific part of the official ruling, the prohibition on the use of condoms, became particularly controversial.

Pope Paul VI's encyclical, promulgated before the appearance of HIV/AIDS, prohibits the use of almost any birth control method. John Paul II, who reigned when the disease was identified, refused to relax the prohibition and permit the use of condoms. He refused it despite the fact that in the context of HIV/AIDS, and with the existence of the contraceptive pill (at least in many developed countries), condoms had often become a means of protection from sexually transmitted diseases rather than a means of preventing pregnancy. In accordance with his theological views on the body and sexuality, John Paul II insisted that the prohibition of the use of condoms applied to married couples as well, even when one partner was HIV-positive. In his view, condom usage was forbidden not only for its contravention of "natural law" through the prevention of fertilization during sex but also for the danger that condom use would promote casual sexual relations, which are forbidden for additional reasons. The struggle against this form of protection was sometimes an active one: in December 2003 Cardinal Alfredo López Trujillo, then the head of the Vatican's "Pontifical Council for the Family," stated in a detailed official document that the HIV virus could permeate condoms, and that their use should be rejected for this reason as well. This cardinal's claims were immediately declared unfounded by many scientists as well as by the World Health Organization.[29] Nevertheless, these claims spread quickly throughout the world, and some believe they brought about a further reduction in condom usage in Africa, Asia, and South America, where the disease is most widespread. Many argue that John Paul II's opposition to the encouragement of condom use and even to acquiescence to such use was destructive. Of course, not every papal injunction is immediately and universally obeyed, and the places most hard hit by HIV/AIDS are generally not areas with a Catholic majority, but it is reasonable to assume that a clear declaration on his part could, at the least, have contributed somewhat to slowing the spread of the epidemic in some parts of the world. One can wonder if one day in the future many Africans will not begin to think of pope John Paul II, regardless of the fact that he was declared a Saint in 2014, the way many Jews think of pope Pius XII, who reigned during the Holocaust: the pope who could have done something to save the lives of many, but did not.

Many Catholics actively involved in the struggle against the epidemic are opposed to the upper hierarchy's stance. According to various estimates, among the many bodies fighting HIV/AIDS and supporting its victims, the Catholic Church is the largest: its emissaries and clinics are treating around a quarter of HIV/AIDS victims. Some of them are doing so in line with the Vatican's instructions, while others ignore them and actively encourage the public to use means of protection, including condoms, in order to avoid infection through sexual relations. Some Episcopal councils around the world and even cardinals have expressed in recent decades reservations about the official stance of the Church on the matter, demanding that it be relaxed at the very least. For a long period, it seemed this had no impact on the Vatican. In fact, in his first years in office, pope Benedict XVI seemed to refuse any discussion of the issue. Suddenly, in an interview published in 2010, Benedict XVI hinted that in some cases the use of condoms might be legitimate. These statements caused worldwide uproar, with reactions ranging from those who tried to minimize it and claim nothing changed, to those who celebrated the statement, to those who were appalled by the fact that it took the papacy almost thirty years to come to what they saw as an ethically obvious conclusion. At the moment, it is hard to know if this statement has had any impact on the practices of Catholics and on the spread of HIV-AIDS.

Pope Francis, elected in 2013, has not declared at the time of this writing any change to the Church's official stance on contraceptive methods and on the use of condoms in the context of HIV-AIDS. Nevertheless, from several statements he has made it seems plausible he will opt for a different, more liberal direction than the one popes Paul VI, John Paul II, and Benedict XVI chose before him. In that case, much of the discussion in the previous paragraphs might become history for the Church.

Abortion

The question of the Catholic attitude towards abortion should be, in theory, an easy one to answer. The Church holds today (though it held other opinions in the past) that life begins at conception, or in other words, at the moment the egg and the sperm unite. As consequence of this, and in line with the prohibition of murder, any act that is intended to destroy the embryo or fetus is forbidden. According to Canon Law, whoever participates in the act, if several conditions are met, is automatically excommunicated.[30]

Considering the fact that in this book the Catholic Church is the sum of all of its members and not only of the hierarchy, the Catholic reality is much more complex. There are many Catholics who support these strict and clear guidelines. Some of them are actively trying to put them into practice, by, for example, opposing certain laws or abortion clinics. At the same time, many other Catholics disagree with this clear-cut stance. What if the conception is the result of a rape, or incest, they ask? Should a child be born from such a union? What are the implications for the child and mother? And what if the embryo suffers from a serious and fatal disease? What if the life of the mother is at risk because of the pregnancy or its complications?[31] Other objections to the rule have a practical nature: if it is clear that women will seek abortion, and that they will do it in dangerous and clandestine ways if no safe and legal alternatives are available, is it moral to stand and not act?

The Catholic hierarchy has tried in recent decades in many places to rally against laws that allow for at least some forms of abortion. In most places these efforts failed, but there are some Catholic-majority countries in which abortion is illegal without exception. Francis, the currently reigning pope, hinted that although this is a serious issue, Catholics should not focus on it exclusively when they defend Catholic doctrine and faith in the public sphere. It is still to be seen if this statement will mark a change in Catholic involvement with this issue in the coming years.

Homosexuality

The issue of homosexuality is particularly difficult for the Catholic Church in comparison to many other Christian groups. On the one hand, the Catholic Church is generally considered, and justly so, a fervent supporter of social justice and minority rights:[32] it is not unusual to see cooperation between the Catholic Church and progressive organizations on such questions. On the other hand, on issues of sexuality the supreme hierarchy of the Catholic Church expressed in recent decades opinions that placed it, at times, close to the most conservative end of the spectrum. With homosexuality, the Church is faced with an additional difficulty: experts today estimate that 5 to 10 percent of humans are attracted to members of their own sex. The consensus among mainstream researchers is that sexual orientation is innate and practically immutable. One does not choose to be homosexual, just like one does not choose to be heterosexual. Since the contemporary Catholic Church, unlike some other religious groups, supports science in all its forms and is officially committed to accepting its findings, it cannot easily dismiss such insights.

In recent decades, various authorities in the Vatican have released documents dealing directly or indirectly with homosexuality. Some of these analyzed the phenomenon, others instructed clergymen on the proper attitude towards gays and lesbians, and others yet touched on the Church's struggle against laws permitting homosexual couples to marry or otherwise attain status analogous to that of married heterosexual couples.

The hierarchy bases its stance on a variety of sources. The most basic of these are, of course, from Scriptures: sexual relations between men are denounced in various parts of the Old and New Testaments.[33] For those who have written these official documents, the verses that appear to treat such relations are crystal clear and binding. Moreover, according to their view, the entire Bible, and specifically the first chapters of Genesis, stipulates the conjugal pair of man and woman, a pairing whose purpose is procreation. Since homosexual relations do not answer the first criterion and quite often do not answer the second one either, according to the Church leadership, they stand opposed to the divine plan as presented in the Scriptures. If this were not enough, the writings of various Church Fathers and the traditional prohibition on same-sex relations in the Church also help to fortify the stance rejecting such relations. On the other hand, some Church thinkers oppose such proscriptive attitudes. Their opposition is partly based in an argument over the interpretation of Scriptures. In their opinion, at least some of the passages quoted as supporting the prohibition of homosexual relations do not do so, or at least do not require a literal and binding reading. According to this alternative reading, the Scriptures forbid sexual relations between an adult man and a minor or slave, relations with an exploitative aspect, which were nevertheless considered legitimate in some ancient societies. In this reading, these verses have nothing to do with the kind of relationship under discussion today, involving consenting adult men or women. Some also ask why such biblical prohibitions are considered valid, while so many other commandments appearing in Scriptures, particularly in the Old Testament, are considered non-binding for Christians. Another line of argument is based on modern scientific opinions on the matter. Since most researchers believe that homosexuality is innate and unchangeable, many theologians argue it must be accepted as part of the divine plan. It is unthinkable that God could have created this orientation in some humans and then prohibited its consummation. Moreover, they claim, a moral examination of the intimate relations between two people has nothing to do with the gender of the partners and everything to do with the way they treat each other.

In practice, there is no doubt that currently many members of the higher hierarchy (even if certainly not all) hold staunchly to the opinion that the homosexual act is wrong and forbidden. Nevertheless, the Church's supreme authorities have declared time and again that people of homosexual orientation are an integral part of the Church. They must not be discriminated against but rather treated with respect, and their spiritual needs must be met. What is more, sin lies not in the orientation but in the act. In other words, the official stance of the Church is that homosexuals should try to change their ways, and if unsuccessful practice celibacy. Frequent recourse to the sacrament of reconciliation may assist them in resisting forbidden acts and thoughts and in staying close to God even if they fail and sin. Members of the Church must assist them, though they should be careful to avoid acts that may be understood as an approval of homosexuality.

In recent years, the Church has found itself faced with a new and related challenge. Many of its leaders understand that the struggle against the right of gays and lesbians to associate, express their desires in public, and fight for their rights has failed in some countries. Homosexuality is gradually becoming a more and more accepted and legitimate phenomenon in many regions. In those places, its rejection has become associated with radical groups at the margins of society with which the Catholic Church is loath to be associated. The central struggle of people of homosexual orientation in parts of Europe and the Americas in these first decades of the twenty-first century regards their right to marry and start a family, including children (in many cases through the use of various fertility technologies and adoption). A significant number of countries already have laws enabling such unions and families, while others will surely adopt them in the coming years.

One should remember, though, that this situation is far from universal: the growing acceptance of homosexuality that has swept large parts of Europe and the Americas in recent years does not reflect worldwide reality. In some parts of Africa and Asia the situation is entirely different, and people with a homosexual tendency have to hide it and live in fear. In those places, the current objection of the hierarchy to gay marriage is rather popular.

Popes John Paul II and Benedict XVI were well aware of the changes in attitude to the issue in Europe and the Americas and saw them as signs of a state of emergency for the Church. If the legal rights of homosexual and heterosexual couples are equalized, the Church's struggle against homosexuality will become much more difficult. No wonder, then, that in 2003 the "Congregation for the Doctrine of the Faith," headed by then-Cardinal Joseph Ratzinger, published a document addressed directly to Catholic politicians, demanding that they clearly and firmly oppose any legislation enabling the recognition of same-sex couples or the granting of legal rights to them. Obviously, in certain respects, the arena of struggle has shifted from public opinion to the opinion of legislators. The current Bishop of Rome, pope Francis, was heavily involved in such a campaign in Argentina before his election to the papacy in 2013, even though it seems he had initially preferred a compromise. The Argentinian Church's campaign failed, and the law allowing gay marriage was adopted. Argentinian commentators suggested that the Church's fight against the law only made it more popular. It is very likely pope Francis learned the lesson, and realizes that the current trend towards allowing such civil unions in many places is unstoppable. The Church cannot of course be forced into celebrating such unions, but it will have to adapt to various legal consequences of them, such as certain rights to spouses of Church's employees, implications for adoption agencies run by the Church, or procedures performed in Catholic hospitals.

Many opponents of the high hierarchy's attitude towards homosexuality can be found within the Church itself. In fact, recent studies have shown that in some countries a significant percentage of Catholics supports marriage rights for homosexual couples. In the US in 2013, this number was already in the range of 50 percent. Since, naturally enough, many Catholics are homosexual (or have friends or relatives who are), and since the Church itself often stands up for the rights of minorities, the debate can be rather fierce. Many groups of homosexual Catholics are openly and unabashedly active. In most cases, the activities of these groups are not endorsed or encouraged by Church officials, though some have achieved a measure of recognition and may even meet within Church buildings.

The question of homosexuality raises an additional, quite sensitive point for the Church: that of its existence within the hierarchy itself. Few today would question the assumption that a higher than average proportion of homosexuals may be found among the clergy. The phenomenon can be explained in psychological, sociological, and other terms. Some studies conducted in several countries in recent years have concluded that about 20 percent of priests are homosexual (that is, two or three times as many as in society at large). Others claim (usually with less solid findings to back their claim, but still often with circumstantial evidence) that the proportion is significantly higher. Whether the percentage among bishops is higher (due perhaps to certain powerful "networks" that work to help those who are part of them to gain prominence in the Church), lower (due to a special attention by Vatican authorities not to recommend priests known as or suspected to be homosexual to the role), or similar, is not known.

One should keep in mind that just because one has a same-sex orientation does not necessarily mean that the person engages in homosexual activity. Many gay priests and bishops are committed to celibacy, and some indeed remain celibate. It is not known if homosexual members of the clergy break their vows in any larger numbers than heterosexual ones. Studies conducted through anonymous questionnaires around the world in recent years have shown that while some priests (both gay and straight) are sexually active, others are faithful to their promise (or in case of members of religious orders, vow) of celibacy.

Canon law does not explicitly state that homosexuality disqualifies a candidate for the priesthood or from joining Institutes of Consecrated Life. Some Church members would like to see such a condition added to the law, while others believe that it would not only be morally and theologically problematic, but that—considering the known high percentage of gay priests and candidates for priesthood—it would also bring about catastrophic results for a Church already suffering from a severe shortage of priests and serve as a grave insult to many active and chaste homosexual priests and members of religious communities, both male and female. At the end of 2005, after years of discussion and preparation, the die seemed to be cast in favor of the stricter position when the Vatican's "Congregation for Catholic Education" promulgated a document on the question of admittance or non-admittance of gay candidates to seminaries. Still, many were surprised (for the better or for the worse): the document did not outright forbid the admittance of gay candidates to seminaries and was less proscriptive than expected.

In July 2013 pope Francis said in one of his first interviews, "If someone is gay and he searches for the Lord and has good will, who am I to judge?" Although at the moment of this writing no practical instruction regarding the topic has come from him, it is rather obvious that his thinking on the matter is dramatically different from the two popes who immediately preceded him. It should not surprise anyone if during his pontificate pope Francis treats homosexuality differently, causing the document issued by Benedict XVI to become obsolete, and if the Church in general and clergy in particular will be instructed to learn to live with the new social realities in which discrimination against gay people is not tolerated anymore in many countries.

Divorce and Remarriage

According to Catholic doctrine, marriage only ends with the death of the husband or wife. This does not mean, however, that couples must continue to live together under all circumstances. The Church recognizes that sometimes this is impossible or undesirable, and in such situations partners may justly decide to separate for practical purposes. The Church recognizes such "separation from bed and board" as legitimate. When in such circumstances a civil divorce proceeding can assist in the distribution of the couple's joint property and in the arrangement of custody over children (if there are any), the Church generally does not oppose it.[34]

Nevertheless, as far as the Church is concerned, a spiritual, sacramental bond continues to link the couple, even if they have broken up for all intents and purposes. This link is only dissolved upon the death of one of the partners, and so long as it remains both are forbidden to marry another person. In other words, Catholics can divorce, and in many parts of the world they do divorce at rates similar to the rest of the population. On the other hand, Catholics whose previous marriages were valid, sacramental,[35] and consummated are not allowed to remarry under Church law so long as their ex-partners are alive. In reality, many divorced Catholics remarry without Church involvement. This phenomenon raises questions that many in the Church feel have yet to be properly addressed.

The Church's positions on divorce have not come out of nowhere. The New Testament denounces divorce in various passages. For example, in the Gospel according to Matthew, Jesus says the following:

> It was also said, "Whoever divorces his wife must give her a bill of divorce" (Deut. 24:1). But I say to you, whoever divorces his wife, except on the ground of *porneia,* causes her to commit adultery, and whoever marries a divorced woman commits adultery.[36]

The Greek word *porneia* given in the above quotation has been understood in many ways. In current translations to English, it is often translated, among other things, as "sexual immorality," "fornication," "prostitution," "unchastity," or "unlawfulness." Indeed, it is the same word upon which the English word "pornography" is based.

Many Biblical commentators and scholars are of the opinion that the statements in this and other related passages in the New Testament are less evident than they may seem. Is this a practical prohibition or a moral ideal that may be unattainable, like many other statements in the same chapter, such as "whoever is angry with his brother will be liable to judgment,"[37] or "do not store up for yourselves treasures on earth"?[38] What does the term *porneia* mean in this context? And whatever the term might mean, if the marriage was dissolved because of it, may the partners—or at least the one among them who is without sin—marry another? Practice in the first few centuries of Christianity leaves many questions unanswered. Many Christian communities who undoubtedly knew these passages well practiced both divorce and remarriage. Even today the Catholic Church recognizes that many other Christian Churches see the words attributed to Jesus on the matter in a different light. In the Orthodox Churches, to which the Catholic Church considers itself quite close, divorcés may remarry. While the second marriage is not considered a sacrament, those who remarry do not lose their rights in the Church. In most Protestant Churches there is no prohibition or stigma associated with remarriage. Among Evangelical pastors, the rate of divorce (and eventual remarriage) is known to be particularly elevated.

In spite of these intellectual caveats, the Catholic Church has for hundreds of years considered as indissoluble any valid marriage stamped with the "divine seal" of the sacrament and consummated through sexual relations. Only the death of one of the parties can undo the bond between them. The traditional wedding vows in which each partner pledges to be faithful "for all the days of my life" (or "until death do us part"),[39] and the celebrant's declaration, "What God has joined, man must not divide," express this idea clearly and categorically. The marriage bond is as permanent as Christ's bond with his Church.

Despite all this, like any system of religious law that is not strictly fundamentalist, The Church's law includes several loopholes enabling a measure of flexibility. Today, these loopholes are much larger than they were before the Second Vatican Council for at least three reasons. One of these is the general liberalization in Church law; the second is Church leaders' realization that the general rise in the divorce rate must be accommodated somehow. A third and no less important reason is the concept espoused by the Council that one of the purposes of marriage is self-realization and mutual growth for both partners. According to some at least, this conception implies that a marriage in which such an element was never present may not have been a true marriage, even if it appeared so from the outside.

In various situations an ecclesiastical court may decide that the marriage was never valid to begin with. Thus, for example, if it is proven that the marriage was forced, or that the partners are too closely related to one another by family ties, or that they were still validly married to others, a Church tribunal may declare the marriage null, as it was impeded in principle from the beginning. Similarly, the marriage can be annulled if it is proven that the partners were below a certain age or insincere in their vows, or that various ecclesiastical rules were not followed during the ceremony though at least one of the partners was Catholic, or that at least one of them did not mean to try and bring children into the world, or that their mental maturity and preparation for marriage were insufficient. In other situations, the existence of a valid marriage might not be denied, but a decision of another kind can mandate its dissolution: thus, for example, if one of the partners was not baptized, the marriage is not fully sacramental even if valid. The Church believes that it has special powers, or "privileges," to dissolve the marriage bond in certain situations of this kind. Proof that the marriage was not fully consummated may also make it possible to dissolve it.

In the past, cases of annulment were quite rare. Following the reforms associated with the Second Vatican Council, the procedure became much simpler and more accessible. This change, together with the rising divorce rate, has made annulment a practical option for many, especially in certain Western countries. Some see this in a positive light, while others regard it as a grave injury to the Catholic concept of the sanctity of marriage.[40]

Those choosing to begin the process of annulment turn first to their parish priest or to a relevant official in the diocese. It is not necessary to receive consent from one's spouse in order to do so, though he or she must be notified of the procedure and provided with the opportunity to express his or her side. After preparation of a legal file, which may include personal questionnaires, testimonies, and more, the file is sent to a special tribunal at the diocese. The legal process may be complicated and sometimes emotionally demanding, but it is generally not insurmountable for most. Its cost is also not prohibitive for most residents of developed countries: in the US, the average cost of filing for annulment is around $1,000, and processing takes a year or two. After filing, the case is examined by members of the court (among whom may be laypeople, including women trained in Canon Law), and after a decision is reached the file is passed on to a higher-level court at the (arch)diocese, which also discusses it. If the courts agree in their decision, the petitioner receives a verdict determining the status of the marriage. If the two courts differ in their opinion, the case needs to be passed on to the *Rota,* one of the Vatican courts, for a final decision.

Usually the decision to annul or dissolve a marriage is based upon a determination that the wedding was not sacramental (that is, if one of the partners was not Christian), upon proof that its performance was flawed (for example, if a Catholic partner did not receive authorization from his or her bishop to marry in an non-Catholic ceremony), or upon the court's satisfaction that the declarations of the partners and their vows of fidelity were invalid (for example if they did not truly intend to marry for "all the days of their lives," if they were considering betraying their spouse, etc.). This procedure has its advantages but also many drawbacks. Primarily, there is a problem of moral principle: many are reluctant to pronounce a marriage, even one that has come to an end, as null and void. Would it be right to announce that what both partners and society believed to be a "real" marriage was in fact false? In many cases, such marriages have produced children. Though the Church insists that the annulment of a marriage does not impinge in any way upon the children, many fear that it does. The legalistic nitpicking over a marriage that has in practice ended, often following a long secular procedure filled with its own challenges, is also emotionally difficult for many. The expense involved, and even more so the issue of access to legal information and legal culture also act as a barrier for many Catholics around the world. As in many other fields, residents of the developed world are privileged in comparison to those in developing countries, and tribunals in different places exercise quite different standards of judgment. Seventy-five percent of annulments in the world today are performed for American Catholics, who make up only 6 percent of the world Church. Eighty percent of requests for annulment in the US are accepted by the local courts. In Italy, in comparison, less than 40 percent of petitions are answered in the affirmative. The legal road is therefore more open for particular sectors of the Church. In its current form, it does not answer the needs of many others.

Most people who desire an annulment or dissolution of their marriage today do so for one of two reasons. The first is the case of couples that have separated in a civil proceeding, and at least one of whom is seeking the Church' recognition of the separation. Usually the petitioner is interested in marrying another person and in being declared eligible for marriage according to Church law. Another common situation is that of people who have already married others without ecclesiastical authorization and would now like to declare their previous marriages invalid or null. In such cases, the purpose is a certain legitimization of the current marriage as well as permission to receive the Eucharist at Mass. Since in the Church's eyes a person in this situation is, de facto, cohabiting with someone who is not his or her lawful spouse, his or her new life is considered a form of adultery—even if many would avoid explicit use of the term. As one guilty of a grave, public, and ongoing sin, he or she is prohibited from receiving the body and blood of Christ.[41]

The prohibition on the partaking of the Eucharist is a great detriment to the religious lives of many remarried divorcés. Many of them feel that remarrying after the failure of their previous marriage was the right thing to do, spiritually and morally speaking, and that it is far removed from adultery. Some may even argue that their decision has rehabilitated not only them but also their children. The fact that the Church regards them as sinners and therefore denies them its most important sacrament pains them greatly. It also draws the fury of many Church members who sympathize. On the other hand, many conservative-leaning Church members believe that despite the pain, this ruling is just. Whoever defies a grave prohibition publicly and continually should not expect to be received by the Church with open arms.

In recent decades, this subject has become one of the hottest topics in the Church in various places. The debate reached its peak in 1993, when three senior German bishops (two of whom were appointed cardinals within the next decade) published a document in which they stated that pastoral discretion, that is, priests' judgment on the right way to lead their congregation, should be brought into consideration in the question of granting the Eucharist to remarried divorcés. If after sincere discussion the parishioner and priest both reach the conclusion that the previous marriage was invalid, even if, for whatever reason, the parishioner is uninterested in undergoing the legal procedure of annulment, the priest may decide that he or she is worthy of the Eucharist, even without commitment to separate from the new partner or to live together while practicing absolute celibacy (to live "as brother and sister").[42]

This statement caused great tension between the German bishops and the Vatican. Catholics around the world, supporters and opponents of the position alike, awaited the expected response. A year later, Cardinal Joseph Ratzinger, then head of the "Congregation for the Doctrine of the Faith" (later pope Benedict XVI) declared that the subject was not up for debate: priests as well as bishops have no powers of discretion in such matters. People who have remarried after being wed and whose first marriage was not annulled or dissolved by a legal Church organ deserve compassion and aid, and are not excommunicated from the Church (as was the case, at times, in the past). On the other hand, they are ineligible to receive the sacrament of the Eucharist, as they are living in ongoing, public sin.[43]

In spite of this declaration, many priests around the world continue to grant the Eucharist to those who ask for it, even when they know them to be remarried divorcés. In their opinion, the prohibition is not only unjustified but also severely spiritually damaging. Many bishops and even a number of cardinals continued to hold to this position even after the publication of the 1994 document, and continue to do so even after an additional statement on the matter was issued in 2000. Thus, for example, in 2011 hundreds of priests in Austria declared they will not refuse communion to whoever asks for it. Other priests and bishops may prove less flexible and refuse the Eucharist, justifiably as far as the official stance of the Vatican is. In fact, every once in a while a case of a strict priest appears in the world media, where such behavior is rarely appreciated.

In 2013 the Vatican announced that pope Francis plans to reconsider the ban during a synod of bishops in late 2014. If the absolute prohibition on remarried Catholics to receive communion is lifted, one aspect of the painful question of how the Church should deal with divorce and remarriage might be solved. It would certainly not be the first time that pressure from grassroots Catholicism has affected the high hierarchy, but it nevertheless would provide a concise and current example.

Coming to Terms with the Past

Like every large and old human association, the Catholic Church must deal with the actions of its members in both the recent and distant past, and with much of which it cannot be proud. The list is long: the persecution of "heretics," humiliation of and violent acts towards Jews, crusades against Muslims and other groups, attacks on Eastern Christians, witch hunts, torture and killing of apostates, oppression of heterodox thinkers, active participation in colonialism, collaboration with oppressive regimes, approval of slavery, forced conversion of believers of other religions, discrimination against homosexuals, discrimination against women, abuse of children and other vulnerable members of society, and more. Historically conscious

Catholics often find themselves struggling with the tension between a feeling of responsibility for the negative actions of their forbears, and a sentiment of pride over the positive things accomplished in the name of the Catholic Church: founding universities, creation of health and education systems, patronage of the arts, development of important concepts about human dignity, establishment of charities for the poor, and more. The question of one's responsibility for the actions of previous generations makes the issue that much more complex.

Pope John Paul II made countless public references throughout his last years to harmful acts carried out by members of the Church, and asked for forgiveness for these. This was apparently due to his own personality, but also due to the symbolic significance of the end of the second millennium CE and the beginning of the third. Yet his apologies were for sins and crimes committed by members of the Church, not by the Church itself: in his view, and that of many theologians, as a mystical entity the Church cannot sin. In spite of this characteristic of his statements of contrition, most were accepted by bodies representing the offended parties. There is no doubt that these bodies and many others will continue to watch over the actions of the Catholic Church and its members in order to see how the new approach affects them now and in the future.

Secularization

For a few centuries, the Catholic Church has been dealing with the process of secularization in the world in general, and in countries previously considered Catholic in particular. Nevertheless, it seems that a growing indifference to institutionalized religious worship, in the developed world at least, has presented the Church with an especially high hurdle in recent decades: it is this indifference, rather than the onslaughts of any anti-religious ideology, which causes many members of the Church to forsake it. In some countries in Europe and North America, the percentage of those who were raised Catholics but who have left the Church reaches 20 to 30 percent. In quite a few places, the fact that Catholic immigrants join the local parishes is the only thing that keep these churches alive.

During the second half of the twentieth century, the Catholic Church has come to realize that the centuries-old distinction between "Christendom" and the yet-to-be Christianized rest of the world has become irrelevant. In European countries previously considered "Catholic," the levels of participation in worship have dropped so low that these countries have become targets for re-Christianization, or, as some would put it, "mission countries."

Some in the Church today ask themselves if there is any point in trying to attract non-Catholics or even people who were baptized in the Catholic Church as infants (and may baptize their own children) but who do not maintain day-to-day contact with the Church; some feel that resources would be better invested in those already close to the Church. Others strongly disagree, reminding that one of Jesus' central commandments to his disciples, as described at the very end of Matthew, for example, was, "Go, therefore, and make disciples of all nation." Mission efforts is what the Church is about. This debate is also related to the very complex practical and theological question of whether the Church is better off as a body of members whose level of commitment is high (such as, perhaps, in the myth-shrouded early Church), even if their numbers are not great, or whether quantity is of equal importance.

In recent decades, practically all popes have pushed for a new missionary zeal. The idea was highlighted by Paul VI in 1975. John Paul II, who was elected in 1978, made it one of the central pieces of his papacy, calling it "New Evangelization." His immediate successor, pope Benedict XVI, gave it a more institutionalized form and support. The pope reigning as these words were written, pope Francis, also seems to give it a central place. Major parts of his first actual, original encyclical, published in late 2013, were about this issue.[44]

At the same time, it should not be forgotten that even if the popes and many Catholics would like to see more "Catholicism" in the surrounding culture, the vast majority of Catholics, including the hierarchy, are fully and absolutely committed to principles deeply linked with the secularization process, such as the separation of Church and State, freedom of worship, and freedom from religious coercion. In fact, looking back, these modern concepts have been so beneficial to the Church that hardly any person aware of history would like to see a massive return of religion to political life. On the other hand, many would probably be happy to see a measure of return to religion, or at least to principles deriving their inspiration from religious traditions, in civil society.

The Catholic Church and the Jews

The question of the correct relation to Jews and Judaism has been an important concern of the Church since its foundation, and will certainly remain so in the future.

The Holocaust, and the realization that the hatred of Jews led to heretofore unimaginable levels of violence and bloodshed, was a key turning point in the relationship between the Catholic Church and the Jews. Pope

John XXIII, who reigned from 1958 until his death in 1963, was without a doubt a major player in this change, though it probably would have occurred sooner or later, with or without him. Shortly after his election he ordered that the liturgy for Good Friday, two days before Easter, be expunged of anti-Jewish statements. This order turned out to be the first major step in a veritable reform of the Church's relation to the Jews, a reform that reached its culmination only after his death.

When he called the Second Vatican Council, and under the influence of a meeting with the French Jewish historian Jules Isaac,[45] John XXIII insisted that the Council promulgate an official position on the Jews. Such a position was finally included in the declaration on the Church's relation to non-Christian religions, which was ratified and promulgated during the reign of his successor, pope Paul VI.[46]

The fourth article of the declaration is dedicated to the Church's relationship with the Jews. The article declares the Church is cognizant of the Jewish origin of Jesus and most of his disciples, and states that God has not forsaken the Jews. This is a departure from an ancient theological principle, according to which the Church has replaced the Jews in the divine plan. According to the article, the Jewish collectivity both in the past and at present is not responsible for the death of Jesus on the cross, even if some Jews, particularly in leading positions, were involved in his execution. Jesus went to the cross of his own free will: the various Jews who participated at the time were, in a sense, only instruments of the divine plan. The article strongly condemns all manifestations of anti-Semitism and calls for "fraternal dialogue" and mutual respect between Jews and Christians, which should be specifically grounded, according to the declaration, in Biblical studies and theology. The declaration does not express hope for the Jews' conversion to Christianity, even at the End of Days, though it does express hope that humanity will turn to God together as one.

Though many problems can be located in the declaration, its importance is immense. An ecclesiastical council, attended by all the world's bishops, thereby declared its rejection of ideas current in the Christian world for many centuries.

In the years following the Council, the Catholic hierarchy in Rome and elsewhere continued to publish documents on the topic. Many were in fact extensions and explications of the Council's declaration, suggestions for its diffusion among the public, etc. John Paul II, the first significant pope whose entire reign postdated the Council, chose to emphasize the implementation of the Council's instructions to commence a "fraternal dialogue" with the Jews. While his positions and actions on many topics were a constant source of tension within the Church and outside it, it is hard not to credit him with a contribution—perhaps greater than that of all his predecessors—to the practical amelioration of the Church's relations with Jews and other religious groups. In addition to his many statements on the topic, three events in particular should be mentioned: his visit to the great synagogue of Rome in 1986, the Vatican's recognition of the State of Israel in 1993, and his visit to Israel in 2000.

In spite of the generally positive atmosphere, not all of John Paul II's statements on the Jews were received positively by Jewish leaders. The document *We Remember: A Reflection on the Shoah,* published in 1998 on his orders, which deals with the Church's part in incitement to hatred of Jews and in the Holocaust, met with both approval and disapproval among Jewish organizations. Some argued that the document was an important step towards accountability on the part of the Church with regard to its attitude towards the Jews; others were enraged, claiming the document underplays the Church's institutional guilt in promoting anti-Jewish feelings, while denying any responsibility on its part for modern anti-Semitism, as it emerged in the nineteenth century and was often supported by Catholic institutions and newspapers. Acts such as the canonization of Edith Stein, a Carmelite nun of Jewish origin, murdered by the Nazis in Auschwitz, angered many, because they saw it as a Church statement declaring that only a Jew who converted to Christianity was a worthy model to follow.

The opening of a canonization process for pope Pius XII, who reigned during World War II, was also seen by many to be inappropriate at best. In recent decades widespread criticism has been directed at the actions, or lack thereof, of this pope during the Holocaust. This criticism garnered more attention after German author Rolf Hochhuth published his play *The Deputy* in 1963. *Hitler's pope,* the sensational title of historian John Cornwell's 1999 book on Pius XII, and the 2002 film *Amen* by Constantinos Gavras certainly did nothing to improve his public image. Most attacks concentrate on two charges: one, that as a cardinal he contributed, perhaps unknowingly, to Hitler's rise and the consolidation of his rule; and two, that as pope he never publicly and directly denounced the persecution of the Jews, although by 1942 he had detailed information on the goings-on in the Nazi concentration and extermination camps.

Some claim, in Pius' defense, that he was afraid public statements would further worsen the situation of Catholics and Jews. Others adamantly argue that his instructions to churches and monasteries saved the lives of hundreds of thousands of Jews—a feat that would have been impossible had he acted publicly. To this last argument, some answer that the many Catholics who rescued Jews did so without any encouragement from the pope. In a radio address on Christmas of 1942, Pius XII did call for defending the rights of the persecuted, but did not mention the fact that Jews were the main target. Even his protestation against the deportation of a thousand Roman Jews in October 1943 was feeble.

In 1999 a commission of Jewish and Catholic historians was convened to investigate the topic. At the end of 2001, after publishing an interim report a year earlier, the members of the committee announced they were halting work as a result of disagreements over access to materials in the Vatican archives. Since then, a number of independent studies that have attempted to analyze Pius XII's behavior in the light of the information at his disposal and the historical context have succeeded in casting some light on the matter.[47] Conclusions are hard to come by, but it appears that Pius XII could have done more, perhaps much more. If he had acted publicly and not only through diplomatic channels, many more Jews may have survived. Even if another man had reigned at the Holy See at the time, it is doubtful that the Jewish Holocaust would have been prevented. Nevertheless, one may surmise that the lives of many Jews, perhaps a great many, could have been saved.

Pope John Paul II has often referred to Pius XII as a "Servant of God." This appellation is normally used for candidates for the status of "Venerable," which precedes "Blessed" and then "Saint." For John Paul II, a man who experienced Communism firsthand and saw it as evil incarnate, Pius XII, who also confronted Communism (and according to John Paul II, Nazism as well) for many years while living a modest and ascetic life, was without a doubt a worthy candidate for sainthood.[48]

In spite of these justifications, the fact that Pius XII may be well on the way to canonization has understandably brought about a great deal of consternation in some segments of the Jewish world. John Paul II's realization of the harm the canonization could cause to the Church's relations to world Jewry, which he worked carefully to foster throughout his reign, probably halted the process. John Paul II died in 2005 without having declared Pius XII Venerable, Blessed, or Saint.

Pope Benedict XVI, who in his previous role as a lead cardinal was involved in almost every decision made by John Paul II, seemed to be attempting to follow the same path of reconciliation with the Jews marked out by his predecessors, but he was definitely less successful. Perhaps he was also less sincere. Despite his visit to a synagogue in his homeland of Germany in the first year of his reign, his years as pope were not been without incident from a Jewish point of view. One controversy arose when a bishop he rehabilitated was discovered to be a Holocaust denier; another followed his speeches during a visit to Israel in 2009, which were certainly less amiable towards the Jewish people than those of his predecessor. At the same time, the canonization of Pius XII was only slightly advanced during his reign.[49]

The contribution of the Jewish people to the improvement of its own relations with the Church is not always easy to identify. Some may point to the lack of a central representative body for the Jews, while others say it will take many years for centuries-old injuries to heal. There are also those that explain this by claiming that nothing has really changed in the Church. It is also not unreasonable to think that some Jewish groups wish to continue to draw the dividends of victimhood, even when these no longer have any basis in reality.

Despite all this, various Jewish bodies have indeed recognized the changes. One important eventuality is the growing number of interreligious meetings at various levels in recent decades, the establishment of diplomatic relations between the State of Israel and the Holy See, and the publication of *Dabru Emet* ("Speak the Truth"), a manifesto published in 2000 by rabbis and Jewish academics calling for Jews to change their attitude towards Christianity and to welcome the reconciliatory acts of the Catholic Church. While non-believing Jews, who are unquestionably a significant part of world Jewry, may find it impossible to sign this religious manifesto (as well as many religious Jews, but for other reasons), in any case it is an interesting Jewish response to the steps taken by the Catholic Church and other Christian groups.

Islam

In recent decades, and even more so in the past few years, the Catholic Church has had to devote a great deal of thought and attention to the question of Islam. As the professed religion of about 1.5 billion people, some Christian theologians find the theological significance of its existence and success a question worth addressing. Moreover, the proximity of residence between Catholics and Muslims in several parts of the world, and the long history of tense and often bloody relations between members of the two religions have forced the modern Catholic world to reformulate its relation to Islam and Muslims.

The Second Vatican Council declared the respect of the Church for Muslims and their faith: the one God they believe in, the creator of earth and heaven who was revealed to humankind, is the same God in which the Church believes. The Council reminded its faithful that the Muslims, while not recognizing Jesus as God, accept him as a prophet and venerate his mother Mary. Their beliefs in divine retribution, the day of judgment, and the resurrection of the dead are close to those of the Church. The Council urged members of both faiths to let go of past conflicts between Christians and Muslims and to focus on the future and possibilities of cooperation for justice, freedom, progress, and peace.[50] Almost thirty-five years later, in a special Mass held in March 2000, pope John Paul II asked for forgiveness and atonement of the sins of members of the Church in past generations. Though this was not said explicitly, many believed that some of his words were meant as an apology for the Crusades, most of which included attacks on Muslims.

In recent years, the Church has been dealing with a new reality: in places where the dominant religion for hundreds of years has been Christianity, in Europe and elsewhere, Muslim communities are growing. What does this mean for local Churches? In cases where both religious communities support the same causes, should they work together? Of what significance is the fact that many of those aided by Catholic charitable associations of various kinds are Muslims? Should the Church support liberal immigration policies, in accordance with its belief that the weak and needy must be succored, or should it oppose them, in order to prevent demographic changes in favor of Muslim communities? What should the Church do to deal with cases of persecutions of Christians, whether Catholics or others, in some countries of Muslim majority? And what about the steady decline in the numbers of Christians in the Middle East, in the very places where Christianity emerged, which is often related to their difficulties as a minority among Muslims?

Horrific terror attacks organized by extremist Muslim groups around the turn of the twenty-first century made the discussion regarding Islam a yet more difficult topic. Opinions differ on the subject within the Church, as they do outside it. Pope Benedict XVI had a more pessimistic outlook than his predecessor, John Paul II, on the chances for dialogue between the Christian and Muslim worlds. The pope reigning while this book was being finalized, pope Francis, has a record of excellent relations with Muslims in his home country of Argentina. How this will affect his papacy remains to be seen.

It might take some time before we can tell whether the twenty-first century will bring a more or less peaceful coexistence between adherents of these two religions, or whether conflict shall reign. Although certainly not omnipotent, the Catholic Church is doubtlessly in a position to contribute, at least to some extent, to either outcome. Many commentators point out that pope John Paul II's staunch opposition to the American invasion of Iraq in 2003 and his attempts to prevent it greatly attenuated Arab conceptions of the war as a Christian crusade against Islam. The Muslim world also remembers that in 1999, when Muslim religious leaders presented John Paul II with an ornate copy of the Quran, the pope bowed in respect and kissed the book. Muslims worldwide believed, probably correctly, that this gesture was sincere. Many of them suspected that his successor's position was less fraternal.

At this point in history, although in many places the relations between local Christians and Muslims are good, this is not the case everywhere. Religious tensions are high in many places, and they lead not uncommonly to discrimination against, at best, and outward persecutions, at worst, of followers of the other faith. One can only hope the situation will improve in the foreseen future, and that mutual respect, cooperation, and peaceful coexistence will characterize the coming years.

Ecumenism

In a Christian context, the term "ecumenism" (from the Greek *oikoumene,* meaning "the inhabited world") has two meanings. The first meaning, in expressions such as "Ecumenical Council," signifies that the council (or decision, or document) reflects the opinions and attitudes of bishops from around the world and not just of a particular area. The term's second sense points to the desire and attempt to find ways to unite or at least bring closer together various Christian denominations. The following will deal with this second sense.[51]

The ecumenical movement arose in the second half of the nineteenth century as a Protestant movement for the unification of the various Christian Churches created in the wake of the Reformation. Beginning in 1910 the movement gained great steam, but still only among Protestant denominations. In 1920, the Patriarch of Constantinople called for Christian unity, thus paving the way for the Orthodox Church to join the movement. The Catholic hierarchy continued to denounce it vociferously: in 1928, pope Pius XI published an encyclical forbidding Catholics to participate in its meetings.[52] He declared that the union of believers in Jesus exists only in the Catholic Church, and that the only way to Christian unity lies in the "return" of all Christians to the Catholic bosom.

Pope John XXIII held a diametrically opposed view. In 1960, less than two years after his election, he announced the formation of an administrative body to be known as the "Secretariat for Promoting Christian Unity." One of the purposes of the Second Vatican Council he convened was, he explained, promoting relations with other Churches. Even before the Council, he authorized the participation of an official Catholic mission in the third convention of the World Council of Churches, the central ecumenical body created twelve years earlier. His next visible step was to invite representatives of various Christian Churches to attend the Council as observers. The observers were seated at the front of the Basilica of St. Peter in which the Council met, and their needs—especially translation from Latin to various languages—were catered for. His successor, pope Paul VI, also saw the issue as very important. On the day before the Council adjourned, he and the Patriarch of Constantinople, Athenagoras I, both declared the anathemas imposed by the heads of the Western and Eastern Churches in 1054, which formally inaugurated the schism between the Catholic and Orthodox worlds,[53] null and void. For many, this declaration symbolized another step towards the ecumenical reconciliation desired by the Council, as expressed directly and indirectly in several of its documents.[54]

Pope John Paul II continued and even redoubled the Church's commitment to Christian reconciliation, through, among other things, symbolically charged meetings with leaders of various Christian groups. Thus, for example, while visiting Great Britain in 1982, he prayed together with the then head of the Anglican Church, the Archbishop of Canterbury, Robert Runcie. He met additional leaders of Christian Churches, both in visits to other countries and at home in Rome. In 1986 he convened representatives of several dozens of religious groups—about three-quarters of whom were Christians—to the first "World Day of Prayer for Peace" in the town of Assisi in Italy.[55]

In spite of these acts of John Paul II, the improvement in relations between the various Christian Churches, which began in the 1960s, did not always proceed smoothly. In 1992, when the Anglican Church decided to ordain women for the priesthood, and once again at the beginning of the twenty-first century, as the ordination of openly gay men as Anglican bishops was discussed and then realized, the many disagreements between the two Churches were highlighted and the degree of cooperation fell off.[56]

In 1995, pope John Paul II published a long encyclical letter, taking its name from Jesus' call as attested in the Gospel According to John, "that they may be one."[57] The letter reemphasizes the Second Vatican Council's call for promotion of the ecumenical effort, including a detailed description of his predecessors' efforts and his own in this cause. The encyclical of Pius XI, who opposed all ecumenical efforts less than seventy years prior, received no mention whatsoever in John Paul II's text: a fascinating and rather stark demonstration of the changes undergone by the Catholic Church during the twentieth century. The new letter defined new ways to promote what John Paul II saw as the proper road to unification of Christendom. It emphasized the aspirations to unification of Catholicism and Orthodoxy, but without leaving out the various other Eastern and Western Churches. Among other things, the letter called for discussion of the ways in which the bishop of Rome could be transformed from an obstacle to unity in the eyes of many non-Catholics, to a contributor to such unity. This last point is rather critical. Indeed, many in the Church today see the various doctrinal differences between the Catholic Church and several other major Churches as bridgeable. Even questions seen as central points of difference for hundreds of years, such as the question of "justification" which bothered Luther so very much,[58] or the issue of the various natures of Jesus (which brought about schism with several Eastern Churches), are now officially treated by all concerned as topics which do not in themselves justify schism.[59] On the other hand, the absolute authority of the pope remains one of the central issues upon which other Churches clash with Catholicism. Many believe that greater collegiality within the Catholic Church, providing more independence for local Churches, though not complete autonomy,[60] would shorten the long and difficult road to unification. Many non-Catholic Churches are concerned that the gigantic Catholic Church would impose its opinions and practices upon them if they unite with it. If this fear could be dispelled, and if these Churches were assured that the pope would not meddle in their internal affairs, it is possible that some Churches, whose sacraments and basic theological positions are similar to those of the Catholic Church, would be willing to form some sort of federation of Churches headed, at least formally, by the bishop of Rome.

As always, the papal document drew mixed reactions within the Church and outside it. Many lauded its appearance as evidence of John Paul II's strong commitment to intra-Christian reconciliation and recognition that the current definition of the status of the bishop of Rome is a stumbling block for the unification of the Christian world. Others opposed the document for various reasons: those with a conservative tendency were concerned by the doubts expressed by the pope with regard to the current definition of his status; those on the progressive side were frustrated by the lack of more concrete suggestions.

Will the relations between the Catholic Church and other Christian Churches (or "Ecclesiastical Communities," as some are officially referred to by the Catholic hierarchy) improve in coming years and decades? Many certainly hope so. The most optimistic foresee some sort of unification, while realists are content, at least in the near future, with cooperation and growing close relations. In many senses, the Churches closest to Catholicism are the Orthodox Churches, whose sacraments it considers valid. While the Orthodox and Catholic Churches are not in "full communion," a state that would, among other things, enable the members of one Church to partake without limitation of the Eucharist of the other, they are not too distant from this state either. The Anglican Church and some of its offspring are farther off, primarily because the Catholic Church doubts the validity of their chain of ordination, but a strong bond links Catholicism and Anglicanism as well. These two major Christian groups will doubtlessly remain the two main targets for unification as far as the Catholic Church is concerned. With many other groups, it is content to create cordial relations and cooperation on issues on the Christian and world agenda.

The challenge remains: all agree that the ecumenical process at both local and global levels has not yet reached its climax, although it improved dramatically relations between Christians, reducing stereotypes and hatred, and opening the door to cooperation of many kinds, including intermarriages of members of different Churches. Though it is unlikely that we will see dramatic unifications of large non-Catholic Churches with Catholicism in the coming decades, a strenuous effort may bring about "full communion" between the Catholic Church and Eastern Churches, as well as better relations with other Western Churches.

Notes

1. During certain historical periods, the Catholic Church experienced the concept of "Conciliarism," according to which general councils have authority over the pope. The most dramatic example of this concept was probably the Council of Constance of the fifteenth century, which ended the reign of two claimants to the title of the pope, one in Rome and one in Avignon, thus finalizing the "western Schism." The principle of Conciliarism is not accepted today and is thus irrelevant at this point of history. At the same time, theologically speaking, one must remember that a pope cannot ignore or explicitly contradict a conciliar statement, even if he can "re-interpret" or "explain" it in a way that might alter its original meaning.
2. See also in the discussion about the interpretation of the Second Vatican Council, pp. 193–195.
3. Liberals are likely to say that these priests left because the Church did not go far enough with reforms. Conservatives will say they left because of their objection to the reforms that were done. Most probably, both sides are wrong in simplifying a much more complex matter.
4. This is probably one of the reasons (there are unquestionably others) that the percentage of homosexual men who become priests is larger than their share in the general population, a fact demonstrated by many studies. See also pp. 224–228.
5. For a quite different example of reasoning regarding the causes for this shortage, coming from what might be classified as a very conservative point of view, see Michael S. Rose, *Goodbye, Good Men: How Liberals Brought Corruption Into the Catholic Church* (Washington, DC: Regnery Publishing, 2002).
6. It should be remembered that Catholics usually see the priesthood as a vocation to which one is called "from above," not a profession like any other.
7. This occurred, for example, when a large number of Anglican priests decided to become Catholic, following (among other reasons) the Anglican Church's decision to ordain women. See also pp. 227–228, n. 56.
8. The reader will remember that ordination is a one-time sacrament that leaves a mark upon its receiver. Even if the person has left the priesthood for all intents, and even if he is under a disciplinary prohibition preventing him from performing sacraments pertaining to priests only, such an ex-priest is still doctrinally entitled to lead the celebration of such sacraments and does not need to be re-ordained in order to do so.

9. For well-argued examples of calls to changes of this kind, coming unsurprisingly from two scholars-priests from the progressive side of the Catholic map, see Donald B. Cozzens, *The Changing Face of the Priesthood* (Collegeville: Liturgical Press, 2000); Andrew M. Greeley, *Priests: A Calling in Crisis* (Chicago: The University of Chicago Press, 2004); Donald Cozzens, *Freeing Celibacy* (Collegeville: Liturgical Press, 2006).

10. See also in the Introduction, pp. 16–18.

11. One of the most glaring examples is the discussion on collegiality, as expressed in *Lumen Gentium,* the "Dogmatic Constitution on the Church." Article 22, for example, contains an exceedingly intricate mix of statements on the power of the bishops as a body and declarations subordinating any and all acts by the bishops to the consent of the bishop of Rome. Some would say that the entire article, which the progressives hoped would clearly embody the power of the bishops, is lacking in practical significance. The *Nota explicativa praevia* ("Preliminary Note of Explanation") appended to the end of the document a few days before its promulgation further weakened the progressive interpretation of collegiality.

12. The phrase *The Smoke of Satan* has since become the title of an interesting book on the ultra-conservative groups that have seceded from the Church (or not). See Michael W. Cuneo, *The Smoke of Satan: Conservative and Traditionalist Dissent in Contemporary American Catholicism* (Baltimore: The Johns Hopkins University Press, 1999).

13. See pp. 199–203.

14. For his insights about the Council as recorded in 1966, see Joseph Ratzinger, *Theological Highlights of Vatican II* (1966; reprint, Mahwah: Paulist Press, 2009).

15. Jorge Mario Bergoglio, the future pope Francis, had formally joined the Jesuit Order two years before the council opened. He was ordained a priest and professed his perpetual vows after the council was closed, in 1969 and 1973 respectively.

16. *Ordinatio Sacerdotalis* by John Paul II, May 2, 1994.

17. On this dogma, see earlier, pp. 73–74.

18. This includes, for example, the translation of biblical terms such as "brothers" to "brothers and sisters," replacement of the word "men" with "humans" or "people" when referring to all human beings, avoiding the imputation of male gender to God, and so on. A new Missal, used in the American Church since 2011 by order of the Vatican authorities, seems to systematically fight, among other things, the calls for inclusive/gender-neutral language.

19. For a good review of contemporary Feminist Christian theology, see Anne M. Clifford, *Introducing Feminist Theology* (Maryknoll: Orbis Books, 2004).

20. Many have pointed out that this historic support is far from unequivocal. Two well-known examples, which raise a number of issues, are related to the interpretation of some of the roles attributed to women in Romans 16 and to the meaning of the text of 1 Timothy 3:11. Others said that if the Church must appoint only priests that are similar to the apostles, an equally valid claim would be that all priests must be minimally educated Jewish fishermen from the Galilee.

21. Of the many descriptions of this sad topic, I believe one of the best is by James M. O'Toole, *The Faithful: A History of Catholics in America* (Cambridge: Harvard University Press, 2008), 268–284.

22. Some of the information provided here is based on the most comprehensive study of those cases, the 2010 report "The Causes and Context of Sexual Abuse of Minors by Catholic Priests in the United States, 1950–2010: A Report Presented to the United States Conference of Catholic Bishops by the John Jay College Research Team." This report was preceded by a preliminary one presented in 2004.

23. 1 Corinthians 7:5.

24. See for example the classic work of John T. Noonan Jr., *Contraception: A History of Its Treatment by the Catholic Theologians and Canonists* (Cambridge: Harvard University Press, 1986). See also Christine E. Gudorf, "Contraception and Abortion in Roman Catholicism," in *Sacred Rights: The Case for Contraception and Abortion in World Religions,* ed. Daniel C. Maguire (New York: Oxford University Press, 2003), 55–78.

25. See for example the sixth chapter of Melissa J. Wilde, *Vatican II: A Sociological Analysis of Religious Change* (Princeton: Princeton University Press, 2007).

26. See, among others, Robert McClory, *Turning Point: The Inside Story of Papal Birth Control Commission* (New York: Crossroad, 1995); Leslie Woodcock Tentler, *Catholics and Contraception: An American History* (Ithaca: Cornell University Press, 2004).

27. For two examples, one relatively recent and one somewhat older, see Charles F. Westoff and Elise F. Jones, "The End of 'Catholic' Fertility," *Demography* 16, no. 2 (1979): 209–217, and Renzo Derosas and Frans van Poppel, eds., *Religion and the Decline of Fertility in the Western World* (Dordrecht: Springer, 2006), 17, who say that during the last decades of the twentieth century "countries where the Roman Catholic Church had been strongest had reached the lowest fertility in the world."

28. Pope John Paul I, who reigned between them, died about a month after his election: his legacy on the issue is therefore negligible. There is reason to believe that if he had had the chance, John Paul I may have taken a more liberal stance than those who came before and after him, but his early death made the point moot.

29. A similar controversy, though perhaps even more telling, broke out in March 2009 when the editorial of leading British medical journal *The Lancet* attacked pope Benedict XVI for making similar claims.

30. In theory only a bishop can absolve this mortal sin after confession, although in practice many bishops grant this power to their priests.

31. If the mother has a serious medical condition that can be treated only by, for example, removing the uterus, Canon Law might allow this in some cases even during pregnancy, but not in all.

32. For a good source on this topic see Pontifical Council for Justice and Peace, *Compendium of the Social Doctrine of the Church* (Washington, DC: United States Conference of Catholic Bishops, 2009). See also p. 30.

33. See for example Genesis 19; Leviticus 18:22; Leviticus 20:13; Romans 1:26–7; 1 Corinthians 6:9–10. Each of these texts can obviously be interpreted in various ways, but it is clear that each may be used quite easily as a scriptural basis for the prohibition of same-sex relations.

34. Beside the Vatican, the Philippines is the only country in which divorce (which permit remarriage) still does not exist, at the time that this book was being written. It is therefore the last bastion worldwide in which the Church's opposition to divorce is still affecting the law of the land.

35. That is, enacted as part of a valid sacrament.

36. Matthew 5:31–32. The translation given here is an adaptation of the NAB translation generally used in this book. Note that in the parallel in Mark 10:12 it is also said that "and if she [the wife] divorces her husband and marries another, she commits adultery." According to Roman law, a woman could divorce her husband. Scholars are not unanimous on the question of whether some Jews also maintained such traditions (in later rabbinic tradition, the answer is definitely not). See also Matthew 19:1–12 (particularly verse 9). In Mark 10:1–12, and in 1 Corinthians 7:10–11, the entire "exception" clause found here is absent.

37. Matthew 5:22.

38. Matthew 6:19. Those who see the prohibition on divorce as binding may also cite Matthew 19:1–12 and Mark 10:1–12, where the issue is discussed in more practical-sounding terms.

39. See also pp. 130–131.
40. For an example of the first type of view, see Joseph P. Zwack, *Annulment: Your Chance to Remarry Within the Catholic Church* (New York: Harper & Row, 1983). For a very different opinion on the matter, see Robert H. Vasoli, *What God Has Joined Together: The Annulment Crisis in American Catholicism* (New York: Oxford University Press, 1998).
41. The prohibition is based on the Code of Canon Law, canon 915.
42. The three bishops were Saier, Kasper, and Lehmann. Some documents related to the debate were published in *Origins* 24 (October 2004).
43. Congregation for the Doctrine of the Faith, "Letter to the Bishops of the Catholic Church Concerning the Reception of Holy Communion by the Divorced and Remarried Members of the Faithful", September 14, 1994.
44. Three of the most important papal documents on the matter are these: *Evangelii Nuntiandi,* published in 1975 by pope Paul VI, *Novo Millennio* by pope John Paul II in 2001, and *Evangellii Gaudium,* issued in 2013 by pope Francis.
45. 1877–1963.
46. Declaration on the Relation of the Church with Non-Christian Religions (*Nostra Aetate,* "In Our Time"), October 28, 1965.
47. For a recent example, see Hubert Wolf and Kenneth Kronenberg, *Pope and Devil: The Vatican's Archives and the Third Reich* (Cambridge: Harvard University Press, 2010).
48. It should be kept in mind that John Paul II declared more people Servants of God, Venerables, Blessed, and Saints, than all popes since the sixteenth century combined. Under his reign, 1,338 men and women were declared "Blessed," and 482 were canonized. The number of "Venerables" and "Servants of God" is even greater. In this context, the opening of the canonization process had a different significance than it would have had under a more parsimonious pope.
49. In December 2009, Benedict XVI declared Pius XII as "Venerable," the second of four steps on the way to canonization.
50. *Nostra Aetate,* art. 3.
51. Some give the term a third meaning, which will not be discussed here—the attempt to reach concord and understanding among all religions.
52. *Mortalium Animos.*
53. See pp. 13–14.
54. Especially in the "Decree on Ecumenism," *Unitatis Redintegratio,* promulgated November 1964.
55. The choice of Assisi was of course related to the figure of St. Francis, its most famous past resident, who was described by John Paul II in his address to his guests as "a man of peace." In popular Catholic culture, a now well-known and no doubt beautiful "Prayer for Peace" is attributed to Francis of Assisi. It should be noted though that this prayer was not known and probably did not exist before 1912. Its attribution to St. Francis happened only a few decades later.
56. In November 2009 an Apostolic Constitution entitled *Anglicanorum Coetibus* was promulgated by pope Benedict XVI. This text is a set of new regulations enabling entire groups from the Anglican Communion to join the Catholic Church while maintaining their unique liturgy, their male clergy (including married priests), and their bishops. Conservative Anglicans who are opposing many changes in their Church in recent decades are indubitably the main target of these regulations. No one yet knows what the practical outcome of this announcement will be, how many will accept the invitation, and how this will affect the relations between the two Churches. In January 2012 more specific instructions concerning members of the Episcopal Church (one should remember that the Episcopal Church is the American wing of the Anglican Communion) were

revealed. By the time this book was finalized, some Episcopal communities already joined the Catholic Church using these new regulations.

57. *Ut Unum Sint.* See John 17:21.

58. The issue of justification has to do with the question of whether a sinner can gain salvation and "justification" through actions ("work") or whether this is a matter of divine grace to which humans can contribute nothing. The statement signed by the Lutheran and Catholic Churches in 1998 (and joined by the Methodist Churches in 2006) declares that today there is no real difference of opinion on this question, which, one should remember, was for hundreds of years considered a major bone of contention.

59. In 1984 the heads of Churches descended from those Churches in disagreement with the decisions of the Council of Chalcedon of 451 (formerly called "monophysites") published a joint document together with pope John Paul II, in which they declared that the controversy at Chalcedon was fuelled mainly by cultural and theological differences of formulation, and that there is no significant theological difference in the conception of Jesus Christ between those Churches which accepted the declaration of Chalcedon and those who did not.

60. On collegiality, see pp. 186–188.

Appendix 1
Eastern Catholics

A number of groups from Eastern Europe and the Middle East who were thought to belong to the Orthodox world have split from it and joined (or "returned" to) the Catholic Church at various times over the last 500 years, or even earlier. Among them were groups who declared that they had never left the Catholic Church. Some other groups that indeed had never been part of the Orthodox world also declared their loyalty to the Catholic Church for one reason or another. Today these Churches are called "The Eastern Churches in full communion with Rome," or simply, the Eastern Catholic Churches. This latent reunion did not do away with the major cultural differences between East and West, as a result of which their customs are distinguishable in many ways from the Western Catholic customs. The fact that Eastern Catholic priests may be married, while Latin Catholic priests, in general, may not, is just one well-known example of the difference between Eastern and Western Catholicism. Other differences have to do with the hierarchical structures of these Churches, their liturgies and prayer melodies, their internal legal system ("Canon Law"), the priestly dress codes, and more. Eastern Catholics number about twenty million men and women, making up about 2 percent of the Catholic Church. Since the Catholicism one is more likely to encounter in Europe and the Americas is the Western one, most of the discussion in this book focuses on this type of Catholicism, which is also known as "Roman," or "Latin," due to the city and the language that have been its main reference for centuries. Yet we would be remiss not to remember the other branches of the Church, twenty-two in number, grouped under the name of "Eastern Catholic

Churches." The number of their adherents is small in comparison to the Western Church, yet their existence is theologically significant. Among other things, their existence supports the Church's desire to live up to the meaning of the term "catholic": universal.

Most Eastern Catholic Churches are culturally proximate to the great ecclesiastical traditions historically associated with the Christian centers of Alexandria, Constantinople, Antioch, and Jerusalem, and not to Rome.[1] Since most Eastern Catholic Churches have developed in non-Roman traditions, their similarities to non-Catholic Eastern Churches are often greater than those they share with Roman Catholicism.

The historical circumstances which led to the formation of these Churches many centuries ago, and those which have brought them to join (or declare they never left) the Catholic Church in more recent times, are very complex and will not be discussed here. I shall only remark that in some cases the reunion was effected by Catholic missionary work, while in other places it came about as a result of political changes, which turned Orthodox groups into minorities in Catholic-majority countries. Legally, the document known as "Laetentur Caeli," created by a Council that convened in Florence in the fifteenth century, forms the basis for the unions (which occurred much later in many cases) between some of these Churches and Rome. That Council decided that Eastern Churches interested in union must accept the authority of Rome and Roman doctrines, but may maintain their liturgy and distinct traditions.

In many ways, the "Eastern" Churches are no more similar to each other than they are to the Western Church. Except for their location to the east of Rome, they lack a common denominator. Their administrative collection under one heading at the Vatican has more to do with the fact that they all do not do celebrate their rituals according to the western, "Roman," custom and with a western "orientalist" worldview, than with what they actually are.

In the past, the Eastern Catholic Churches were called "uniate," referring to their union with Rome. Most of these Churches today consider this term derogatory. In recent decades, one of the reasons the term lost currency is due to the fact that many Orthodox Christians claim the existence of these "defecting" Churches makes the unification of the Christian world more difficult, not easier.

The Western Catholic Church is today characterized by one dominant "rite," meaning a certain manner of performing the religious rituals, whose origin is in Rome.[2] The Eastern Catholic Churches, all of which are an order of smaller magnitude, pertain to five liturgical traditions or "rites." The Alexandrine liturgy is used by two Eastern Catholic Churches: the Coptic Catholic Church and the Ethiopian Catholic Church. Traditionally, the very ancient Coptic (or Egyptian) and Ethiopian Churches trace their lineage to Mark, the presumed author of one of the Gospels. Together, the members of these Churches number 400,000. The Antiochene liturgy is used by three Churches: the Syro-Malankara Catholic Church (a branch of the Indian Church preserving ancient Eastern traditions), the Maronite Church (centered in Lebanon and without a non-Catholic equivalent), and the Syrian Church. About 3.5 million people are members of these Churches. Only one Catholic Church, the Armenian-Catholic, uses the Armenian liturgy. About 500,000 Catholics worship this way. The largest congregations of this Church are in Lebanon and Syria, but like many Christian communities in the Middle East in recent years, many of their members emigrated to Europe and North America. The Chaldean-Assyrian liturgy is maintained by two Churches belonging to the Catholic family: the Chaldean and the Syro-Malabar (a branch of the Indian Church influenced by the Latin rite of the Portuguese colonialists). These groups consider the Apostle Thomas to be their founder. Together, these groups number about 4 million. The Byzantine (or "Constantinopolitan") rite is used by the greatest number of non-Latin Catholics: around 7.5 million. The Churches using it all come from an Orthodox environment and have rejoined the Catholic Church (or claimed, justly or not, to never have left it). The Byzantine ritual is used by many Churches, among them the Greek (or "Melkite"), Slovak, Ruthenian, Italo-Albanian, Albanian, Belorussian, Bulgarian, Hungarian, Romanian, Russian, and Ukrainian Catholic Churches.

In different periods, attempts have been made by Western Catholics to induce Eastern Catholics to assume Western traditions. This was done by Western Catholics in the East as well as in the West with regard to Eastern immigrants: immigration has in recent decades brought millions of Eastern Catholics to North America and Europe, creating large diasporas. Attempts at such influence, known as "Latinization," are today viewed negatively as condescending and wrongheaded. The Catholic hierarchy has explicitly denounced them, calling upon Eastern Catholics to maintain their traditions and to adhere to them, regardless of where they settle.

Notes

1. In this they are distinguished from the Western Christian Churches, Catholic and Protestant alike, who have always seen Rome as the center to which they turn, or, in the case of the Protestants, against which they define themselves.
2. The only two other ancient rites to survive in the Western Church are the rite named after Ambrose of Milan and the "Mozarabic" rite of Toledo. Though the number of adherents

Appendix 2
Catholics in the United States

Roughly a quarter of Americans identify themselves today as Catholics. This short appendix will try to describe briefly some aspects of this significant group.

Leaving the earlier Norse explorations of North America aside, almost all of the first Europeans to arrive in areas that are now part of the United States were Catholics. Simply put, until the Protestant movement began, no matter if we date it to Luther's theses of 1517 or to the moment the term "Protestants" appeared in 1529, European Christians were supposed to be, at least nominally, Catholic. Whether the first European Christians to land in what is now the United States did it in 1513 or a few years earlier is of no difference: they were Catholics, and Luther's revolution was still in the future. Nevertheless, the situation changed radically about a century later, as Europeans started to actually settle this area in the 1620s. In the intervening period, Protestantism swept over large parts of Europe, and the Church of England was founded. For this reason, many of the early European settlers in the areas that are now the United States, and in particular those who settled in what was to become the first thirteen colonies, were not only non-Catholics—a significant number of them came to the New World because of their opposition to the Church and to its real or presumed power. Nevertheless, among the newcomers there were also Catholics. Some of them lived as a minority among other non-Catholic settlers, while others settled together, founding Catholic communities in places such as Pennsylvania, Maryland, and Florida. Their number was still very small, and only a very few of them had churches to attend. By the time of American Independence in 1776, only a small fraction of the population of the colonies, estimated to be not more than 2 to 3 percent (about 35,000 people), was Catholic. It took another fourteen years until they had their first American-born Bishop in 1790. One should remember, however, that in other states and territories that joined the Union later, where many of the residents were of Spanish or French origin, the number and percentage of Catholics was significantly higher.

A little more than a century later, by the end of the nineteenth century and when the United States comprised forty-five states, Catholics became the largest religious group, numbering well over ten million people. This outstanding jump was in part due to the annexation of states with a high number of Catholics, but was mostly the result of huge waves of immigration, particularly from Ireland (where about two-thirds of the immigrants were Catholics), Germany (about a third of immigrants were Catholics), and Italy (almost all immigrants were Catholics). During this century of expansion, a large number of churches were built, dioceses founded, and priests ordained.

By 1899, this success had caused some anxiety in Rome. In an encyclical, pope Leo XIII condemned what he called "Americanism." He was primarily targeting ideas that many Catholics in the US indeed valued: freedom of press, liberalism, and separation of Church and State. The condemnation had very little impact—many American Catholics probably did not even know about it at the time. The real or imagined control of the Vatican over American Catholicism had almost come to an end; a few years later, in 1908, pope Pius X declared the American Church to be independent and no longer under the authority of one of the Vatican's congregations.

The fact that the American Catholic Church was now large and able to decide for itself how to act in many domains did not mean that all hurdles were removed from its path. In the same nineteenth century, anti-Catholic sentiments were extremely common in the United States. Some of these sentiments were related to an all-too-common fear and stigmatization of newcomers, particularly when they arrive in significant numbers. Other negative sentiments were fueled by long-lasting theological and historical confrontations between Protestants and Catholics. The fact that the Catholic hierarchy did not condemn slavery, and that pope Pius IX recognized the legitimacy of the soon-to-lose Confederacy in 1863, did not help the Catholic cause. At the same time Catholics were afraid that sending their children to public school and exposing them to Protestant teachers and peers might harm them spiritually, so they began developing an impressive network of private schools. Protestants considered this separatist impetus yet further proof that one should not trust Catholics. Often tensions remained high, and many would say that it was not until the election of the Catholic John

F. Kennedy as president in 1960 and later cooperation between conservative Catholics and Evangelicals in the 1980s, that most Protestants accepted Catholics as equal citizens.

Today, Catholics are obviously found in every corner of the United States, although their percentage varies greatly between regions and states. Their representation is particularly strong in the Northeast, the Midwest, and the Southwest. In some states their representation is greater than the national average: California, Connecticut, Delaware, Illinois, Louisiana, Massachusetts, Nevada, New Hampshire, New Mexico, New Jersey, New York, Pennsylvania, Rhode Island, Texas, and Wisconsin. In some states, such as Alabama, Mississippi, and Tennessee, they comprise a small minority.

Currently when taken as a group, the voting patterns of American Catholics are not significantly different from the general population. About half of them vote for Democrats and about half for Republicans. Still, according to some studies, in some sub-groups there is a dividing line between Catholic and Protestant voting patterns: thus, for example, Latino Catholics are much more likely to vote for Democrats compared to Latino Protestants. Within the parties themselves, one can find Catholics on both sides.

It should be remembered that due to its nature and history, "ethnic" lines of many kinds run through the American Catholic Church. The Church includes people who see themselves as part of many cultures: they can be Mexican, Dominican, Italian, Irish, Polish, Native American, Nigerian, Filipino, African American, or part of many other ethnic and cultural groups. Some of these lines remain significant in the daily life of many of these Catholics; others are reflected in only a few fading family traditions. Moreover, although the vast majority of American Catholics are of the Western, Roman, rite, there are also American Catholics who are members of one of the Eastern rites, as well as a small but potentially growing group of those who keep elements of the Anglican rite.

The three most impressive contributions of Catholics to US culture are probably the education system, health-care facilities, and charity organizations they created. The education system includes anything from childcare facilities to elementary schools, and up to some of the most respected colleges and universities in North America. Catholic health-care networks treat about one out of every six patients in the country. Finally, Catholic charitable organizations are found everywhere and range from small, local soup kitchens to national, multi-billion-dollar organizations.

The official body that is supposed to represent Catholic interests in the United States is the United States Conference of Catholic Bishops (USCCB). This body is made of all the bishops (and currently an additional member who is not a bishop but who is in charge of Catholics who keep the

Anglican rite). In recent decades, the USCCB has often expressed opinions that were more in line with the moderately conservative side of the Church. With pope Francis now in charge, one can expect some changes in content and tone. One should remember, though, that opinions expressed by the bishops as a collective or by individual bishops are never a good indication of the opinions of all or even most Catholics. The American bishops often find themselves in a complicated situation because they control only a small part of the Catholic world in the US, and require the cooperation and support of organizations that are not under their jurisdiction. These necessary partners include some parts of the vast Catholic education system, media outlets and spokespeople, charitable organizations, health-care institutions, and more. Many of these bodies are run by lay Catholics or are under the wings of Institutes of Consecrated Life. Tensions between these different bodies and the USCCB are not rare.

The percentage of Catholics in the United States, which stands around 25 percent, has remained rather stable for decades. This is not because of retention: in fact, the American Catholic Church loses a significant number of those who were raised in it. Rather, the percentage remains stable because of immigration: almost half of new US immigrants are Catholic. In the coming decades, the US Catholic Church will become dramatically less "White," and more Hispanic.

Six out of the nine judges in the US Supreme Court are, when these lines were written in 2014, Catholics (the other three are Jews). What this fact can tell us about the standing of Catholicism in the United States today is something we will leave the reader to meditate upon.

Recommended Bibliography

Adsera, Alicia. "Religion and Changes in Family-Size Norms in Developed Countries." *Review of Religious Research* 47, no. 3 (2006): 271–86.

à Kempis, Thomas. *The Imitation of Christ*. New York: Dover Publications, 2003.

Alberigo, Giuseppe. *A Brief History of Vatican II*. Maryknoll: Orbis Books, 2006.

Alberigo, Giuseppe, and Joseph A. Komonchak, eds. *History of Vatican II* (5 volumes). Maryknoll-Leuven: Orbis-Peeters, 1995–2001.

Allen, John L. Jr. *The Catholic Church: What Everyone Needs to Know*. New York: Oxford University Press, 2013.

Amen. DVD. Directed by Constantinos Gavras. 2002; New York: Kino International, 2004.

Beal, John P., James A. Coriden, and Thomas J. Green, eds. *New Commentary on the Code of Canon Law*. Mahwah: Paulist Press, 2000.

Benedict of Nursia,. *The Rule of Saint Benedict*. Edited and translated by Bruce L. Venarde. Cambridge: Harvard University Press, 2011.

Boff, Leonardo. *Sacraments of Life, Life of the Sacraments*. Translated by John Drury. Portland: Pastoral Press, 1987.

Brown, Raymond E. *An Introduction to the New Testament*. New York: Doubleday, 1997.

Buckley, Michael, and Tony Castle, eds. *The Catholic Prayer Book*. Ann Arbor: Servant Books, 1986.

Catechism of the Catholic Church, 2nd ed. New York: Doubleday, 2003.

Clifford, Anne M. *Introducing Feminist Theology*. Maryknoll: Orbis Books, 2004.

Cloutier, David, ed. *Leaving and Coming Home: New Wineskins for Catholic Sexual Ethics*. Eugene: Cascade Books, 2010.

Compendium of the Catechism of the Catholic Church. Washington, DC: United States Conference of Catholic Bishops, 2005.

Coriden, James A. *An Introduction to Canon Law*. New York: Paulist Press, 1991.

Cornwell, John. *Hitler's pope: The Secret History of Pius XII*. New York: Penguin, 1999.

Cozzens, Donald B. *The Changing Face of the Priesthood*. Collegeville: Liturgical Press, 2000.

Cozzens, Donald. *Freeing Celibacy*. Collegeville: Liturgical Press, 2006.

Cuneo, Michael W. *The Smoke of Satan: Conservative and Traditionalist Dissent in Contemporary American Catholicism*. Baltimore: The Johns Hopkins University Press, 1999.

Cunningham, Lawrence S. *An Introduction to Catholicism*. New York: Cambridge University Press, 2009.

Danielou Jean. *The Angels and Their Mission According to the Fathers of the Church*. Translated by David Heimann. 1953. Reprint, Notre Dame: Ave Maria Press, 1996.

Derosas, Renzo, and Frans van Poppel, ed. *Religion and the Decline of Fertility in the Western World*. Dordrecht: Springer, 2006.

Dolan, Jay P., *The American Catholic Experience: A History from Colonial Times to the Present*. Notre Dame: University of Notre Dame Press, 1992.

Dues, Greg. *Catholic Customs & Traditions, a Popular Guide, Revised and Updated*. Mystic: Twenty-Third Publications/Bayard, 2000.

Dulles, Avery. *Models of the Church, Expanded Edition*. New York: Doubleday, 2002.

Dulles, Avery. "The Population of Hell." *First Things* (May 2003): 36–41.

Eco, Umberto. *The Name of the Rose*. Translated by William Weaver. Orlando: Harcourt, 1994.

Ehrman, Bart D. *A Brief Introduction to the New Testament*. New York: Oxford University Press, 2004.

Ehrman, Bart D. *Did Jesus Exist? The Historical Argument for Jesus of Nazareth*. New York: HarperOne, 2013.

Ferguson, Everett. *Baptism in the Early Church: History, Theology, and Liturgy in the First Five Centuries*. Grand Rapids: William B. Eerdmans, 2009.

Flannery, Austin, ed. *Vatican Council II, The Basic Sixteen Documents: Constitutions, Decrees, Declarations: A Completely Revised Translation in Inclusive Language*. Dublin: Dominican Publications, 1996.

Foley, Edward. *From Age to Age: How Christians Have Celebrated the Eucharist (Revised and Expanded Edition)*. Collegeville: Liturgical Press, 2009.

Fox, Thomas C. *Sexuality and Catholicism*. New York: George Braziller, 1995.

Frazee, Charles A. "The Origins of Clerical Celibacy in the Western Church." *Church History* 57 (Supplement: Centennial Issue, 1988): 108–26 (Article originally published in *Church History* 41, no. 2 (1972)).

Gillis, Chester. *Roman Catholicism in America*. New York: Columbia University Press, 1999.

Gordon, Mary. "Women of God." *The Atlantic Monthly* (January 2002): 57–91.

Greeley, Andrew M. *The American Catholic: A Social Portrait*. New York: Basic Books, 1977.

Greeley, Andrew M. *The Catholic Imagination*. Berkeley: University of California Press, 2000.

Greeley, Andrew M. *Priests: A Calling in Crisis*. Chicago: The University of Chicago Press, 2004.

Grün, Anselm. *The Seven Sacraments*. Translated by John Cumming. New York: Continuum, 2003.

Gudorf, Christine E. "Contraception and Abortion in Roman Catholicism," in *Sacred Rights: The Case for Contraception and Abortion in World Religions*, ed. Daniel C. Maguire, 55–78. New York: Oxford University Press, 2003.

Hahnenberg, Edward P. *A Concise Guide to the Documents of Vatican II*. Cincinnati: St. Anthony Messenger Press, 2007.

Hanson, Eric O. *The Catholic Church in World Politics*. Princeton: Princeton University Press, 1987.

Hayes, Michael A., and Liam Gearon, eds. *Contemporary Catholic Theology: A Reader*. New York: Continuum, 1999.

Hinze, Christine Firer. "A Distinctively Catholic Patriotism?" in *God and Country?: Diverse Perspectives on Christianity and Patriotism*, eds. Michael G. Long and Tracy Wenger Sadd, 129–46. New York: Palgrave Macmillan, 2007.

Hochhuth, Rolf. *The Deputy*. 1963. Reprint, Baltimore: The Johns Hopkins University Press, 1997.

I Confess. DVD. Directed by Alfred Hitchcock. 1953; Burbank: Warner Home Video, 2004.

Jenkins, Philip. *The New Anti-Catholicism: The Last Acceptable Prejudice*. New York: Oxford University Press, 2003.

Johnson, Luke Timothy. *The Creed: What Christians Believe and Why it Matters*. New York: Doubleday, 2003.

Johnson, Maxwell E. *The Rites of Christian Initiation: Their Evolution and Interpretation*. Collegeville: Liturgical Press, 2007.

Kärkkäinen, Veli-Matti. *An Introduction to Ecclesiology: Ecumenical, Historical & Global Perspectives*. Downers Grove: InterVarsity Press, 2002.

Kasper, Walter, ed. *The Petrine Ministry: Catholics and Orthodox in Dialogue*. New York: Newman Press, 2006.

Keating, James, ed. *The Deacon Reader*. Mahwah: Paulist Press, 2006.

Lakeland, Paul. *The Liberation of the Laity: In Search of an Accountable Church*. New York: Continuum, 2004.

Lamb, Matthew L., and Matthew Levering, eds. *Vatican II: Renewal Within Tradition*. New York: Oxford University Press, 2008.

LaVerdiere, Eugene. *The Eucharist in the New Testament and the Early Church*. Collegeville: Liturgical Press, 1996.

Madigan, Kevin, and Carolyn Osiek. *Ordained Women in the Early Church: A Documentary History*. Baltimore: Johns Hopkins University Press, 2005.

Marchetto, Agostino. *The Second Vatican Ecumenical Council: A Counterpoint for the History of the Council*. Translated by Kenneth D. Whitehead. Scranton: University of Scranton Press, 2009.

Marienberg, Evyatar. *Katoliyut Akhshav: Mavo le-Havanat ha-Knesiyah ha-Katolit bat Yamenu*. Jerusalem: Carmel Publishing House, 2010.

Marthaler, Berard L. *The Creed: The Apostolic Faith in Contemporary Theology (Third Edition)*. New London: Twenty Third Publications, 2008.

McBrien, Richard P. *Catholicism: New Edition*. New York: HarperCollins Publishers, 1994.

McBrien, Richard P. *The Church: The Evolution of Catholicism*. New York: Harper One, 2008.

McCartin, James P. *Prayers of the Faithful: The Shifting Spiritual Life of American Catholics.* Cambridge: Harvard University Press, 2010.

McClory, Robert. *Turning Point: The Inside Story of Papal Birth Control Commission.* New York: Crossroad, 1995.

McInerny, Ralph M. *What Went Wrong with Vatican II: The Catholic Crisis Explained.* Manchester: Sophia Institute Press, 1998.

Metzger, Bruce M. *A Textual Commentary on the Greek New Testament, Second Edition.* Stuttgart: United Bible Societies, 1994.

Miller, Maureen C. *Power and the Holy in the Age of the Investiture Conflict: A Brief History with Documents.* New York: Bedford/St. Martin's, 2005.

Moss, Candida. *The Myth of Persecution: How Early Christians Invented a Story of Martyrdom.* New York: HarperOne, 2013.

Mullin, Robert Bruce. *A Short World History of Christianity.* Louisville: Westminster John Knox, 2008.

Nichols, Aidan. *Holy Order: The Apostolic Ministry from the New Testament to the Second Vatican Council.* Dublin: Veritas Publications, 1990.

Noonan, John T. Jr. *Contraception: A History of Its Treatment by the Catholic Theologians and Canonists.* Cambridge: Harvard University Press, 1986.

O'Collins, Gerald, and Mario Farrugia, *Catholicism: The Story of Catholic Christianity.* New York: Oxford University Press, 2003.

O'Malley, John W. *What Happened at Vatican II.* Cambridge: Harvard University Press, 2008.

O'Toole, James M. *The Faithful: A History of Catholics in America.* Cambridge: Harvard University Press, 2008.

Pontifical Council for Justice and Peace. *Compendium of the Social Doctrine of the Church.* Washington, DC: United States Conference of Catholic Bishops, 2009.

Priest. DVD. Directed by Antonia Bird. 1994; New York: Miramax, 1999.

Rapp, Claudia. *Holy Bishops in Late Antiquity: The Nature of Christian Leadership in an Age of Transition.* Berkeley: University of California Press, 2005.

Ratzinger, Joseph. *Theological Highlights of Vatican II.* 1966. Reprint, Mahwah: Paulist Press, 2009.

Rausch, Thomas P. *Catholicism in the Third Millennium* (second edition). Collegeville: Liturgical Press, 2003.

Reese, Thomas J. *Inside the Vatican.* Cambridge: Harvard University Press, 2003.

Rose, Michael S. *Goodbye, Good Men: How Liberals Brought Corruption Into the Catholic Church.* Washington, DC: Regnery Publishing, 2002.

Rubin, Miri. *Mother of God: A History of the Virgin Mary.* New Haven: Yale University Press, 2009.

Rynne, Xavier (Francis X. Murphy). *Vatican Council II.* 1963–1966. Reprint, Maryknoll: Orbis Books, 1999.

Salzman, Todd A., and Michael G. Lawler. *The Sexual Person: Toward a Renewed Catholic Anthropology.* Washington, DC: Georgetown University Press, 2008.

Scott, Robert A. *Miracle Cures: Saints, Pilgrimage, and the Healing Power of Belief.* Berkeley: University of California Press, 2010.

Steinfels, Peter. *A People Adrift: The Crisis of the Roman Catholic Church in America.* New York: Simon & Schuster, 2003.

Stone, Darwell. *A History of the Doctrine of the Holy Eucharist*. 1909. Reprint, Eugene: Wipf and Stock Publishers, 2007.

Sullivan, Francis A. *From Apostles to Bishops: The Development of the Episcopacy in the Early Church*. New York: Newman Press, 2001.

Tentler, Leslie Woodcock. *Catholics and Contraception: An American History*. Ithaca: Cornell University Press, 2004.

Tierney, Brian. *Origins of Papal Infallibility, 1150–1350; A Study on the Concepts of Infallibility, Sovereignty and Tradition in the Middle Ages*. Leiden: E. J. Brill, 1972.

Tomkins, Stephen. *A Short History of Christianity*. Grand Rapids: William B. Eerdmans, 2005.

van Gennep, Arnold. *The Rites of Passage*. Translated by Gabrielle L. Caffee and Monika B. Vizedom. London: Routledge, 2010.

Vasoli, Robert H. *What God Has Joined Together: The Annulment Crisis in American Catholicism*. New York: Oxford University Press, 1998.

Walsh, Michael. *Roman Catholicism: The Basics*. London: Routledge, 2005.

Westoff, Charles F., and Elise F. Jones. "The End of 'Catholic' Fertility." *Demography* 16, no. 2 (1979): 209–217.

White, James F. *Roman Catholic Worship: Trent to Today*. Collegeville: Liturgical Press, 2003.

Wilde, Melissa J. *Vatican II: A Sociological Analysis of Religious Change*. Princeton: Princeton University Press, 2007.

Wiltgen, Ralph M. *The Rhine Flows into the Tiber: A History of Vatican II*. 1967. Reprint, Illinois: TAN, 1985.

Winroth, Anders. *The Making of Gratian's Decretum*. Cambridge: Cambridge University Press, 2000.

Wolf, Hubert, and Kenneth Kronenberg. *Pope and Devil: The Vatican's Archives and the Third Reich*. Cambridge: Harvard University Press, 2010.

Woodhead, Linda. *An Introduction to Christianity*. Cambridge: Cambridge University Press, 2004.

Woodhead, Linda, *Christianity: A Very Short Introduction*. Oxford: Oxford University Press, 2004.

Zwack, Joseph P. *Annulment: Your Chance to Remarry Within the Catholic Church*. New York: Harper & Row, 1983.

Index

201 Bane & H.V.

203 abortion